UNARMED AND UNAFRAID

UNARMED AND UNAFRAID

Glenn B. Infield

THE MACMILLAN COMPANY

COLLIER-MACMILLAN LTD., LONDON

The Macmillan Company
866 Third Avenue, New York, N.Y. 10022
Collier-Macmillan Canada Ltd., Toronto, Ontario

Library of Congress Catalog Card Number: 74-97758

First Printing

Printed in the United States of America

To Peggy

Acknowledgments

It would be impossible to list all those persons who contributed information, effort, and personal photographs for this book. While everyone cannot be listed by name I am certain that they are well aware of the value of their contribution to such a complex subject. Special thanks, however, are due to Major P. N. Nadashkevich, Don Forke, Colonel Robert R. Smith, Dave Ecoff, Major David P. Blackbird, George Humbrecht, Clark Sykes, R. E. Currie, Fred Hargesheimer, General Russel Berg, Hassell Stump, Major Jerry Lents, and Wilbur Householder, all pilots who have helped develop aerial reconnaissance techniques from the hand-held camera to the sophisticated concepts in use today. In addition, the help of Lieutenant Colonel Gerald M. Holland and his staff at the Magazine and Book Division of the Office of the Assistant Secretary of Defense has been invaluable, as was the assistance of Royal D. Frey and his staff at the Air Force Museum, Robert R. Roalef at the Air Force Avionics Laboratory, and Lieutenant Michael W. Loder of the 91st Tac Recon Squadron. Each contribution, small or large, was greatly appreciated by the author.

G. B. I.

Contents

Illustrations follow p. 148

UNARMED AND UNAFRAID

1

No Place to Hide

WHEN Ambassador W. Averell Harriman of the United States and Minister of State Xuan Thuy of North Vietnam met in Paris for the first peace talks on May 14, 1968, one of the demands made by Xuan Thuy shocked a great many people. Most interested individuals were well aware that North Vietnam would demand a halt to the bombing of the north by U.S. planes but few were prepared for the strong emphasis Xuan Thuy placed on another type of flight over North Vietnam—reconnaissance flights. To the uninformed the American aircraft flying over Hanoi and Haiphong and other areas of North Vietnam armed only with cameras could do little or no harm to the enemy. Why then was Xuan Thuy so adamant in his demand that the aerial reconnaissance flights stop immediately before any further peace negotitions take place?

The answer is obvious to those who know the accomplishments of U.S. reconnaissance aircraft and pilots, the fliers whose motto is "Alone, Unarmed, Unafraid." The enemy can hide nothing from them. Using cameras that can detect a golf ball on a fairway from an altitude of nine miles or take clear pictures at supersonic speed when the aircraft is at treetop height, the reconnaissance pilot brings home more secrets in less time than any other type of intelligence in the military. During the 1967 Tet "truce" period, for example, when the ground warfare in Vietnam was supposedly halted and the North Vietnamese were claiming to observe the truce agreement, reconnaissance pilots, who did not take a break, discovered:

—North Vietnam moved 25,000 tons of supplies toward the south.
—Some 2,200 trucks were used.
—At least 970 vessels moved south in coastal waters; about 600 moved north, apparently to pick up supplies and personnel.
—Over 300 foreign ships—many positively identified as French, British, Yugoslav, or Greek—were in Haiphong and other North Vietnamese ports.
—Some 300,000 laborers were put to work clearing up earlier bomb damage.

It is little wonder that one of the first and most determined demands Minister of State Xuan Thuy made at the Paris peace talks was to halt all flights of reconnaissance planes over North Vietnam.

The "secret war" of aerial reconnaissance recognizes no truce, takes no breaks, never knows peace. The actors in it rarely surface; its battles are won or lost without benefit of much publicity. There isn't much glory for the reconnaissance pilot, but no flier—fighter ace or strategic bomber commander—has a more important job or a more dangerous one. It is an assignment that demands resourcefulness, accuracy of detail, technical skill, and devotion to duty; a mission that is usually flown alone, not in a formation; one that is anticipated by the enemy, who is usually waiting to pounce upon the reconnaissance aircraft or bracket it with intense antiaircraft fire or rockets.

In order to join this elite group, a pilot must meet exacting requirements that deal not only with his flight hours and the types of planes he has flown but also with his personal characteristics. In many ways he must be a lone-wolf type of flier, exactly opposite from today's fighter pilot, who must always coordinate his aerial combat tactics with his wingman and other members of his unit. The reconnaissance pilot is strictly on his own most of the time. Other armed aircraft may be assigned to escort him to the target and back in some instances but even then it is up to the reconnaissance pilot to make the necessary decisions on procedure, altitude, airspeed, and other factors involved in successfully obtaining the required photographs or electronic intelligence. He adapts his tactics to the situation without having to consult with other pilots or his own headquarters.

In fighter-bomber missions over North Vietnam, for instance, a strike force usually consisted of sixteen to twenty F-105 Thunderchiefs. Flying escort to protect the Thunderchiefs from Migs were at least eight F-4D Phantoms, while four other F-105s were assigned to flak and SAM suppression. The force was also supported by EB-66 radar-jamming aircraft and by EC-121 "College Eye" warning planes, carrying radar observers to report SAM site activity and track enemy fighters from the moment they take off. In contrast, reconnaissance pilots and crews go to the same areas in North Vietnam alone. They go high or on the deck, maintaining radio silence, ECM pods shut off until the moment they are needed, and at speeds from 500 to 900 knots. Many go at night, some disappearing into the darkness never to be seen again. They disappear without a trace. Were they shot down over the target? Did they plow into a mountainside or plummet into the sea? Most of the time the questions are never answered.

It is to answer other questions, however, that the reconnaissance pilot, the photo interpreter, and the highly skilled technician are vitally important. It is the far side of the earth—not the far side of the moon—that is the greatest threat to peace and freedom, and knowledge of what is going on on the opposite side of the globe is a necessity. In 1955 President Dwight D. Eisenhower, in an effort to promote disarmament and abolish secrets between Russia and the United States, presented his famous "open skies" proposal. He declared essentially that peace could be secured only by eliminating all secrecy between nations and keeping each other informed on all military activities. His immediate aim at that time was to provide an accurate inventory of all armies in order to reduce the chances of miscalculation by top leaders, to end the talk of weapon gaps, and to halt the constant escalation of war resources. President Eisenhower's method provided for mutual overflights by the United States and Russia, with a free exchange of reconnaissance photographs. The Russians promptly rejected the plan, knowing that they had much to lose and that there was little they could not gain by other means from the open-door policy of the United States. It was this rejection that necessitated less open methods of gathering vital information by the United States and that set off the "secret war" of aerial photography and electronic espionage.

Basically, there are two main types of reconnaissance flights—strategic and tactical. Strategic reconnaissance became important with the coming of global total warfare. In modern war long-range aircraft and nuclear weapons can strike at the enemy's homeland and destroy his means of production, disrupt his transportation, break his morale, and render his military establishment impotent. To do this successfully, however, it is necessary to know what and where the vital targets are, the disposition of his troops, aircraft, and ships, and recent developments and tests of a military nature. In peacetime there is a continuing need for long-range reconnaissance to prevent enemies of the nation from secretly developing weapons that might enable them to attack the United States successfully, from massing their military might for a surprise attack, from making any maneuver detrimental to the security of the nation without Washington's knowing about it. These functions are known as strategic reconnaissance. Aerial strategic reconnaissance is the greatest single source of overt intelligence the United States has today.

Tactical reconnaissance deals principally with support of front-line armies during periods of actual combat. It is needed fast to assist military commanders in seeking solutions to their command and control problems. The "lean and hungry eye" of the aerial camera looks over the next hill or across the DMZ or into the jungle for the ground commander and helps him formulate his immediate plans for offensive or defensive warfare.

The vital need for strategic aerial reconnaissance became immediately apparent at the beginning of World War II. Less than one-tenth of the earth's surface had been mapped, and bomber crews, especially in the Pacific theater, were assigned missions for which there were no target folders, no accurate navigational maps, no detailed information to help perform the task successfully. Commanders had no way of assessing the actual bomb damage caused by their aircraft except by the visual examination of the area by the combat crews. These reports were often inaccurate for obvious reasons. The bomber was sometimes under enemy fighter attack or intense antiaircraft fire and the crew was too busy defending itself to be concerned about accurate assessment of bomb damage. Human memory cannot absorb and retain the quantity of detail that is required and often the human tongue cannot adequately report what the eye sees, so it became obvious that aerial photography was needed.

By June of 1942 the USAAF Second Air Force was training the pilots and technicians who were assigned the task of obtaining the strategic aerial reconnaissance so desperately needed. The training program was on an around-the-clock basis at the main aerial photography school located at Lowry Field. Aircraft used by the school were B-18s, F-2s, F-4s, and B-25s. Within a few months aerial reconnaissance units were operating in every combat area, bringing back to the commanders the information that eventually enabled the U.S. military forces to halt the Axis advances and begin the offensives that ultimately ended in victory. The Army Air Force alone took 171,000,000 negatives during World War II.

By the end of World War II the expanded geographic scope of aerial warfare had made the need for more strategic-reconnaissance capability increasingly obvious. More long-range B-29s were modified as reconnaissance aircraft so that photographs of territory far from the mainland of the United States could readily be obtained. At the same time the Research and Development Branch of Wright Patterson Air Force Base devised new cameras that could photograph from high altitudes. These new cameras were ideal for use by the RB-29 and later the Boeing RB-50.

The RB-50 was the first aircraft suitable for high-altitude, long-range reconnaissance missions of the type needed during the initial stages of the cold war. It filled the role admirably until the first multijet aircraft capable of performing strategic reconnaissance missions, the North American RB-45, appeared on the scene. Later the huge Convair RB-36 was built and its extremely long range made all previous Strategic Air Command reconnaissance planes outdated for missions on the opposite side of the globe. No spot on earth was out of reach of this aircraft, and with the newly developed high-altitude cameras available for use on the RB-36 the problem of keeping the nation's leaders informed by aerial reconnaissance seemed to be solved.

It seemed that way but it soon became apparent that solution was a long way off. The RB-36, while having a long range, did not have the speed necessary to fly it to some targets that had to be photographed. If the U.S.S.R. had agreed to President Eisenhower's open skies proposal and had permitted overflights without opposition, the RB-36 would have been ideal. However, Russia had no desire to allow American reconnaissance planes over, or even near, its territory, and the RB-36 was much too big and much too slow for any covert missions in such areas.

In-flight refueling converted the swift RB-47s from medium-range to long-range reconnaissance aircraft and for a while these planes accomplished the dangerous, delicate along-the-Iron-Curtain missions. Despite their speed and low- and high-altitude capabilities, however, Communist military authorities were well aware of the prying eyes of the cameras aboard the RB-47s and had the guns and aircraft to stop such flights. After Russian Migs had forced down several American reconnaissance planes and shot down others, precipitating an international crisis, the flow of intelligence to the Department of Defense from aerial reconnaissance was reduced to a trickle. It was at this time that the Strategic Air Command requested special high-performance reconnaissance aircraft to handle the secret missions required to maintain national security. The modified bombers from the RB-29 to the RB-47 had done a good job but were no longer suitable for the task ahead.

A designer named Kelly Johnson at Lockheed Aircraft Corporation came up with the answer to the question of how the United States could keep tabs on developments inside Russia—the U-2. It was a better answer than anyone had expected. The U-2, with a wingspan of more than 80 feet, an altitude capability of at least 90,000 feet, and a flight duration of eight hours, was by far the best reconnaissance aircraft ever built by any country. It was a glider with a jet engine, a plane that could half fly and half glide for four thousand miles at a height that protected it from enemy rockets and fighters. When all efforts failed at obtaining Russian cooperation in the exchange of information and it became necessary for survival to learn more about Soviet military plans, the U-2 was assigned the mission. Until 1960, when Francis Gary Powers was shot down on an overflight of Russian territory, U-2 pilots located missile stations, military airbases, troop maneuvers and concentrations, nuclear-test sites, and other establishments that threatened the survival of the free world. This overflight program came to an end when Powers was knocked out of the sky in May 1960 while piloting his U-2 over Russia for the Central Intelligence Agency.

The downing of the U-2 near Sverdlovsk, nine hundred miles east of Moscow, and the political aftermath of the incident emphasize the role of aerial reconnaissance in the twentieth century and the importance attached to it by world leaders. President Eisenhower, after admitting that the flight over Soviet territory had been authorized by him and that he assumed full responsibility for it, the first time that a nation had ever admitted it was involved in espionage, explained his reasons. "Our deterrent must never be placed in jeopardy. The safety of the whole free world demands this. As the Secretary of State pointed out in his recent statement, ever since the beginning of my Administration I have issued directives to gather, in every feasible way, the information that is required to protect the United States and the free nations against surprise attack and to enable them to make effective preparations for defense."

In Russia Premier Nikita Khrushchev also acknowledged the importance of the overflights by his actions. In the Hall of the Kremlin Palace at the opening of the meeting of the Supreme Soviet he announced that an American U-2 spy plane had been shot down over the Soviet Union and warned all countries where there were United States air bases that they were "playing with fire" for permitting reconnaissance aircraft to take off and land on their territory. Subsequently he canceled the scheduled summit meeting with President Eisenhower in Paris after bitterly attacking the United States for its spy flights. It was the Russian judges who tried Francis Gary Powers, however, who gave the most vivid account of the importance of the overflight. They said that Powers "photographed important defense objectives and recorded signals of the country's antiaircraft defense radar installations. The developed films established that Defendant Powers photographed from the U-2 plane industrial and military objectives of the Soviet Union—plants, depots, oil storages, communication routes, railway bridges and stations, the dislocation of troops and military techniques."

After the U-2 incident the Eisenhower Administration declared that there would be no more overflights of the Soviet Union. The statement was later reaffirmed and endorsed by the Kennedy Administration. The U-2, however, continued to make both high-altitude air-sampling flights to detect radioactivity and weather-reconnaissance missions in various parts of the world. While the United States has never admitted the fact, it is apparent that the U-2s were also used secretly along but outside the borders of the Soviet Union to pick up on tapes electronic emissions of Communist radio and radar and to take slant-range photographs of Soviet frontier areas from great distances and altitudes. Periodically China and the Soviet Union charge the United States with overflights of their territory by U-2s, but there has been no official comment on most of these accusations and the Communist countries have not been able to prove the charges. It is a known fact, however, that U-2s make regular reconnaissance flights over North Vietnam and furnish the Pentagon and White House with photographic evidence of enemy activity as well as bomb-damage evaluation of targets assigned United States aircraft.

On February 29, 1964, President Johnson announced at a White House news conference that an advanced experimental jet airplane capable of flying more than 2,000 miles an hour in sustained flight at an altitude of more than 70,000 feet had been developed. He said that its performance "far exceeds that of any other aircraft in the world today." The plane was initially designated the A-11 and later the YF-12, with the reconnaissance version known as the SR-71. Officials refused to elaborate on the details of the secret plane which like the U-2, was designed by Kelly Johnson at the Lockheed Aircraft Corporation's "Skunk Works." However, a photograph of the new plane revealed a long, rocketlike fuselage with the cockpit near the front and stablizing wings and rudder back near the engine exhaust. It carried a crew of two and some experts immediately decided that the main mission of the A-11 was as a long-range interceptor, one that could launch missiles to stop an enemy attack.

Later, however, it was learned that besides being designed by Kelly Johnson, the man who had developed the U-2, the A-11 also had engines designed and built by the same manufacturer, the Pratt and Whitney Aircraft Division of the United Aircraft Corporation, that had built the engines for the U-2. Putting two and two together, military observers came to the conclusion that the SR-71 version of the A-11 was a follow-up of the U-2. After it was revealed that the new aircraft could scan 60,000 square miles of the earth's surface per hour from an altitude of 80,000 feet, all doubts about the effectiveness of the SR-71 as the successor to the U-2 were erased. Officially, little is said about the SR-71 or its mission, but the all-black "rocket with wings" with its sophisticated observation equipment, electronic and photographic, watches the trouble spots of the world for the Strategic Air Command. There is ample evidence of its success.

The explosion of Red China's first nuclear bomb—and of subsequent bombs—came as no surprise to Washington. The United States experts were able to estimate the bomb's yield, the "dirt" in its fallout, and dozens of other key details the Chinese would have liked to keep secret. How did the United States obtain these important facts? Undoubtedly the answer is spy planes. Almost from the start of China's atomic project, pilots in reconnaissance planes spotted the distinctive nuclear factories on the mainland of China and the remote testing site near Lop Nor in Sinkiang Province near the Russian border. Whether the U.S. SR-71 overflies China or not has never been officially revealed, but ever since the Soviet Union stopped supplying the Red Chinese with the latest Russian missiles China has been almost helpless against high-flying photographic planes.

Months prior to China's first test the United States was aware that roads were being constructed deep in the Sinkiang Desert, that supply depots and houses were being built in the same area. Then, just before the first tests, Chinese weather stations went on the alert to monitor radioactive fallout; air traffic increased greatly; and radio communication volume nearly doubled. Reconnaissance pilots revealed this information to Washington just as they did the facts about the shock waves of the exploded bomb. These waves were recorded by sensitive electronic devices on their planes. Later, various reconnaissance aircraft of the United States gathered air samples over Asia and the Pacific Ocean. These samples were analyzed to determine the explosive fuel used in the bomb, its size, how it was made, and its design complexity. China didn't know any more about its own test than did the United States by the time the reconnaissance aircraft finished their missions.

Shortly after Russian surface-to-air missiles were installed around New Delhi, India, the Pentagon knew it. The missiles, the same as those given to North Vietnam and Cuba by the Soviet Union, were one of India's most closely guarded secrets, but Washington even knew how many of the SAM-2s were in position and exactly where. The reconnaissance planes also revealed that there were additional missiles at Ambala, the key Indian air force base 115 miles north of New Delhi, as well as between twenty and thirty Mig-21 fighter planes assembled by the Russians. The high-flying aircraft also reported that the Indians had established an unpublicized training program under Russian supervision at Baroda, five hundred miles south of New Delhi.

Late in 1967 Communist China equipped two of its largest submarines with missile launchers for nuclear weapons. Hardly had the Chinese finished the installation project than Washington knew that the submarines were at Dairen in southern Manchuria and that each sub had three vertical launching tubes capable of hurling missiles 380 miles—probably the nuclear-tipped missiles reconnaissance planes had revealed were tested successfully October 27, 1966. Once again there was no place to hide from the prying eyes of the aerial reconnaissance planes.

When the Soviet Union exploded a nuclear device in the

Semipalatinsky area of eastern Russia in violation of the test-ban treaty signed by Russia, the United States, and more than a hundred other nations, reconnaissance planes noted the blast and reported it to Washington. After the North Koreans captured the U.S. Navy intelligence ship *Pueblo*, U.S. reconnaissance aircraft kept track of the vessel. Washington knew immediately when it was moved from Wonsan Harbor to Chong Jin and revised plans accordingly. Perhaps the most important assignment of the reconnaissance planes was given them after a B-52 bomber carrying four nuclear weapons crashed in an ice field near Thule, Greenland. The crash created such adverse propaganda for the United States that then Defense Secretary Robert S. McNamara halted the Air Force's airborne alert program in which a small number of planes with nuclear weapons aboard were kept constantly in the air. This was a safeguard in case of a surprise attack by enemy planes or missiles. Once this program was stopped a new technique had to be developed to prevent surprise attacks. The details are supersecret but it is known that aerial reconnaissance plays a major role in the alert system. Washington is depending upon these planes and crews to provide instant reports of any launchings of missiles, long-range aircraft, or weapons from Russia's new fractional orbital bombardment system.

While these planes roam the world gathering intelligence, there is also a need for tactical reconnaissance to obtain up-to-the-minute information of immediate targets and enemy dispositions within a commander's striking distance. This type of aerial reconnaissance requires a different series of aircraft, different cameras, and, most of all, speed—not only speed in the air but speed in the delivery of the photographs to the technicians on the ground, their development and printing, and ultimate delivery to the ground, air, or naval commander who then makes his decisions based on the intelligence gained from the pictures.

Korea was the first important test for the newly developed tactical reconnaissance techniques and equipment. With the

United Nations ground forces greatly outnumbered, aerial reconnaissance was the one positive method by which the enemy's back yard could be studied. Not only were the photographs of vital importance to the U.N. ground-force commanders but the pictures allowed the Far East Air Forces to keep abreast of the Communist air order of battle, both within North Korea and at the Manchurian airfields on the opposite side of the Yalu River. Aerial reconnaissance permitted FEAF to bomb Communist airfields in Korea when they were reaching serviceable status, plot the changing locations of enemy antiaircraft batteries, plan airstrikes against North Korean targets using the photographs in air-objective folders, and assess the success or failure of bombing tactics and techniques.

Initially the FEAF reconnaissance aircraft operated against virtually no opposition over North Korea, but gradually the Communist air defenses took effect. When the fast, maneuverable Mig-15 appeared over North Korea the outdated RF-80A reconnaissance plane that United States pilots had been using became outclassed. It was more than 200 miles an hour slower than the Mig and much less maneuverable. Flak defenses also increased greatly and added to the hazards the reconnaissance fliers faced over enemy territory. In an effort to equip the tactical reconnaissance units with a more efficient aircraft, the RF-84, a swept-wing version of the Thunderjet fighter, was scheduled to replace the RF-80A, but for various reasons these planes were never readied in time to see action during the Korean conflict. Instead, the RF-86A was introduced. A camera was mounted parallel to the longitudinal axis of the Sabre with a mirror arrangment to secure vertical coverage of enemy target areas. While this unique arrangement didn't produce the quality of pictures desired, the RF-86A was able to penetrate Mig alley with a minimum loss rate.

RB-26s were used for night reconnaissance missions but they, too, met obstacles not anticipated by those who had organized tactical reconnaissance techniques during the peacetime years between the end of World War II and the beginning of the

Korean War. These night missions were usually route surveillance sorties that normally included photography of briefed objectives along the route. In order to accomplish such missions successfully it was necessary to have very precise navigation and the artificial illumination carried aboard the RB-26 had to be reliable. Unfortunately neither of these requirements was met. The cartridge-ejection illumination system which used A-14 magazines and M-112 flash cartridges was used initially but proved troublesome and inefficient. Another basic defect in the night-reconnaissance procedure was that planes using the flash equipment available had to fly at 3,000-foot altitudes, which was not high enough to be safe from mountains or enemy antiaircraft fire.

Before the reconnaissance crews could photograph their objectives at night they had to locate them, and it soon became apparent that the navigational equipment available was not accurate enough. The shoran receivers could not pick up the beams at the altitude their flash equipment forced them to maintain. As a result the RB-26 crews were forced to operate at the dangerous low altitude without proper navigation capability and the effectiveness of the missions was limited.

Despite these handicaps, the reconnaissance record of the Korean War far outstripped the reconnaissance performance during World War II. The highest number of sorties flown in one month during World War II was 1,300, while during the Korean War the record was raised to 2,400. The average sortie rate per month in the earlier conflict was 604, but in the Korean War it was 1,792. Three times as many negatives were produced during the Korean conflict. These statistics give the impression that all reconnaissance requirements were met during the years of war with the North Koreans and Chinese, but this was not the case. In fact, the Eighth Army contended that only 75 percent of its requests for photographs were filled. Representatives from this unit warned that in future wars at least 5,000 negatives a day would be required by ground commanders.

Once the battles came to an end in Korea, however, this warning was promptly forgotten and aerial reconnaissance was neglected in the military budget and on the planning boards. Not until 1962 did tactical reconnaissance become of primary importance to the national security once again. When intelligence sources received information that the Soviet Union had positioned medium-range missiles in Cuba, tactical reconnaissance pilots were immediately assigned the task of providing the evidence. Covering the island with both high- and low-altitude reconnaissance flights, these fliers brought back thousands of photographs—over 30,000 feet of film in all. These aerial pictures proved beyond a doubt that the rockets were in Cuba, that ingenious launchers to pick the rockets off the loading trailers were in large supply, and that Russian crews were manning the missile sites.

After President Kennedy signed the proclamation that put the quarantine of Cuba into effect, reconnaissance planes spotted incoming ships and notified the U.S. Navy. Later, after the Soviet Union agreed to remove the missiles, it was the reconnaissance aircraft that kept a continuous aerial watch on the island and verified that the missile sites were being dismantled. After the crisis had passed President Kennedy stated, "The camera, I think, is going to be our best inspector."

At the conclusion of the Cuban crisis, the Air Force quickly recognized the need for a central agency designed to keep the reconnaissance forces fully prepared and updated to meet the demands of the military forces. The Tactical Air Reconnaissance Center at Shaw AFB, South Carolina, was founded on this idea on February 8, 1963. The TARC does the testing and evaluation of tactical air reconnaissance equipment and systems. It develops and field-tests new policies, doctrines, organizations, tactics, and techniques. Many of the center's projects are aimed at future reconnaissance capabilities but the immediate needs of the conflict in Southeast Asia hold first priority.

Aerial reconnaissance missions over the seven segments of

North Vietnam into which the Military Assistance Command, Vietnam, has divided the enemy territory are the most hazardous of any air tasks in Southeast Asia. North Vietnam's defenses are more concentrated and far more sophisticated than those encountered by any air forces in World War II or in Korea. To combat these defenses, the United States reconnaissance equipment and procedures are constantly being updated. Photo cameras, infrared cameras, and side-looking radar are all installed on the RF-4C. Night missions are especially dangerous. When reconnaissance crews tried to use flash cartridges in the Hanoi area at night their planes were immediately silhouetted and the loss rate was much too high. Consequently they switched to infrared cameras and obtained the necessary pictures, thanks to the testing and evaluation of this camera at the TARC. "Real" time is getting closer and closer. This term, which means different things to different people, can be explained briefly as the time it takes for the intelligence information gathered by the aerial reconnaissance crew to reach the hands of the "customer." Some forms of tactical reconnaissance may take a number of hours between the time the scene is recorded and a detailed analysis is accomplished by a trained interpreter. However, in Vietnam the air doctrine provides for near "real" time by the use of recording sensors. The pilot can make an initial visual airborne report. Then, while the photo interpreter is developing the pictures after the pilot lands, there are provisions for a voice "flash" report by the interpreter made from wet negatives to speed up the time cycle of tactical reconnaissance. Also in use are aerial developers, which develop the photographs while the plane is still in the air; the pilot then drops a cassette with the pictures in it to a ground commander. There is no question that the aerial surveillance in Southeast Asia is the most sustained and highly sophisticated system in military history.

The detailed information that can be obtained by aerial reconnaissance touches the lives of every citizen of the United

States. There is no place to hide from the aerial camera. From 40,000 feet one plane can photograph a strip 490 miles wide and 2,700 miles long—from Los Angeles to New York—in less than four hours. An analyst, studying this strip of film, could state with surprising accuracy what the relative economic status of citizens in any certain area is; could describe the construction of the houses; tell the relative age of the community; and say whether any certain home had a telephone or not. He could reveal whether the homeowner used a rotary or reel-type lawnmower to cut his grass and whether he had an underground septic tank; he could describe the items of apparel hanging from a clothesline in the back yard. Some pilots have even photographed—in detail—sunbathers who think they are completely concealed from prying eyes because they have a high fence around their property. There are no secrets from the aerial camera.

Russia, too, maintains an extensive aerial surveillance program. Soviet TU-16 Badger medium bombers with photographic and electronic sensors fly near, and sometimes over, Point Barrow, Alaska. There have been unpublicized Soviet overflights of the United States although Washington refuses to verify the fact. Russian reconnaissance planes constantly spy on U.S. Navy ships on the open sea. On May 25, 1968, a TU-16 Badger made four passes over the U.S. aircraft carrier *Essex* in the North Sea, and on the last pass the Soviet pilot was so low that when he attempted to bank away from the ship his wingtip hit the water and the aircraft crashed. Russia did not protest the "incident" since to do so would be to admit the spying. The Russians frequently have protested U.S. overflights while insisting they never engage in such operations themselves.

The incidents will continue. Aerial surveillance and electronic eavesdropping will continue as long as the cold war goes on and hot wars erupt in various parts of the world. No nation can dispense with it without taking a very long gamble with the lives of its citizens.

2

Balloons and Biplanes

EARLY in history reconnaissance was limited to the ground and was usually carried out by a lone scout on foot. In June 1793, however, with nearly all of Europe united against it, the French republican government added an "air arm" to its military might. This revolutionary organization consisted of captive balloons from which observers high in the air scouted the movements of the enemy. Colonel Jean-Marie-Joseph Countelle, the first commander of the French air arm, made his initial ascent at Maubeuge on June 2, 1794, and his ability to observe enemy movements northeast of the city permitted the French forces to win the battle in that area. Immediately, a second company of balloonists was formed and Napoleon himself became a staunch supporter of aerial observation. He sent balloonists to Italy in 1797 and to Egypt in 1789 to help his military forces.

After the development of the camera it was only a matter of time until human observation from the air was replaced by the lens. History shows that in 1849 Colonel Aimé Lassudat, an officer in the French Corps of Engineers, began experimenting with aerial photography as a means of preparing topographic maps. His experiments included attempts to use glass plates suspended from kites. Another Frenchman, Gaspard Félix Tourchon, is credited with taking the first successful aerial photographs from a balloon. He wrote a letter to the military explaining his views on the new type of reconnaissance: "The village belfry from which the officers of the General Staff can made observations is of great strategic importance to the commanding general. I have such a belfry at any point and thanks to my photographic apparatus I am in a position to send to the General Staff the most trustworthy intelligence every fifteen minutes in the form of a positive."

Tourchon proved his point in 1858 by using a balloon to photograph a village from an altitude of 250 feet.

In Russia, aerial photography was introduced after Kovanko, commander of a balloon crew, took aerial photos of the Kronstadt and Petersburg fortresses. Since Kronstadt is an island and Petersburg a port, Kovanko is credited with the first naval aerial reconnaissance. Later the Russians developed further balloon-camera techniques in the Russo-Japanese War of 1905 and used them successfully.

The first official attempt to use balloons for military reconnaissance in the United States was during the Seminole Indian War in 1840. Colonel John H. Sherburne was dispatched by the U.S. government to Florida to transfer the Seminole Indians from their homeland to a reservation in the West. The Indians weren't in favor of the move and promptly hid in the Florida swamps where for five years they evaded the troops. Sherburne wrote to Secretary of War Joel Poinsett suggesting that each column of infantry be equipped with a hot-air balloon to be used for aerial observation. He explained that observers could ascend in the balloons at night, mark down the location of enemy campfires, and by detailed plotting and triangulation of these locations the positions of the Seminoles could be established. Troops could then surround the Indians and surprise them.

Sherburne, while waiting for official authorization, contacted balloonist Charles Ferson Durant, known as "the first professional American aeronaut." Durant offered to sell the colonel a used balloon for $600 and make a new one for $900. The official authorization for use of the balloons in the Seminole Indian War never came, however. The U.S. Army commander in Florida, General W. K. Armistead, rejected the idea and the first attempt to use aerial reconnaissance in a military operation in the United States was dropped.

Five years later, during the Mexican War, a Pennsylvania balloonist by the name of John C. Wise offered to ascend in a balloon to observe and, if necessary, bomb Mexico City. The War Department never answered his letter and General Winfield Scott successfully attacked the fortress guarding Mexico City by land, unaware of the idea proposed by Wise.

The Civil War was the first time that aerial reconnaissance for military purposes was actually used. Within hours after the rebellion began, many of the best-known balloonists of the day offered their services. One of these was John Allen, who had had four years of balloon experience prior to the Civil War. He was a member of the Rhode Island 1st Regiment and was convinced that the military commander with the best reconnaissance had an advantage over the enemy forces opposing him. Taking two of his balloons, Allen and his helpers went to Washington on April 19, 1861, and contacted the U.S. Army. After convincing the military that he could be of service, he was ordered to make a reconnaissance flight south of the Capitol. Allen, Henry L. Abbot of the Topographic Engineers, and several others tried to launch the balloon but a strong gust of wind slammed it into a telegraph pole. There was a tearing sound and moments later the balloon sagged to the ground ruined. The military ignored Allen after that initial attempt and he returned home discouraged.

John Wise, the Pennsylvania balloonist who had wanted to help during the Mexican War, was ordered into Federal service as a military balloonist on July 1, 1861. At a cost of $850 he and his son constructed a balloon of India raw silk. One unique feature of the new aerial vehicle was a thick sheet of iron on the bottom of the wicker basket to protect the observer from enemy ground fire, the first known use of armor plate for lighter-than-air craft. On July 19 General McDowell prepared to engage the Confederate forces at Manassas. Wise was ordered to be at the general's headquarters ready for duty with his balloon by dawn of the twentieth. Unfortunately, the orders didn't reach him in time and Wise didn't even start for the front lines until the morning of the twenty-first. With helpers who knew very little about handling a delicate balloon, Wise supervised the movement of the craft to Georgetown, up the Chesapeake and Ohio Canal, and across the Potomac River to Fairfax Road. There, Major Albert J. Meyer, chief signal officer, was waiting impatiently for the arrival of Wise and his balloon. The major ordered the balloon tied to an army wagon as soon as Wise arrived and then whipped the horses to a gallop. Despite Wise's pleas for him to stop, the major continued whipping the horses until they were racing at full speed. The balloon swung back and forth across the road and finally slammed into a tree. A long gash was ripped in its side and the gas escaped. That was the end of Wise's first attempt at aerial reconnaissance.

A second try was made several days later after the balloon was repaired. Wise ascended high enough in his balloon to spot numerous Confederate detachments scouting Union lines and reported enemy artillery pieces being positioned about three miles distant. General McDowell quickly realized the importance of aerial reconnaissance and ordered Wise to be at Ball's Cross Road outside Washington at dawn the morning of July 25. This time Wise wasn't so fortunate. A stiff breeze blew his balloon into some nearby trees and telegraph wires sliced into his tow ropes. As the balloon floated free and headed for the Confederate lines, the Pennsylvanian ordered it shot down. Major Amiel W. Whipple, chief of the Topographic Engineers, rebuked Wise angrily and at length. Dejected and bitter, Wise returned home.

John La Mountain was another balloonist who offered his services and equipment to the Union Army. One day after John Wise quit, La Mountain made his first ascent for the army at Fortress Monroe in his balloon which he had named the *Atlantic*. During the following fifteen days he made five additional ascents but little information was obtained during the flights. During August 1961, it was decided to have La Mountain operate from a transport ship anchored off Hampton Roads. On his initial mission from the ship the balloonist spotted a heavy concentration of artillery and gun emplacements aimed directly at Fortress Monroe. The guns were quickly captured and La Mountain's prestige climbed rapidly. During a night ascent from another ship La Mountain gave an accurate estimate of the enemy troops in the area by counting the number of campfires visible from his balloon.

Despite the success of his aerial reconnaissance missions La Mountain wasn't satisfied. He wanted to make some free ascents instead of always having his balloon tethered to the ground or a ship. Finally in the fall of 1861 he was attached to the headquarters of Brigadier General W. B. Franklin, who gave him permission to attempt free flights. Several times the daring La Mountain ascended in his balloon, permitted the wind to drift him over the Confederate lines where he would sketch the scene below, then throw out some ballast, climb to where the wind would blow him back to friendly lines, and land. On November 16, however, a high wind broke the ropes mooring his balloon and it disappeared. Without a balloon and unable to get another one he was forced to halt his reconnaissance flights.

Before he gave up entirely, La Mountain tried to get his military superiors to borrow a balloon from Thaddeus S. C. Lowe but Lowe refused. Lowe and La Mountain, two of the best-known balloonists at the time of the Civil War, had disagreed earlier over the use of balloons and Lowe flatly refused to permit La Mountain to fly one of his balloons. Lowe was undoubtedly the most successful of the Civil War balloonists and many of his ideas formed the basis for later aerial reconnaissance developments. He was a flamboyant showman with a scientific education and many important contacts in Washington. He had started making aerial flights in 1860 when he built a balloon and announced that he was going to fly the Atlantic Ocean. The following year, just a week after the Civil War began, Lowe decided to make a practice flight in preparation for his proposed Atlantic crossing. The takeoff point was Cincinnati but unfortunately for Lowe a strong wind was blowing and he drifted eastward at full speed; also unfortunate was the fact that he carried several copies of the Cincinnati *Commercial*, a morning newspaper. He took the newspapers along to verify that he had taken off from Cincinnati that morning, not taking into consideration that there was a war being fought and that he might land in southern territory. He did just that. Nine hours after lift-off his balloon settled to the ground outside Unionville, South Carolina, where a group of whites and their slaves took one look at the northern newspapers and rushed him off to the Unionville jail as a spy. Fortunately for Lowe, just about the time the mob started talking lynching, some faculty members of South Carolina College recognized him. He was quickly released and given safe conduct back through the Confederate lines to Cincinnati.

Lowe's experience started him thinking about using his balloon for aerial reconnaissance and on June 6, 1861, he was in Washington offering his services to the War Department. President Abraham Lincoln was intrigued with the idea and authorized the Secretary of War to allot Lowe $250 for expenses involved in a demonstration for the military forces. Twelve days later Lowe ascended to 500 feet in his balloon *Enterprise,* taking with him in the basket an official of the telegraph company and an operator. At an altitude of 500 feet he had the operator relay a message to the ground, the first time an electrically transmitted message was ever sent from an aerial vehicle. From the air Lowe sent the following telegram to the White House:

Balloon Enterprise, Washington, D.C. June 18, 1861.
To the President of the United States
Sir: This point of observation commands an area of nearly 50 miles in diameter. The city with its girdle of encampments presents a superb scene. I have pleasure in sending you this first dispatch ever telegraphed from an aerial station and acknowledge indebtedness for your encouragement for the opportunity of demonstrating the availability of the science of aeronautics in the service of the country.

T. S. C. Lowe

Lincoln was delighted with the demonstration and immediately sent Lowe to General Winfield Scott, the senior Union Army general. Unfortunately, Scott scoffed at the idea and repeatedly ignored Lowe. It wasn't until Lincoln went with Lowe to the general's office and insisted that he be given a chance to use his balloon on a reconnaissance flight that Scott finally relented. Lowe made his initial reconnaissance ascension for the Union Army on August 29, 1861.

Lowe's contributions to the Union forces were substantial and set the pattern for aerial reconnaissance flights in World War I and World War II. He learned to ascend in his balloon, watch the puffs of smoke as the Union Army artillery shells exploded behind enemy lines, and telegraph the battery commander what corrections were necessary to hit the target. This was the first time that artillery had ever been directed from the air. His missions in August and September of 1861 were so successful that the quartermaster general, General Montgomery C. Meigs, ordered Lowe to construct four additional balloons. Lowe also added some new aeronauts to his staff and the Balloon Corps of the Potomac was established.

By New Year's Day, 1862, the newly established corps had seven balloons in its inventory. General Hooker had aeronaut William Paullin attached to his unit; balloonist John B. Starkweather accompanied General Sherman into battle; and a German aeronaut, John H. Steiner, was assigned to General John Pope's Army of the Mississippi. Lowe remained in the Washington area with General Fitz John Porter, a corps commander for

Major General George B. McClellan. The extra balloons were used wherever needed.

General Porter was extremely enthusiastic about the importance of aerial reconnaissance, so enthusiastic that it nearly cost him his life. Porter often flew with Lowe as an observer but he was always so intent on scouting enemy positions and gun emplacements that he never learned how to maneuver and control the balloon. Early one morning in April 1862, he led his corps to the outskirts of Yorktown and wanted to see what lay ahead of his men if they advanced farther. Hurrying to Lowe's camp just before daylight, he spotted a balloon already inflated. Since it appeared ready for ascent and was well tethered, the general leaped into the basket and yelled for the ground crew to let out the ropes.

Unfortunately for Porter the moorings had not been checked. When the balloon, with the general in it, reached an altitude of 50 feet, the single rope tying it to the ground snapped. Suddenly Porter found himself in free flight drifting straight toward the enemy lines. As soon as the Confederate soldiers spotted the drifting Union balloon they started using it—and Porter—for a target. The only fact about balloon flying that the general remembered was that the more ballast he got rid of the higher he would go, so, wanting to get away from the enemy guns, he tossed half of his sandbags overboard. Safely out of range of the Confederate guns, Porter calmly took out his long black spyglass and started jotting down the positions of the enemy troops.

When he completed his reconnaissance to his satisfaction, the general continued to do the only thing he knew to do when in a balloon. He tossed out the remaining sandbags. It was one of the best moves he ever made during his long, successful career. The balloon promptly climbed to a higher altitude where luck was with the general. A westerly wind slowly drifted him back to the Union lines where Lowe, using a megaphone, yelled for him to release some of the gas. Porter released too much and made a rough landing but was uninjured. He calmly stepped from the basket, nodded to the excited Lowe, and went back to his headquarters where he sketched what he had seen during his wild balloon ride.

All together Lowe made over three thousand flights and spent several hundred hours in the air on reconnaissance missions during the Civil War. Perhaps his greatest feat of aerial reconnaissance occurred on May 31, 1862, during the Battle of Fair Oaks. At noon on that day Lowe ascended in his balloon to check the surrounding area. He immediately saw wagon trains of equipment and large numbers of Confederate troops moving from Richmond toward Fair Oaks. By two o'clock he had determined that the enemy was marching to attack the Union troops under Heintzelman on the right bank of the Chickahominy River before the completion of a temporary bridge that would permit reinforcements to cross. General Heintzelman's army would be destroyed if this happened.

Lowe reported what he had seen to General McClellan. The general sent additional men to help complete the bridge, and just before the Confederate forces arrived additional Union troops crossed the river to support the men with General Heintzelman. Lowe was credited with saving the Union forces from a tragic defeat.

Lowe advanced aerial reconnaissance to a niche in the military that it had never reached before but, sadly, the Balloon Corps of the Potomac didn't remain as a permanent organization. From the very moment of its conception, the corps was plagued with troubles that would have made a less determined "Chief Aeronaut" than Lowe quit. There was never enough equipment or men or supplies or money. Most of the time Lowe had to pay for supplies and services with his own money and then fight for weeks to get a refund from Washington. Many of the Union generals remained unconvinced that aerial reconnaissance was of any value and ignored Lowe's plea for men and equipment. Even Porter and McClellan, two of the strongest backers of the Balloon Corps, were often discouraged because of the time lag between their orders for Lowe to make a reconnaissance flight and the time they received information from him. The same complaint is still heard in the twentieth century, although the lag is measured in minutes now.

Between June 1861 and June 1863 the corps was under three different commands: the Topographic Engineers, the Quartermaster Corps, and the Corps of Engineers. When the chief engineer of the Army of the Potomac reduced Lowe's pay from $10 a day to $6 Lowe decided he had had enough. He stayed on until early May 1863, then left the scene. That was the end of the U.S. Army's first aerial reconnaissance organization. Lowe left his imprint on the military with his brilliant innovations. He had proved that messages could be sent by telegraph from a balloon; devised a calcium light that could be used at night without being spotted by the enemy; developed a signal system of phosphorescent balloons; introduced aerial artillery-fire adjustment; used a barge on the Potomac River to launch his balloon from over water; used a camera successfully from a balloon; and perfected an enlarger that the famous photographer Matthew Brady used to blow up aerial photographs from three inches to twenty feet.

Despite Lowe's experimental use of a camera from a balloon during the Civil War, most of his intelligence from the air was gained by visual observation. Cameras were just reaching the reliable stage during these years. J. W. Black, a Rhode Island photographer, successfully photographed Boston from a balloon at an altitude of 1,200 feet in 1860 and proved that under ideal conditions pictures could be taken from a balloon. In 1862 a Union Army balloon photographed on one plate all the countryside between Richmond and Manchester to the west and the Chickahominy to the east. However, by far the largest amount of reconnaissance information gathered during the Civil War was done by the human eye.

England, France, Germany, Spain, Russia, Italy, and Japan established balloon corps for their military forces during the years immediately after the Civil War, but the United States made no move to do so after Lowe resigned from the Army. The balloon reverted back to the "country fair" status during these years and in all probability would have been completely ignored in the military if it had not been for one man—Adolphus V. Greely.

When Lowe was making his spectacular reconnaissance flights during the Civil War, Greely was a teen-age enlisted soldier. He managed to survive the fighting, rising to the rank of a brevet major, and when the war ended he accepted a commission in the regular army. In 1891, after an expedition to the Arctic which made him famous and many other assignments, he was appointed chief signal officer of the Army. Greely was by then a brigadier general with enough authority to do what he had been wanting to do for several years—investigate the potentials of aeronautics.

He sent a staff officer, Lieutenant William A. Glassford, to France on a twofold mission: to study the latest balloon developments and to buy a balloon for the Signal Corps. Glassford did both and after his return to the U.S. in 1892 established an air arm for the Signal Corps, exhibiting his one-balloon force during the Chicago World's Fair. William Ivy, a famous balloonist, was his pilot. During some of the numerous flights made at the fair, Glassford used a telephone to communicate with the ground, the first time such a device was used from the air.

Ivy and Glassford were still the sole members of the air arm on February 15, 1898, when the battleship *Maine* exploded in Havana Harbor. By this time the balloon Glassford had brought from France was no more, and Ivy was using one he and his wife had constructed of silk. As soon as hostilities started in Cuba between Spain and the United States the balloon was sent to Cuba. Ivy, Lieutenant Colonel Joseph E. Maxfield, Lieutenant Colonel George M. Derby, Lieutenant W. J. Volkman, and General Castillo of the Cuban Army took turns making reconnaissance flights in the silk balloon.

When General William Shafter planned to attack San Juan Hill he asked Derby and Maxfield to go up in the balloon and look the situation over. Early on the morning of the famous battle, after the fighting had already begun, the pair ascended; but the daring Derby decided they were too far away from the battle scene to do any effective reconnoitering. He moved the balloon to within 600 yards of the Spanish barricades and went up again. This time Derby spotted a new trail leading up San Juan Hill which General Shafter used to send up a second force to reinforce his initial group of attackers. Maxfield and Derby also corrected the aim of the artillery guns on El Pozo Hill against the Spanish positions on San Juan Hill. Many military experts credit the American victory to these two men in the reconnaissance balloon.

The use of the balloon for aerial reconnaissance during the Spanish-American War was the final gasp of the gas bags for the United States as far as military use was concerned. Within four years Wilbur and Orville Wright achieved the first successful airplane flight and though it lasted a mere twelve seconds it ushered in the heavier-than-air era of flight. The United States, however, was extremely slow to take advantage of the Wright brothers' development. Great Britain and France both were negotiating with the Wrights for their plane when President Theodore Roosevelt intervened and ordered the Secretary of War, William H. Taft, to investigate the possibilities of the new aircraft. Taft called for bids for an airplane that could carry two persons at a speed of at least 40 miles an hour for 125 miles. In 1909, after being delayed by a crash in 1908, the Wright brothers' aircraft was accepted by the War Department as "Airplane No. 1, Heavier-Than-Air Division, United States Aerial Fleet."

By 1911 the Signal Corps had established a flying school at College Park, Maryland, and one of the courses fostered at the new school was aerial photography. This was instigated by the fact that in January of that year the first shots from a powered airplane had been taken over San Diego, California, by Major H. A. Erickson. The plane had been piloted by Charles Kenney Hamilton. The pictures were very good and high-ranking military officers immediately saw the advantage of using the newly developed airplane for reconnaissance photography.

Use of the aerial camera lagged, however, and most reconnaissance was accomplished by the pilot's sharp eyes on flights over suspect territory. Lieutenant Benjamin D. Foulois, the pioneer military pilot, made a number of reconnaissance flights during February and March 1911. The first official military reconnaissance flight in an airplane was made by Foulois on March 3, 1911, in a Collier Wright-B plane. The flight was accomplished in conjunction with the exercises of the newly formed Army Maneuver Division on the Mexican border. Foulois was ordered to reconnoiter along the Rio Grande River from Laredo to Eagle Pass, a distance of about 110 miles, and look for "enemy" troops. With Phil O. Parmalee as observer, he completed the flight in two hours and ten minutes at an average altitude of 1,200 feet, but they didn't spot the enemy. However, the reconnaissance flight was considered a success, mainly because the trip was completed without a forced landing or an accident and because Foulois and Parmalee, by carrying aloft a total weight of 1,400 pounds, established an American record for weight and distance.

On subsequent flights along the border during the maneuvers, Foulois had a small radio installed in his plane so that he could communicate with Signal Corps stations along the route. With the radio he could send position reports and also indicate any enemy activity he saw from the air. While this was not the first time radio communication had been accomplished from an aircraft in flight, it was the first practical use of radio and was the beginning of the development of airborne radio communication for military aircraft.

Because the reconnaissance missions failed to reveal the expected information about the enemy troops, those officers who opposed military flying because they thought it impractical were elated with the results. The next year, however, Foulois was ordered to take part in Army field exercises in Connecticut, and this time it was a different situation. The pilots and their observers operated first with the Red Forces and then with the Blue, and in each case were able to give the force to which they were attached a decided reconnaissance advantage over the other. They proved that aerial reconnaissance could prevent surprise mass attacks by providing information on enemy troop buildups and movements much faster than it had ever before been available.

By 1913 the Signal Corps had a total of eleven planes and was making use of them in various ways. In November of that year, Lieutenant Henry H. "Hap" Arnold, later to become the first general of the Air Force, directed artillery fire from an airplane for the first time in history. He also set an Army altitude record of 4,674 feet. Captain Paul Beck managed to keep his plane in the air for four hours and twenty-three minutes, an unofficial endurance record. That same year political unrest in Mexico led to serious border fights and threatened the peace between that country and the United States. However, it wasn't until three years later, on the night of March 9, 1916, that Pancho Villa led a force of about a thousand men across the Mexican border and raided Columbus, New Mexico. The following day President Woodrow Wilson ordered Brigadier General John J. Pershing into Mexico to assist the Mexican government in tracking down Villa. That same day Secretary of War Newton D. Baker instructed Pershing "to make all practical use of the aeroplane for observation."

The orders directing the 1st Aero Squadron, Benjamin D. Foulois commanding, to join Pershing at Columbus, New Mexico, arrived on the afternoon of March 12. Foulois had his unit ready for action at New Mexico three days later and on that same day made the first reconnaissance flight. He and Captain Townsend flew thirty miles into Mexico searching for Pancho Villa and his men but saw no sign of them. This was the first aerial reconnaissance flight by a United States military airplane over foreign territory.

The work of the 1st Aero Squadron during the search for Villa was important not because of any outstanding reconnaissance achievements but because it clearly illustrated to the nation the great need for new aviation equipment to accomplish an important task. The pilots, flying inadequate machines, did a great amount of scouting over country in which cavalry and infantry could not operate and took many aerial photographs using a Gem camera manufactured by the Gem Engineering Company of Philadelphia, Pennsylvania. The missions accomplished by the 1st Aero Squadron proved to the skeptics that aviation was out of the experimental and freakish phase, that it was a military tool to be used to great advantage. On August 29, 1916, largely because of the fine work of the unit in Mexico, Congress appropriated the first large sum of money ever voted in the United States for aviation—$13,281,666.

Unfortunately, on the eve of America's entrance into World War I, Foulois and his Signal Corps Aviation Section still had only thirty-five rated pilots and fewer than three hundred aircraft, including training planes.

3

World War I Aerial Spies

WHEN hostilities opened in Europe in 1914, aerial reconnaissance and the airplane began to prove their true value. The United States, however, still lagged far behind the European countries even though the opening months of World War I illustrated to those interested the importance of air power. While Germany was allocating $28,000,000 for military aeronautics in 1914, the U.S. Congress appropriated a mere $350,000.

"Why give more to develop a ridiculous contraption which will only be of minor use for reconnaissance," one congressman snorted.

Even the high brass of the U.S. military had reservations about the expansion of the air arm. They found many of the aviators too outspoken and brash in their statements about the old and established conventional military customs. The same characteristics that made the fliers so outstanding and daring in later years worked against them during the early struggle for a strong military air service. The trait that produced great combat pilots—eagerness to fight—caused disagreement, dissension, and dissatisfaction in the U.S. Army.

Fortunately, as the feats of men such as Germany's Red

Knight, Baron Manfred von Richthofen, French ace René Fonck, British fliers Edward Mannock and William Bishop, and Belgian fighter pilot Willy Coppens became known to the public, pressure began to build up in the U.S. for an equally strong air service to produce American aviators of equal ability. Congress, with its back to the wall, finally opened its purse strings in August 1916 and provided the then huge sum of $13,281,666 for military aeronautics. With this money Army aviation began to expand. A new school to train military pilots was opened at Essington, Pennsylvania. At Mineola, New York, officers of the reserve and National Guard were taught flying. Some Army officers such as Major William Mitchell, assistant chief of the Aviation Section, even paid for their own training. Mitchell commuted weekends from Washington to the Curtiss school at Newport News, Virginia.

In 1916, too, the War Department authorized seven more aero squadrons of twelve planes each—four for continental United States and three for deployment overseas. The old 1st Aero Squadron, which had had a near-fiasco in Mexico, the 3d, 4th, and 5th were to remain in the country while the 2d Aero Squadron was to be stationed in the Phillipines, the 6th in Hawaii, and the 7th in Panama.

Despite these grandiose plans, however, the Aviation Section had only 131 pilots and student pilots and 1,087 enlisted men when the United States entered the war in April 1917. Perhaps the most embarrassing fact was the complete lack of knowledge about combat tactics and techniques. When the United States declared war on Germany only one important air officer was in Europe studying the air arms of the other Allied countries and the strength of the enemy, and that was Colonel William Mitchell, one of the earliest advocates of air power. With few men and no combat planes, the American Air Service*

* This name, used to describe the air arm of the A.E.F. during World War I, became the official designation of the air wing of the U.S. Army with the Army Reorganization Act of 1920.

was not ready to fight the more experienced Germans but there was no choice.

Despite the more romantic interest of the public in the feats of the air aces during the early years of World War I, reconnaissance was the most important function of the military air arm. Military leaders no longer had to rely on the limited view from the "high ground." Observation balloons, which had provided valuable information during the Civil War and the Spanish-America War, were too vulnerable to enemy aircraft in World War I. Slow, stable aircraft from which pilots could photograph and study the terrain below were in demand, just the opposite from the demands for reconnaissance aircraft today. The German High Command actually restricted production of speedier planes at the beginning of the war because such aircraft hampered good camera work. At first few of the reconnaissance planes were equipped with guns. Consequently when Allied reconnaissance fliers met German reconnaissance pilots in the air they usually waved at each other and went about their assignments unhampered. As the war continued, however, the British, French, Germans, and Americans realized that aerial intelligence was actually changing the course of the war, dictating tactics, and affecting planning. When they came to understand the immense value of these daily unarmed flights, each side became determined to stop the other. As a result, pilots on both sides began carrying everything from pistols to machine guns to prevent the enemy from gathering such vital information. This was the beginning of the "fighter pilot."

Photographs taken from the air were not new at the opening of World War I but it was during this period that aerial camera work had its principal development. In 1893 U.S. Patent 510758 was taken out by an American named Adams for a method of making maps from aerial photographs from a balloon. By 1911 the eight-lens Scheimpflug-Kammerer camera was in use by German army balloonists. Oblique and vertical photographs both became common. Oblique photographs were made with the axis of the lens inclined to the surface of the earth while the vertical pictures were taken with the lens at right angles to the earth's surface. Both types of photographs presented problems for the pioneer aerial cameramen and pilots. Some of the fliers strapped their cameras to their bodies and leaned out into the freezing airstream to get their pictures. Others cut a hole in the bottom of the cockpit, aimed the lens of the camera through the opening, and snapped the shutter. Later, some of the more inventive pilots and aerial cameramen devised a mount on the side of the cockpit to which they attached the camera. Using trunion brackets and universal joints, they were able to swing the camera in all directions. While this eliminated the tiresome job of hand-holding the heavy camera, the fliers soon discovered that the vibration of the aircraft ruined most of their pictures. This problem was solved by one ingenious cameraman when he cut an inner tube into pieces and installed them under the mount to help dampen the vibration. Later more suitable rubber cushions were manufactured for this purpose.

A camera was developed that had one lens in a vertical position while several other lenses clustered around it were aimed at oblique angles to cover a wide area. Another company constructed a multiple-lens camera that used prisms or mirrors to reach out in all directions from the vertical. These multiple-lens cameras weighed as much as 600 pounds and had to be mounted. Some of the single-lens cameras, however, weighed only 55 pounds and could be held by hand if necessary.

Unlike today, during World War I the pictures were taken not by the pilot but by an observer. The complicated but excellent remote-control units and automatic-sequence devices that can be operated by the pilot in today's RF-101 or RF-4C were still far in the future in 1917–18. Consequently the two-man crew of the reconnaissance aircraft required a great deal of training before they could work together as a team.

The reconnaissance pilot, after being accepted for duty in the Air Service, was sent to ground school set up at eight large engineering colleges. These schools—Massachusetts Institute of Technology, Cornell University, Ohio State University, University of Illinois, University of Texas, University of California, Princeton University, and Georgia School of Technology—had an eight-week curriculum at the start but later increased it to twelve. The students were instructed in theory of flight, principles of radio, code, aerial photography, meteorology, map reading, and aerial tactics.

Next, the pilots were sent to one of eighteen flying fields for their actual flight training. Some of these fields, such as Chanute, Selfridge, Kelly, and Scott, are still famous today. The future reconnaissance pilot received from four to nine hours of dual flying, followed by approximately twenty-four hours of solo time. After a 60-mile cross-country flight and an altitude test at 10,000 feet, he received his wings.

Aerial observers who did most of the camera work received comparable training in their specialty. The observer took a four-week course and was required to send and receive eight words a minute by radio, take at least a dozen good aerial photographs, and locate and direct artillery fire against enemy batteries.

Once an observer and a reconnaissance pilot were brought together teamwork became essential. Before taking off on a mission they had to discuss in detail what they were going to photograph and how they were going to do it. It was one thing to practice over the suburbs of Paris where many a feminine sunbather had her picture taken from the air, much to her embarrassment, and another to photograph enemy trenches while under attack by German aircraft and guns on the ground. Beginners usually made the mistake of taking their pictures at too high an altitude. Experience proved that good oblique shots had to be taken at 1,500 feet or less and at this height any good enemy marksman could hit the aircraft.

Most observers wanted to take pictures with their cameras pointing nearly into the tail of the plane. This meant that the pilot had to fly over the target to be photographed at a constant altitude and maintain a predetermined airspeed and course. In most cases interphones were not available so other signals had to be devised by the reconnaissance team. Usually the pilot would move his control stick from side to side rapidly, rocking the aircraft to notify the cameraman to get ready. Once this signal was received, the observer checked to make sure his camera was all set, aimed it toward the tail, and the pilot flew over the target. In some aircraft the technique had to be altered because of severe vibration. If the plane was in poor condition and the observer indicated that he could not get sharp pictures because of excessive vibration, the pilot would cut the throttle as he reached the target area and for approximately five seconds glide while the photographer snapped his pictures. The pilot would then gun the engine and circle around for another run over the target while the cameraman wound his film and got ready for the next exposure.

The first American reconnaissance flight over the enemy lines was made on April 15, 1918, by Major Ralph Royce of the 1st Aero Squadron. However, British, French and American pilots flying for the Allies prior to the entrance of the United States into the war had started their aerial observation missions much earlier. During the initial weeks of the war reconnaissance pilots such as Captain Joubert de la Ferte, and Lieutenant G. W. Mapplebeck of the British Royal Flying Corps, made many visual observations of enemy positions. The French, however, soon started experimenting with the use of cameras and the British followed suit. By March of 1915 Lieutenant J. T. C. Moore-Barbizon had a small Royal Flying Corps photographic unit organized at the front and a trench map he made from pictures taken over enemy lines proved valuable during the attack on Neuve Chapelle.

Just exactly how the aerial camera came into prominence during World War I is speculative. One report indicates that during the early days of the war a private in the infantry managed to obtain a flight in a plane over the front. At the time there was a strict rule that no cameras could be carried on such flights but he ignored the regulation and took a small hand camera with him. He photographed whatever happened to interest him during the trip. When the aircraft landed it was discovered that the passenger had carried the camera and the films were quickly confiscated. Instead of destroying the films, however, the authorities developed the pictures and were amazed to discover the accurate and detailed information they revealed about the enemy area, information that the trained eyes of an observer had previously missed. The private had unwittingly provided a permanent record that could be studied and interpreted by many eyes and many minds.

Another report credits Germany with the introduction of aerial photography in the war. The British and the French had been carrying out a few experiments pertaining to the use of the camera from the air, but it wasn't until a camera on a captured German aircraft revealed vital military information that a thorough investigation of the merits of aerial photography was made. One fact that gives credence to this report was the discovery that a number of German flying pupils who went to England before the war were discovered to have carried cameras during their advanced practice flights. It is thought that the system of sending German pupils to England to learn to fly at this time was a clever espionage trick, showing much foresight and perhaps a considerable knowledge of aerial photography.

A study made by the Air Material Command, USAF, about reconnaissance aircraft and aerial photography during World War I states:

> The outbreak of WW I in Europe found the Central Powers best equipped technically for work in aerial photography. For one example. the Germans had learned to heat their cameras with electricity to assure more efficient performance of the apparatus at higher altitudes. After a short while it became common practice on the part of the Germans to photograph the entire active Western Front every

two weeks. In 1918 the German army alone had in use 2000 mapping cameras and 100 automatic film cameras for large size pictures and were taking about 4000 photographs per day.

Great Britain and France were quick to follow the actions of the Germans in putting the camera to work for them once hostilities began. Britain acquired some experience in the aerial photographic field in the course of making aerial pictures for maps of Egypt and the Suez Canal zone. As a result they, too, were able to put aerial photographic organizations into operation on the Western Front in a comparative short time.

The first British photo groups were put together in a somewhat hasty and disorganized fashion. However, under the direction of Major J. T. C. Moore-Barbizon who was a pioneer in the field of aerial photography and who later became head of the photographic activities in France, the organization and equipping of aerial photographic units was steadily improved. Major T. M. Campbell, in charge of photographic activities in London, helped. Cameras were tested and new designs conceived and put into production. Within a short time the Royal Air Force was delivering an average of 1000 exposures and prints daily.

The French probably acted with greater celerity than the British for they were the first to try out aerial photography in the field and to use the results for military purposes. The French photographic section was largely under the control of camera designers and scientific men and as a result apparatus of a more complex nature than that of the British was developed. Cameras of French design served as the basis of much of the United States production in succeeding months.

During the first two years of the war in Europe, the 1st Aero Squadron was carrying out aerial reconnaissance on the Mexican border in support of General Pershing, but once the United States entered the conflict the situation changed.

On May 20, 1917, the 1st Aero Squadron received orders to prepare for immediate foreign service. On August 9 it arrived at Fort Hamilton, New York, where Major Ralph Royce joined the squadron and took command. The unit set sail on August 13 on the S.S. *Lapland* from Pier 6, North River, at about 6 P.M. and reached Liverpool, England, on September 2. A few days later the squadron was in France. During the next several months the pilots and observers went through a training program managed largely by the French, and it wasn't until April 11, 1918, that the 1st Aero Squadron began operations over the front lines.

It didn't take long for Major Royce and his men to discover that they needed all the lessons they had learned from the French textbook on reconnaissance. On April 12, one day after they started combat operations, Lieutenant A. J. Coyle crossed the enemy lines for a look at the German trenches. His plane was immediately attacked by several German aircraft and returned to the field with bullet holes in its fuselage and wings. Fortunately, Coyle was uninjured but it impressed upon the American fliers that the experienced German pilots were waiting for them on the opposite side of the front-line trenches.

Lieutenant Fred E. D'Amour, one of the best-trained photographers in the 1st Aero Squadron, tells what it was like to fly a mission during the early weeks of operations. His report of the July 29, 1918, mission in a plane piloted by Lieutenant E. G. Wold gives a vivid description of the action the American airmen faced while attempting to take pictures of enemy positions and installations:

Protection had been promised by the First Pursuit Group. We landed at Saints where the fighters were based and agreed to meet their patrol over Conluise at 1000 meters. Rendevous made. Started for the front. Low clouds blocked our flight path and we lost our fighter protection. Went ahead anyway to get the assigned pictures. The photographs were to be obliques of strong points in the rear of the German lines. The first film magazine was taken of the target area without incident but after five pictures were exposed on the second magazine the camera jammed. I changed magazines but the camera still refused to operate. On investigating I found that broken glass had worked into the shutter and the camera was definitely out of commission. Since we were already deep behind enemy lines, we decided to make a reconnaissance of the enemy rear area in an effort to locate pill-boxes in the area and any new construction. After noting the position of these installations, we started home at an altitude of 600 meters with average ground fire being fired at us. As we neared the front lines on our return flight, however, the ground fire became extremely active. When we were still about 12 kilometers inside the German lines an anti-aircraft shell exploded directly underneath the motor, tearing a large piece off the end of the propeller blade and stopping the motor. We started down. Emptied our machine guns on the way down because we had incendiary bullets in them. The German guns increased their barrage and our plane took several more hits. Just as Lieutenant Wold was leveling off preparatory to landing, the motor started again. However, the piece torn off the propeller cut down on our power and we flew the rest of the way out which was about ten kilometers at from ten to forty meters altitude. Tracers from ground machine guns formed a formation all around the ship, tearing away a flying wire and another shell tore a large hole in the elevator. Some days later the Chief of the Army Corps visited the field and stated that the photographs taken that day had given them information of valuable importance and that dugouts sheltering an entire regiment of enemy troops had been located and destroyed by our artillery after being detected on one of our pictures.

On August 10 two of the most famous of the 1st Aero Squadron members, Lieutenant William Erwin and Lieutenant B. V. Baucom, were ordered to fly a photographic mission into the enemy-held section of the Château-Thierry area. "Battling" Baucom, the observer, was one of the most reliable photographers in the unit and could handle the French DeRam camera like an expert. Lieutenant Erwin's combat report about the mission indicates the difficulties faced by World War I reconnaissance crews:

We started out at 7:00 A.M. for pictures just above Père-en-Tardenois in the Château-Thierry sector. The pictures had to be taken regardless of everything as our troops were to advance over that ground the next day and the camera would save many lives by uncovering new battery positions, machine gun emplacements, and the like. Arrangements were made by telephone for a Spad squadron of a neighboring pursuit group to act as protection since the Germans had an overwhelming concentration of air forces in our sector at the time. It wasn't unusual for as many as 40 or 50 German machines echeloned in three formations to patrol the area.

Attaining our altitude we were met by eight Spads and started out for the front lines. Before reaching the lines two of the Spads developed motor trouble and lost the formation. When we reached the place where we were to photograph we were at an altitude of about 3000 meters and, the coast seeming clear, Lieutenant Baucom started filming. I was paying strict attention to my course so that the pictures would be the best possible when I suddenly saw the leader of the Spads dive around my wing. This was the prearranged signal that the Huns were in the air and about to attack. I yelled through the speaking tube to Baucom but he was already on the job. I think he can smell a Hun—I know one never caught him napping. Pulling up into a chandelle, I saw the party had already commenced. Eleven Fokkers had dived out of the sun on the seven of us and a dogfight had commenced in earnest.

One Spad climbed on a Fokker's tail and started down whereupon, apparently from out of nowhere, a Fokker started pouring it into this Spad. I whipped my nose around and started my Vickers pumping a stream of tracers into the German. He dropped off into a kind of half-spin and disappeared under my wing but my bullets came too late. The chap he was shooting at fell out of control and crashed 1200 feet below. I learned later that it was Lieutenant Beauchamp, a chap who had came over from the States with me and we had taken all our training together. Almost at this moment I heard the rat-tat-tat, the song of the Fokker on my own tail and another stream of tracers seemed to be coming from under my right wing. I dove down into this fellow with my own gun firing. Meanwhile, Baucom was giving the glad hand to the one on our tail. I thought, "good old Lewis gun" when one of the German's guns cut out but suddenly both of Baucom's guns jammed. The Fokker on our tail moved in for the kill but Captain Vasconcelles, seeing our plight, attacked and shot the enemy plane down. The others retired.

Lieutenant Baucom had only about 16 pictures whereas our strip required at least 36. After landing and refueling, I started out again at 11:00 A.M. with Lieutenant Earl B. Spenser as observer. We managed to get 12 plates of valuable pictures at 2500 meters when 10 Fokkers cut us off from returning to our lines. I dove under them at full speed but was caught. In the ensuing fight I shot down one Fokker attacking me head-on. However, our plane was badly damaged. The camera was shot full of holes, several wires were cut, our spar was shot through in two places, and Lieutenant Spenser was wounded in the side.

Six pilots were lost in the attempt to get the pictures in order that the boys on the ground might advance with less cost of their own lives. It was costly to us.

The cameras used during World War I caused a great deal of trouble. The French and the British both contributed designs to the United States. The French camera was the DeRam, which was a large camera, had a focal length of 20 inches, weighed about 90 pounds, and took a plate size approximately 7 by 9 inches. The "L" type camera was adapted from a British production model and was used by many of the American aircrews. About 750 of this type were made in the United States, 300 of them being shipped abroad. The basic characteristics of this camera were focal lengths of 8½ and 10 inches, weight 35 pounds, 4-by-5 format, and a magazine capacity of 24 negatives. The Folmer film camera, which was manufactured by the Folmer & Schuing Division of Eastman Kodak, was set up for production with a hundred cameras on contract for delivery scheduled for November 18, 1918, the day the war ended. Roll-film cameras, despite their attractive features and principle, did not work out as well in practice. Film flatness, film definition, and other considerations produced an overwhelming vote for the aerial glass-plate cameras.

The observers were relatively inexperienced in the art of aerial photography although they had attended schools in the United States and had been further instructed by the French after arriving overseas. After a few weeks of combat photography a check list was officially published for use by the observers and those who took time to follow this standard operating procedure eliminated many of their previous troubles. The instructions to observers on photography missions were explicit and had a touch of humor:

BEFORE TAKE-OFF:

1. Before leaving the ground inspect your camera, leaving the shutter closed. Try snuffling the plates of each magazine through once and work the reaching handle and the trigger several times. The rocking handle should be pulled all the way back.

2. If you are using a 52 cm with oblique mounting, slip several plates on and off several times until you are able to change rapidly.

3. Have the area you have to cover plainly marked on your map and be sure the pilot knows it. Plan with him the best route, know the position of the sun, the wind, at what altitude your pictures are to be taken, and what interval of time to allow between each exposure. Spend a minimum of time in enemy territory.

IN THE AIR:

1. If your magazine jams don't jerk it as this will break a plate. Take the magazine off, look in the shutter to see that no broken glass has worked in and put in another magazine.

2. If you are using a 26 cm for oblique be sure that you hold the camera so as not to take pictures of the wings or tail. Do not hold the arms rigid or the pictures will blur.

3. With the present oblique mounting for the 62 cm camera pictures are taken from the right side of the plane. Be sure the right side is towards Germany.

4. It is necessary to steady the 62 cm camera while pictures are taken to prevent blurring. The grip of the magazine is a good place to take hold of for this.

5. Even if the area to be covered is small take plenty of exposures. Some may not be on the objective.

AFTER LANDING:

1. Report any trouble to the cameraman on the field.

2. Show him the area covered and the sequence in which the magazines or plates were used.

3. Keep in touch with the photo department. If pictures are no good find out why.

A mission flown by Lieutenant Harry D. Aldrich with Lieutenant M. Clark as observer on August 11, 1918, depicts the frustration of the airmen when their cameras didn't work properly. Clark reported the details of the operation after landing:

The mission was of great importance and of such urgency that it was attempted as soon as received although it was too late in the day to arrange for fighter protection. Every previous mission during the day had seen many Boche patrols and several had been attacked. As it was getting late, Aldrich and I decided to make the attempt unprotected. As every observer knows, a photo mission without protection is one of the most dangerous missions that could be flown since it is necessary, of course, to fly for a considerable time inside enemy territory and during the time the observer is working he is too busy with his camera to have much time to spare in watching for enemy planes and the inevitable happens. We were no exception. We found ourselves in the midst of a German patrol of nine planes just as I tried to operate the camera. I quickly took 24 exposures while Aldrich kept the plane level. Our rudder controls were finally shot away but he managed to keep the machine upright and we escaped by diving into the clouds. Unfortunately, when we got back on the ground I discovered that the photographs were no good because of a broken mechanism in the camera.

Not all cameramen were so unlucky, however. On September 2, 1918, near Eply, France, Lieutenant Arthur E. Masterbrook took 20 oblique photographs at the extremely low altitude of 100 meters and all the pictures were good. This was the lowest altitude flown until that time on a successful photographic mission and introduced a new technique that was used often in later reconnaissance missions. In fact, as the war progressed, fewer problems were encountered with the cameras and almost all missions were successful if the weather permitted.

The price was often high for the photographs, however. The mission of July 20, 1918, cost the life of one of the best-liked observers of the 1st Aero Squadron, Lieutenant H. St. John "Benny" Boldt. One of his comrades expressed the feelings of them all when it was learned that Benny Boldt had been killed in action.

When I think of Benny Boldt it recalls to mind the sight of him playing nearly every evening at the base at Francheville with a flock of little French kids, every one of whom simply worshiped him. We who knew him knew his warm generous nature and could understand the children's love for him. When on the afternoon of July 20th the plane returned to the field with the dead body of Lieutenant Boldt in the cockpit not a member of the squadron did not feel deeper than words can picture. Lieutenant Boldt's work with the squadron was of the very highest. When on that afternoon he was sent out to locate the position of the front lines, low clouds and approaching darkness made it necessary to fly very low making the plane an easy target for the German machine gunners. Pilot Lieutenant William

Erwin reports that he called to Lieutenant Boldt through the speaking tube but received no response. He then started for home immediately where it was learned that the observer had been killed instantly by machine gun bullets from the ground.

Lieutenant E. G. Wold, whose July 29 mission was detailed earlier, was one of the first American cadets to arrive in France in the fall of 1917. With the rest of the 1st Aero Squadron members he worked to build the great base at Issoudun, then later took his training there at Field No. 7. After getting his wings, Lieutenant Wold went to the front and put in a remarkable number of hours in the air on reconnaissance missions during the short time he was in combat. Always preferring the most difficult and dangerous missions, on August 1 he volunteered for a photography mission several miles inside the enemy lines. Starting out with the usual pursuit protection, he was twice driven out of Germany by overwhelming numbers of German planes. At last, returning to enemy territory alone in an attempt to accomplish the photography mission, he was attacked by five of the enemy. Single-handed he engaged them and by brilliant fighting regained friendly lines but he was so seriously wounded that he became unconscious and crashed into one of the American battery positions from a hundred meters altitude and was killed.

The squadron report on the last flight of Lieutenant James I. Sykes of Charlotte, North Carolina, a typical good-natured southern boy who was friendly with everyone, reveals the hazards of aerial photography missions during World War I.

Lieutenant Sykes was ready to fly on August 1st but he couldn't find his gloves. He borrowed a helmet and gloves from another observer and took off with pilot Lieutenant Walter B. Miller. Lieutenant Sykes had a little black dog named Cazaus which was a favorite among the entire squadron. As Sykes climbed into his ship carrying his camera, he bade Cazaus farewell and exhorted him to be good during his absence. When he had departed, Cazaus sat in front of the hangar with such an unusual look of profound sadness and disappointment for a dumb brute that several of the officers called attention to it. He wouldn't be consoled by anyone no matter how much we tried. I don't know what thoughts were on this dog's mind but Lieutenant Sykes never returned. On their photographic mission Sykes and Miller had with them for protection six Nieuports. They stumbled into a large German formation which was, without a doubt, the Von Richthofen Flying Circus. The entire American group of planes was wiped out. Sykes' and Miller's machine fell on the railroad only a few kilometers north of Fère-en-Tardenois. I think it was near an overhead crossing where the railroad went through a cut. There was an awful crash and the bodies of our comrades were in terribly mutilated condition.

While the 1st Aero Squadron did much of the pioneering work in aerial reconnaissance both before and during World War I, there were other American units in France also. The 8th Aero Squadron was formed on June 21, 1917, from personnel of the 2d Company, I Provisional Aviation Camp at Kelly Field, Texas. On November 22 the unit embarked for overseas aboard the British ship *Carpathian* and sixteen days later arrived at Liverpool, England. After various other stops they ended up in Toul, France, where they remained a little less than a month, but during this stop they did considerable photographic work. The 8th Aero Squadron developed the technique of sending out two photographic planes on a mission instead of just one. If the Boche managed to penetrate the fighter protection there was a chance that one of the two planes might escape and get back to base with the vital pictures. On September 25, 1918, the unit made a string of pictures covering some 40 kilometers, one of the longest strips ever taken by an American reconnaissance squadron on a single mission. Another duty assigned to the 8th Aero Squadron was to photograph the entire 4th Corps area to a depth of 10 kilometers, an area of about 600 square kilometers. This project was completed before the squadron was transferred to the 6th Corps.

On October 9, 1918, Lieutenant Edward Russel Moore and Lieutenant Gardiner P. Allen displayed extraordinary heroism while on a photographic mission. General Orders No. 8 issued on November 7, 1918, awarded each of these officers the Distinguished Service Cross, stating:

. . . for extraordinary heroism in action near Thaiutourt, France. Lieutenant Moore with Lieutenant Allen, observer, took advantage of a short period of fair weather during generally unfavorable atmospheric conditions to undertake a photographic mission behind the German lines. Accompanied by two protecting planes, they had just commenced their mission when they were attacked by eight enemy planes which followed them through their course, firing at the photographic plane. Lieutenant Moore, with both flying wires cut by bullets, the landing wire shot away, the elevators riddled with bullets, and both wings punctured, continued on the prescribed course although it made him an easy target. Lieutenant Allen was thus enabled in the midst of the attack to take pictures of the exact territory assigned. He made no attempt to protect the plane with his machine guns, displaying an entire disregard of personal danger and steadfast devotion to duty. The two officers successfully completed their photographic mission.

The 8th Aero Squadron used the DH-4 airplane, which was relatively new at the time, and on October 22, 1918, the commanding officer of the squadron filed the following report on the use of the airplane for reconnaissance. Even at this early date in the history of aviation no aircraft was specifically designed for aerial photography. Instead, modified fighter or bomber aircraft had to be used and, as this report indicates, the results were not always satisfactory:

The first DH-4 airplanes sent to the front were provided with one oil tank. This supply of oil was not sufficient and a second tank of equal size had to be installed. Because of enemy planes it is often necessary to fly close formation on photographic missions. The upper plane in the American DH-4 blinds the pilot and prevents such formations. By removing tanks an opening can be made over the pilot's head for better visibility. Also, at present it is impossible to obtain enough different size carburetor jets to make fine adjustments of gas flow. This reduces the maximum time of flight at high altitude one hour or more. I request that the squadron be supplied with these jets. The only two planes of this squadron shot through the main tanks both fell in flames. The high tank pressure is dangerous. The British are using a tank that has been more successful because they use a pump in the tank which replaces the pressure system. However, the most serious defect of the DH-4 as an observation airplane is the distance between the pilot and the observer. This difficulty has, in part, been done away with by the interphone. The supply of these interphones has been limited and some planes do not have them. Successful cooperation between the pilot and the observer in the DH-4 without one is almost impossible.

John Gilbert Winant
Captain, Air Service

The British ship *Adriatic* brought another squadron to the battle scene, one that was to distinguish itself in aerial reconnaissance. This was the 91st Aero Squadron. It reached the Toul sector of France on May 24, 1918, and flew its first combat mission on June 3, 1918. The 91st was equipped with the two-place Salmson aircraft, constructed of wood and canvas and with cameras that were mechanically driven by a counter-weighted propeller in the slipstream of the aircraft engine. In mid-September 1918, the 91st aided in the St.-Mihiel offensive by photographing the sector over which the Allied ground troops planned to advance. It encountered so much enemy opposition while performing the reconnaissance missions that four of its members—Lieutenant Leonard C. Hammond, Lieutenant Victor H. Strahm, Lieutenant William T. Bedham and Lieutenant Everett R. Cook—became aces. Strahm and at least two other members of the squadron—Lieutenant George C. Kenney and Lieutenant Asa Duncan—later became generals.

The following figures show the type and amount of activity the 91st faced between June 3 and November 11, 1918, while the squadron was stationed in the Toul sector and Meuse-Argonne:

Destruction of enemy aircraft confirmed	21
Number of air engagements	139
Number of hours behind enemy lines	1,045

Distance in miles beyond enemy lines	17,000
Negatives exposed in enemy territory	4,500
Successful negatives	3,700
Total visual reconnaissance missions	252
Total photoreconnaissance missions	108

One of the most outstanding reconnaissance pilots of World War I was Major Kenneth P. Littauer, the commanding officer of 88th Observation Squadron. Using a Caudron two-seater for most of his missions, "Kepi" Littauer ignored the fact that the temperamental machine was considered a flying death trap and went anywhere at any time. He invariably flew at low altitude, a technique usually avoided by reconnaissance pilots who wanted to survive the war, and just as regularly brought his observer and the observer's photographs back safely. At times when the observer was wounded, Littauer remembered the prime aim of his operation was to get the photographs and other intelligence back to base. With this in mind he would use his skilled flying technique and daring to escape the Boche planes. He was awarded the French Croix de Guerre with two palms, the Belgian Chevalier Order of Leopold, and the American Distinguished Service Cross.

Littauer, Strahm, Royce, Erwin, and the other men of the reconnaissance squadrons of World War I took a total of 18,000 aerial photographs from which 585,000 prints were made. They pioneered an aerial technique that was to grow in importance with every year until finally the survival of the nation depended upon it. The courage of these World War I airmen will never be forgotten.

4

More Words than Pictures

DURING the period between World War I and World War II, reconnaissance techniques were constantly improved despite the fact that the budget for such work was very limited. As soon as the war was officially over on November 11, 1918, the Air Service along with the rest of the military was quickly reduced to a mere skeleton force. Orders for 13,000 planes and 20,000 engines were canceled immediately and trained airmen by the hundreds were discharged and sent home. Among this group were the aerial reconnaissance pilots and photographers who had accomplished such outstanding work during World War I.

Strange as it may seem, most people in the United States had never seen an airplane when the war ended and to them taking pictures from an aircraft was a novelty that daredevils engaged in for the thrill of it. They didn't understand that the security of the nation demanded that aerial reconnaissance techniques be improved, that new and better equipment was not only justified but a necessity. A few men understood this vital fact, however, and among them was George W. Goddard.

Goddard, more than any other man, molded the photoreconnaissance effort in its thirty years from 1920 to 1950. He enlisted as a private in the Aviation Section of the Signal Corps when World War I began and in December 1917 was selected to attend the first Officers' School in Aerial Photography, U.S. School of Military Aeronautics, Cornell University. Upon graduation from the school he was appointed instructor in aerial photographic interpretation.

On August 8, 1918, he was commissioned a second lieutenant and ordered to Taliaferro Field, Fort Worth, Texas, to organize and take to France the 43d, 44th, and 45th Aerial Photographic Sections. However, when the armistice was declared these plans were canceled and Goddard was ordered to Carlstrom Field, Florida, where he obtained his pilot's wings after a rigorous training course. Less than a year later he was transferred to McCook Field, Dayton, Ohio, as officer in charge of Aerial Photographic Research and the U.S. Army never made a better assignment. Since that time he has provided the nation with many outstanding contributions to the advancement of the science of optical recording, measurement, and identification as employed in military aerial reconnaissance.

It was while he was at McCook Field that Goddard started developments in infrared and long-range photography; special cameras for aerial reconnaissance; plans for aircraft designed primarily for photoreconnaissance work; and portable field laboratory equipment. It was there also that he formed the nucleus of the present Photographic Laboratory of Wright-Patterson Air Force Base. It was Goddard who was mainly responsible for the development of huge, long-focal-length lenses that proved so valuable during World War II and have become a United States trademark ever since.

After starting these developments and finishing a few, Goddard, then a lieutenant, was appointed chief photo officer on the Air Service staff by General Billy Mitchell. While on this assignment he received a Presidential appointment as the Air Service representative on the Federal Board of Surveys and

Maps. He organized the first Army Aerial Photographic Mapping unit, which pioneered in mapping Muscle Shoals, the Tennessee River basin, Teapot Dome, the Mississippi River, and other areas.

"Many people think of aerial reconnaissance as a principal service to the ground forces in time of war," Goddard said. "They do not realize that peacetime aerial mapping use of reconnaissance is of great importance."

The aerial photography work that Goddard's mapping unit did in 1920 is credited with pointing the way for the civilian mapping and photogrammetry industry of today.

In 1924 he was once again assigned to McCook Field at Dayton, Ohio, and he was able to continue with the research he had started earlier. In a most unusual move, the military allowed Goddard to specialize in aerial reconnaissance during the remainder of his long career until he retired in 1953 as a brigadier general.

One important development that Goddard first started in 1925 was night aerial photography, a technique that has been used to great advantage ever since. The first experiment was crude in comparison with the procedures used today, but it worked. Goddard attached an expendable glider loaded with 40 pounds of flash powder to his airplane with a tow rope. The powder was ignited over the target and the photograph was taken as the flash reached its peak intensity.

The following year he demonstrated a quick processing technique and the results were published in the Canton, Ohio, *Repository* on September 12, 1927:

> Thirty minutes after an army aerial photographer opens the shutter of his camera over an objective along the Pacific Coast a print of what the speeding army eye saw can be laid before a governmental official in Washington.
>
> The operation is made possible by the development of the film in the plane and its transmission by telephoto over telegraph wires.
>
> The immediate problem of experts in the army air corps laboratories

at Wright Field is to make the feat so completely fool-proof that everybody in the air service can do it. Dr. Samuel Burka, who is working toward a simplification of the process, and Lieutenant George W. Goddard photographed the government prison at Fort Leavenworth, Kansas and 23 minutes later the telephoto print was received in New York during a recent test.

The Air Corps Act of 1926 gave the flying service a temporary boost. It changed the name of the Air Service to Air Corps, which strengthened the conception of military aviation as an offensive, striking arm rather than just an auxiliary service. The most encourging aspect of the act was the allotment of enough funds to permit the planning of a five-year expansion program, which made it possible for this branch of the U.S. Army to compete with the air arm of the U.S. Navy for military assignments. Part of the money was used to further modify the DH-4B aircraft for photo purposes and redesignate it the DH-4M-2. The following year the Air Corps made an aerial photographic survey of the east and west coasts of Florida for the United States Coast and Geodetic Survey. This assignment was accomplished so successfully that the photo crews were asked to continue their work, finally photographing a total of 35,000 square miles in various parts of the nation for government agencies. The additional money enabled Goddard to continue his experiments with the new Bagley Tri-Lens camera, designated the K-3, which made the K-1 single-lens aerial camera obsolete. He also helped develop waterproof paper during these between-war years. Atmospheric humidity had relatively little effect on this paper. It required very little drying and was supplied in large quantities to the British, Russians, and other wartime allies to improve their reconnaissance operations during World War II.

On October 10, 1928, Captain St. Claire Strett, a pilot, and Captain A. W. Stevens, a photographer, set an unofficial world altitude record of 37,854 feet for airplanes carrying more than one person. The following year Captain Stevens photographed

Mt. Rainier from an airplane at a distance of 227 miles from the peak, exceeding by fifty miles any previous record in long-distance aerial photography. In another attention-getting experiment which forecast important future uses of aerial cameras, Dr. Robert Goddard fired a liquid-fueled 11-foot rocket into space at Auburn, Massachusetts, on July 17, 1929. The rocket carried a small camera which was recovered intact after the flight. The same year the Air Corps was given the job of photo-mapping the Rio Grande from El Paso to the Gulf of Mexico and the route of the proposed Nicaragua Canal.

Limited funds, however, seriously hampered progress in aerial reconnaissance and during these poverty days of the Air Corps between world wars only one aircraft designed solely for photo use was purchased. This was the Fairchild F1-A. According to the *Congressional Record* the sum of $137,192.35 was spent for six of these planes with spare parts, an amount that wouldn't be enough to buy the engines of a reconnaissance aircraft thirty years later. Yet it was a step in the right direction during a period when few steps were taken.

During 1931 an agreement was made between the Army's General Douglas MacArthur and the Navy's Admiral William V. Pratt that had a far-reaching effect on the future of aerial reconnaissance. In this compromise agreement it was decided that the Army's land-based air arm would defend the coasts and overseas possessions of the United States while the Navy's air forces would be based on the fleet and move with it at all times. At first the Navy had violently opposed the idea of the Army planes operating off the coasts at sea but General MacArthur's persuasion finally resulted in the important compromise. It wasn't until 1933, however, that the War Department finally gave the Army Air Corps a clear-cut directive that its mission included long-range reconnaissance. General Foulois, then chief of the Air Corps, immediately decided that he should make certain that everyone in the military establishment was convinced that his planes and crews could handle this assignment so he scheduled an extensive exercise to take place in May on the West Coast.

The General Headquarters Air Force (Provisional) under the command of Oscar Westover was the air arm used in the maneuvers and the results of the exercise were of historic significance, with respect not only to bombardment functions but also to the value of aerial reconnaissance. In his report after the completion of the maneuvers on the West Coast, Westover stated that high-speed and high-altitude bombardment aircraft, together with observation aviation of superior speed and range and communications capabilities, could successfully defend the nation. His report also pointed out the need for better reconnaissance planes:

> During these exercises, observation aviation appeared woefully obsolete in performance, as did pursuit aviation in speed characteristics. Since new bombardment aircraft possesses speed above 200 miles per hour, any intercepting or supporting aircraft must possess greater speed characteristics if they are to perform their missions.

One direct result of these maneuvers was the development of long-range reconnaissance planes to perform the clearly defined mission given the Air Corps by the War Department. Eventually these long-range planes—B-17s and B-24s—were used primarily as bombers but if they had not initially been planned for reconnaissance they would not have been ready by the time the nation entered World War II. Projects "A," "B," "C," and "D," started by the Air Corps at this time, progressed through many designs and prototypes until the B-17, B-24, B-19, and B-29 came off the production lines. They all had their beginning, however, in an effort to develop an aircraft that could achieve the necessary long-range reconnaissance required.

In July of 1934 General Foulois decided that he should show the War Department that one of his new long-range planes, the Martin B-10, could accomplish the reconnaissance assignment he had forecast for it. Consequently he ordered Hap Arnold, by then a lieutenant colonel and commanding officer of March Field, California, to lead a flight of ten B-10s from Bolling Field, Washington, D.C., to Fairbanks, Alaska. George Goddard, by this time a captain, went with Arnold and, utilizing the new T-3 Maltese Falcon camera, photographed 20,000 square miles of Alaskan territory. This new five-lens camera produced forty exposures on a single roll of film and he did most of his mapping photography from an altitude of 16,000 feet. The Alaskan Project not only proved the worth of the B-10 but it also gave Goddard valuable experience in the problems of aerial photography at extremely cold temperatures, experience he passed on to other officers working in this field.

In November 1935, Air Corps Captains Orvil A. Anderson and A. W. Stevens climbed to a height of 72,395 feet in a balloon with a specially constructed pressurized cabin. During this flight they took more than 15,000 aerial photographs, learning a great deal about the use of cameras from the "edge of space," knowledge that would become invaluable later as the U-2 and other reconnaissance aircraft began operating at these heights.

Despite the efforts of men such as Foulois, Arnold, Goddard, and many others in the Air Corps, the U.S. Navy was still not convinced that the War Department had made the correct decision when it assigned the long-range reconnaissance task to the Air Corps. The dissension reached such a stage that the War Department issued a pamphlet entitled *Joint Action of the Army and Navy.* Paragraph 4c clearly stated:

> In order that the most effective cooperation may be attained, the following general principles will govern:
>
> (1) Neither service will attempt to restrict in any way the means and weapons used by the other service in carrying out its functions.
>
> (2) Neither service will attempt to restrict in any way the area of operations of the other service in carrying out its functions.
>
> (3) Each service will lend the utmost assistance possible to the other service in carrying out its function.

In actual practice both services, the U.S. Navy and the Air Corps, tried in every way to prove that their equipment and personnel were best suited for reconnaissance—and all other missions that overlapped. Joint Air Exercise No. 4, which took place in August 1937, was a direct result of this interservice conflict.

Basically, Joint Air Exercise No. 4 involved both long-range reconnaissance and bombing. The battleship *Utah* was to penetrate an area between San Francisco Bay and San Pedro Bay extending to a maximum of three hundred miles out to sea from the California coast. This search area covered about 100,000 square miles. The Flying Fortresses of the GHQ Air Force were to locate the *Utah* and bomb it with water bombs if they could. The crews had from noon August 12 until noon August 13 to accomplish the mission.

It was obvious from the beginning that both commands desired to outfox the other in an effort to prove once and for all to the War Department that their respective qualifications were the better. If the GHQ Air Force could not find the *Utah* and drop bombs on it, the future of the B-17 aircraft and the important role of long-range reconnaissance would be in jeopardy. If the B-17s did succeed, they would point out to the public and the War Department both that surface-vessel programs alone were not enough for national security and that land-based reconnaissance aircraft could locate an enemy fleet and direct bombers and other attack aircraft to its position.

In theory, according to those who participated in the exercise, the Navy was supposed to send out reconnaissance planes to locate the battleship *Utah* and report its position to the Flying Fortresses. Most critics believe, rightly or wrongly, that the U.S. Navy had no intentions of contributing to its own defeat by pinpointing the *Utah* for the GHQ Air Force planes. At any rate, the position finally relayed to the Flying Fortresses on the twelfth shortly before dark—there was to be no bombing attempt after darkness fell—proved to be sixty miles in error and the bombers returned to Sacramento Municipal Airport without seeing the battleship.

The following day, August 13, was foggy, so foggy that the

U.S. Navy reported that their reconnaissance planes could not take off and search for the *Utah.* The GHQ Air Force fliers finally decided that they were being given the runaround, that the U.S. Navy reconnaissance planes might take off and find the *Utah* too late for the bombers to reach the battleship before the noon deadline. They made up their minds to search the area themselves. With Curtis E. LeMay, later to become chief of staff of the Air Force, as lead navigator, the B-17s climbed through the fog and began the hunt. General D. C. Emmons, who was commanding officer of the planes searching for the *Utah*, estimated that the battleship would make a feint toward San Francisco, then head south, so that was the direction in which the aircraft headed.

At five minutes to twelve o'clock, flying less than 1,000 feet above the ocean, LeMay and his crew spotted the *Utah*! They got three direct hits on the ship with their 50-pound water bombs, proving that they could locate and attack a surface vessel with land-based aircraft successfully. While it was a hit-or-miss type of visual reconnaissance used by LeMay and his crew members that August day in 1937, it solidified the claim of the Air Corps that it could accomplish the long-range reconnaissance mission and had an important bearing on reconnaissance carried out by USAAF aircraft during World War II.

A year later, just to prove that the *Utah* exercise was no fluke, three Flying Fortresses searched out the incoming Italian liner *Rex* while it was far off the New York coast. LeMay was once again the navigator, while George Goddard went along to take pictures of the interception. So that there would be no question about the achievement, newsmen were in one of the B-17s and there was a radio broadcast scheduled at the exact moment LeMay forecast he would locate the ship, a broadcast to originate from a Flying Fortress. Fortunately, the future chief of staff of the Air Force hit his Estimated Time of Arrival at the *Rex* right on the nose.

Four months after the *Utah* exercise in 1937, formal ceremonies were held to name Lowry Field in Colorado in honor of the state's first aerial observer, who had been killed in World War I. Lowry Field a year later received three hundred men for the Air Corps Technical School, plus thirty freight cars of photographic and armament equipment. On February 28, 1938, photographic instruction began at Lowry in Building 252 in a heatless attic. This first class was composed of four National Guardsmen, one Marine, and five Regular Army students. First Lieutenant Paul T. Cullen, a 1931 graduate of the photo course at Chanute Field, Illinois, was the chief instructor. Cullen rose to the rank of brigadier general and at the time of his death in 1951, when his plane crashed in the Atlantic Ocean, was one of the top experts in aerial photography in the USAF.

As the ominous signs of war appeared more and more imminent in Europe and Adolf Hitler grew increasingly powerful, the need for personnel who could take pictures and who could read the pictures after they were developed became obvious. On August 11, 1939, a new three-month course designed to provide more photographic technicians under the Air Corps Augmentation Plan was started. This course included four weeks of basic photography, five weeks of ground photography work, one week of aerial photography, and one week of mosaics and trailer operations. After the Nazis moved on Poland at dawn on the morning of September 1, 1939, and the actual fighting began in Europe, the photography school at Lowry Field expanded rapidly. Army Engineer Corps personnel were brought to the school to teach topography; a six-month special course for officers was started under the supervision of Master Sergeant Joseph M. Cates; and instruction in camera repair was inaugurated.

In January 1941 a three-month course designed to train aerial photographers for reconnaissance with heavy bombardment units was begun. The United States learned from Great Britain's example, as that country battled the Germans, that reconnaissance was of vital importance in this new war and an increasing number of students were enrolled at Lowry Field. By August 1941 a hundred men each month were entering the photography course, so many that a double shift was necessary to ease the growing pains. Major W. S. Park, an instructor at the school, designed a photographic trainer that simulated actual flight conditions for the fledgling aerial photographers just as the Link trainer did for student pilots, and this helped the overloaded situation some.

Meanwhile, other developments in aerial photography were taking place. During the summer of 1941 Fred Sonne perfected the S-2 strip camera and the Army Air Force purchased thirteen of these units for low-altitude, high-speed photography. The continuous-strip camera eliminated the shutter and controlled the exposure by matching the speed of the film with the speed and height of the aircraft. Major A. W. Stevens continued his stratospheric balloon ascents, during which he became the first man to take a picture showing the earth's curvature and the first to photograph the moon's shadow on the earth during an eclipse. He took what was then the world's longest-distance photograph, that of Mt. Shasta from a distance of 330 miles. George Goddard developed a camouflage detection film that made natural chlorophylls show up red.

In London the naval attaché at the U.S. Embassy, Vice-Admiral Ghormley, visited the British photo interpretation center at Wembley and was so impressed by the intelligence about enemy activities and installations being gathered that he requested an American officer be sent to England immediately to learn how it was done. Lieutenant Commander Robert S. Quackenbush, head of the photography section at the U.S. Navy's Bureau of Aeronautics, was assigned the task. In order to speed up the learning process, two other officers, Captain Charles Cox and Captain Gooderham McCormick, both of the U.S. Marine Corps, went with him. They spent three months at Wembley and Medmenham, another PI center operated by the British, and returned to the United States shortly before December 7, 1941. Quackenbush was lavish in his praise of the work being done by the aerial reconnaissance units in Britain, both in the air and on the ground. He recommended strongly that a school of photographic interpretation be organized by the U.S. Navy and after a few weeks the Chief of Naval Operations approved the idea. The school was to be located at Anacostia. Its purpose was to train PIs for every carrier of the fleet and for every U.S. Navy headquarters.

Shortly before the entry of the United States into World War II Captain Harvey C. Brown, Jr. of the U.S. Army Air Force was sent to England, also, for a photographic course from the British. Brown visited Medmenham where he met the soon-to-be-famous photo interpreter Constance Babington-Smith. When she pointed out to the amazed captain the large amount of valuable information she could obtain from one photograph he, too, became a disciple of aerial reconnaissance and returned to the United States to spread the word. George Goddard flew to England at about the same time and observed the reconnaissance work being accomplished by the RAF. He immediately discovered that the U.S. Army Air Force needed faster photo planes and he did much to promote the construction of such aircraft.

Despite the enthusiasm of these men who had witnessed firsthand in England under actual combat conditions the importance of aerial reconnaissance, Washington wasn't impressed. While the school at Lowry Field kept expanding—on the day of Pearl Harbor 484 students were enrolled—few new reconnaissance units were established in either the U.S. Army Force or the U.S. Navy. Goddard kept up his fight for new photo planes but even the modification of bombers and fighters in existence at the time so that they could be used for aerial reconnaissance proceeded very slowly. Not until the British warned Washington that Japanese planes had been seen flying over the Gilbert Islands and probably had been photographing them did the United States decide it was time for some action, that it would be a good idea if they sent some of their own aircraft to photograph the Japanese-mandated islands, the coastline of French Indo-China, and other Japanese-occupied territory. On November 26, less than two weeks before Japanese planes bombed Pearl Harbor, the War Department notified General Douglas MacArthur that two B-24s equipped for high-altitude photography were being sent to the Philippines within forty-eight hours. The two modified heavy bombers and their crews were ordered to photograph Jaluit in the Marshalls and Truk in the Carolines and to bring back as much information as they could obtain on the location and strength of Japanese military and naval installations. Unfortunately, even these two planes were delayed in leaving the United States because of difficulties encountered in securing and equipping them for the mission. The first B-24 finally reached Hawaii on December 5, but it was decided to hold it there until additional guns could be installed. The second B-24 was still in the United States when the bombs fell on Pearl Harbor. So were the 38th and 88th Reconnaissance Squadrons. Both of these units, assigned to a base on Mindanao, were still sitting on the hardstands at Hamilton Field, California, on December 7, 1941. Consequently there were no reconnaissance planes, visual or photographic, to detect the Japanese aircraft as they proceeded toward Hawaii from their carriers two hundred miles north of Oahu that morning. While the enemy had made regular reconnaissance flights prior to the surprise attack, the United States had depended upon the regular routine patrols of the Army Air Force and Navy planes. This lack of an adequate aerial reconnaissance program in the Pacific during 1941 was at least as much to blame for the disaster at Pearl Harbor as any other factor.

5

Lens in the Sky Against the European Axis (1)

THE advances in techniques used in aerial reconnaissance during World War II were startling compared to those of World War I, yet at the outset of the fighting there was a great deal of groping and experimentation. Most of the aerial reconnaissance in the first war was achieved by nonpilot observers and for a while after the fighting ceased the training of such observers continued at Fort Sill, Oklahoma, where the U.S. Army had a large field artillery school. Gradually, however, this concept changed and by 1940 general reconnaissance and aerial photography both were rated of equal importance with artillery-spotting duties.

At the time of Pearl Harbor the USAAF had several reconnaissance squadrons and a single photographic group in addition to the more familiar old-style observation units. The observation units flew short-range missions in cooperation with the ground forces. They were assigned to the air support commands of each air force. However, the reconnaissance squadrons were each attached to a bombardment group and the "recce" pilots flew the same type of aircraft as the bomber pilots. The primary duty of these squadrons was aerial reconnaissance but they also had the very important secondary assignment of actual combat bombardment. This overall plan, while it filled a gap that desperately needed filling during the early stages of World War II, was not successful. One main drawback was the aircraft. The F-7, which was a modified B-24 bomber equipped for aerial reconnaissance, and the F-9, which was a similarly equipped B-17, were not adequate for the assignment despite the heroic work of the crews. Both types usually carried a total of six cameras: three K-17s in a trimetrogon mount in the nose; another K-17 and a K-18 to take verticals from the belly; and a K-20 hand-held camera operated by one of the crew. Losses were extremely high since the F-7 and F-9, if sent out alone on a reconnaissance mission, were no match for the Me-109 or FW-190. Nor did they have the speed to escape the enemy planes as later reconnaissance aircraft did.

The observation units were in no better shape. During World War I most standard models of aircraft were suitable for visual reconnaissance, just as most standard models were suitable for aerial photography. By the time of Pearl Harbor, however, the new standard planes were much too fast and big to use on the small airstrips available for observation planes attached to ground troops and required to work in close cooperation with them. By 1941 the argument was still going on among members of the General Staff of the USAAF about whether a small, slow, unarmed observation—or liaison, as it was designated in 1941—plane could survive in combat areas. Finally, in January 1942, the USAAF was assigned the responsibility of developing a new series of light planes for liaison duty but it was not until 1944 that an adequate quantity of the fine L-4 and L-5 aircraft was available. These were then assigned to divisions, corps, and armies for observation, artillery adjustment, camouflage detection, and other reconnaissance duties. Until that time, however, obsolete planes such as the O-47 and O-49 had to fill the gap.

In April 1942, after the General Staff of the USAAF realized that the entire reconnaissance concept was outmoded and inefficient, the aerial reconnaissance setup was changed completely. All the units that had been assigned to the bombardment groups were redesignated bombardment squadrons, and new photo-reconnaissance groups were planned for assignment to the respective air forces. An Operational Training Unit for these groups was established at Peterson Field, Colorado, based upon the organization and procedures the RAF had been using so successfully against the Axis. At the same time observation aviation concepts were also modified. Washington was forced to admit that the American observation units in North Africa in 1942 had been very ineffective. Using a conglomeration of aircraft including medium and light bombers, fighters, and obsolete "puddle jumpers," the pilots had done their best with the equipment available but the results were poor. Meanwhile, the RAF, using only their fastest and most up-to-date fighters modified for photorecon missions, had accomplished an outstanding job. Consequently, an Operational Training Unit patterned along the lines of the British organization was established at Key Field, Mississippi.

Later, weather reconnaissance units were organized to provide meteorological reports upon which to base bombing missions, ground attacks, and other military operations. Weather crews were trained in the F-5 and a modified P-38, as well as modified versions of the B-24 and B-25.

Thus, a stable concept was eventually established for aerial reconnaissance by the USAAF although it came late in World War II. The "tac recce" units were the forerunners of today's tactical air reconnaissance units, while the photoreconnaissance groups of World War II did the same work as today's Strategic Air Command reconnaissance units. The photoreconnaissance units went on the long overwater or overland missions to photograph enemy installations for target folders and bomb-damage assessment reports and to expose new weapon developments by the enemy. The new tactical reconnaissance squadrons, equipped with fast fighters modified for reconnaissance work, carried out short-range missions such as adjusting artillery fire and securing tactical information that the ground commander could use immediately. While the new concept came under criticism as soon as the new units went into action, the final results proved that the tac recce and photoreconnaissance groups performed their missions with a high degree of success compared to the slipshod methods and organization available at the start of World War II.

The first American photographic mission flown over the North African battlefield was made by Lieutenant Colonel James Anderson of the USAAF in a modified Flying Fortress. A unit of British Spitfires equipped for aerial photography had flown to Algiers on November 13, 1942, five days after the Allied forces landed on the coast of North Africa, and began operating from the airfield at Maison Blanche. Unfortunately the Luftwaffe bombed this airfield day and night and within a few days the photographic Spitfires were only a mass of wreckage. Since the Allied landings were still not secure it was vital that information about the German defenders and their movements be obtained. Anderson was assigned the job.

He took off early on the morning of the nineteenth with Major Wayne Thurman as co-pilot. Heading for the Kasserine Pass, Anderson maintained a high enough altitude to avoid much of the antiaircraft fire that was directed at him by the Germans. Once he reached the pass, however, he nosed the B-17 down to a mere 6,000 feet, turned on the cameras, and made several long runs back and forth between the hills. After completing his photo work at the Kasserine Pass, the lieutenant colonel calmly flew to Gabes and made three photographic runs over the city before returning to Algiers. All together he was in the air seven and a half hours and miraculously not a single German fighter had challenged him.

After the film was developed, Anderson took the pictures straight to the headquarters of the Twelfth Air Force, where General James H. Doolittle, the commanding officer, studied them for over an hour. There were no photo interpreters at the headquarters so both Anderson and Doolittle analyzed the pictures, pointing targets out to each other as they discovered them on the prints. Within hours American and British planes were attacking these targets with great success.

During the period that most long-range aerial reconnaissance, both visual and photographic, was accomplished by modified bombers assigned to a bombardment group, a mission flown by mild-looking Norman C. Appold must go down in the history of armed reconnaissance as one of the most daring and unique. Appold, a chemical engineering graduate from the University of Michigan, was a small, slightly built pilot who gave his commanding officer, Colonel George F. ("Mickey") McGuire, the impression that the United States was getting very low on manpower when he first saw him. McGuire soon discovered, however, that he had made a mistake by permitting the lieutenant's physical appearance and talkative nature to influence his judgment. He discovered that Appold was not only deadly serious about his part in the war but also intelligent enough to solve a problem that had both the USAAF and the RAF stymied.

In 1942 when Field Marshal Bernard L. Montgomery massed his Eighth Army for one final attempt to drive the Nazis out of North Africa it appeared that his goal was near attainment. If he could cut the German supply route and close the ports to the Nazi convoys, the enemy would have to leave North Africa to avoid disaster. But as the winter of 1942–43 wore on and spring came, the "if" loomed larger and larger. Despite an all-out effort to block the main terminal at Benghazi by the British and American air units, the port was still operating. When the RAF night pathfinders flew over the city and dropped flares, the Germans continually lured the following bombers to phony target flares they set off themselves and the high explosives would drop on a barren beach. When American fliers of the 376th Bomb Group tried to use Norden bombsights, the glare was so bright that the bombardiers became confused and also dropped on the false Benghazi. Appold came up with the idea that solved this problem and enabled the bombers to devastate the city. He volunteered to make a one-plane reconnaissance flight over Benghazi at night, a flight that he promised would show the outline of the real city to the following bombers. Flying his B-24 at 20,000 feet, Appold crossed directly over the black area he thought was the city. He was near enough to the city for the German antiaircraft gunners to open fire and the ground forces immediately lighted the mock target. Appold didn't drop any target flares, however, knowing full well that it was a false target outlined below. He crossed Benghazi, turned and deliberately flew back over it, bringing more ground guns into action. On his third pass over the heavily defended city, with shells bursting all around his B-24 and rocking it violently, every muzzle on the ground was belching orange flame. This was exactly what Appold wanted. The real Benghazi was clearly outlined by the firing guns as plainly as though there were lighted boundary markers all around the city. Appold calmly dropped his target flares and the heavy bombers systematically dropped their high explosives on the important port.

Such hit-or-miss aerial reconnaissance was not satisfactory, however, for at least two important reasons. The pilots were essentially bomber pilots and were not trained in the field of reconnaissance. They made up for this lack of training by displaying great courage and ingenuity but this led directly to the second factor—high losses. More than 25 percent of the original pilots assigned to aerial reconnaissance in North Africa were lost during the first few months of the campaign. It was obvious that a change was needed and the new photoreconnaissance groups, formed in the continental United States and assigned to the various theater air forces, were the hoped-for answer.

The first such group to be sent to Europe was the 3d Reconnaissance Group under the command of Lieutenant Colonel Elliott Rooosevelt. Roosevelt had been active in aerial mapping and surveying photography for nearly two years, finding sites for North Atlantic airbases and later mapping areas in West Africa that were important to the French. Since he was the son of the President of the United States and apparently had some playboy tendencies, Roosevelt's appointment as C.O. of the 3d Reconnaissance Group was criticized by many. Additionally, he had not gone through USAAF flight training to earn his wings as a pilot. Despite these obvious drawbacks, however, it soon became apparent that Roosevelt intended to do everything possible to improve the quality of aerial reconnaissance in the ETO.

The 3d Reconnaissance Group—sometimes designated as the 3d Photographic Group Reconnaissance—was a workhorse from the day it reached Algeria. Committed to supplying photo intelligence to all commanders in the Mediterranean Theater of Operations, the group pioneered in the development of aerial photography to meet the tactical requirements of air, ground, and naval forces. For bomber units it obtained target photographs and made plates for the assessment of damage resulting from bombing attacks. In support of the ground forces it engaged in photographic reconnaissance, canvassing enemy airfields, mapping long strips of road, and procuring front-line coverage. For naval headquarters the 3d Reconnaissance Group provided photographic records of shipping in the harbors of such ports as Bizerte, Tunis, Sfax, and Sousse in North Africa and Cagliari, Sardinia.

During the first three months of operations in North Africa by the 3d Reconnaissance Group, fourteen of the total of fifty-one officers originally assigned to the unit were reported killed or missing in action. Such losses were keenly felt in this early period because they included some of the most experienced fliers.

"We learned many of our tactics the hard way," said George Humbrecht, a veteran pilot who served with the group. Humbrecht told about the hazards the reconnaissance pilots faced during these early months:

"When I returned from my first few missions to the airfield at Algiers I always dove the F-4 (modified P-38) down through the clouds. Sometimes I would break out of the overcast at such a steep angle and going so fast that the British and American antiaircraft gunners would think they were under attack by the Luftwaffe and start firing. Finally their C.O. asked me to let down slowly through the clouds and promised me that if I did his gunners wouldn't fire.

"That seemed fair enough so the following day when I returned from a photo mission checking on Rommel's advance, I showed down, dropped my flaps, and began a very shallow descent through the clouds. I broke out of the bottom of the overcast very gently—directly into the path of six FW-190s on their way to bomb a British airfield. The six FW-190s were escorted by nine Me-109s.

"Fortunately they were as startled as I was and for a few moments nothing happened. As soon as I recovered from my shock I raised my flaps, slammed open the throttle, and leveled off. The FW-190s dropped their bombs, thinking I was leading a group of fighters which intended to attack their formation. The bombs exploded harmlessly on the desert below while I circled frantically trying to stay out of the line of fire of the German planes. I had no guns and no way to fight back. Meanwhile I called my airbase and requested some help.

"I was able to outmaneuver the Luftwaffe pilots for the ten minutes it took for the American fighters to arrive. Once they engaged the Germans in a dogfight, I tried to slip away, wanting to get my photos of the Souk el Khems Beja area back to headquarters, but an Me-109 pilot spotted me and opened fire. My hydraulic lines were shot away, part of my controls, and the left engine started to burn. With only the elevators working as they should I descended in a wide circle and crash-landed at a British airfield while one of the P-38 pilots knocked the Me-109 out of the sky. Fortunately, the pictures were not damaged."

Humbrecht, who later was commanding officer of the 7th Reconnaissance Group in England, soon learned the necessary techniques needed for the survival of a reconaissance pilot and became an expert at obtaining photographs. When no one could locate the secret airfield that was keeping Rommel supplied during his advance against the British in North Africa, Humbrecht was assigned the job. It took him several days but he finally located the well-camouflaged field. After making a successful photo run over it, he flipped his F-4 around to make a second pass—and nearly rammed an attacking Me-109. As usual, his recon plane was unarmed. He immediately jettisoned his drop tanks. As these loaded gasoline tanks dropped away, the F-4 shot 500 feet higher, and Humbrecht was able to escape from the German aircraft and get the pictures back to base. The next day American and British bombers destroyed the secret airbase.

On another occasion, Colonel Lauris Norstad, Director of Operations, Headquarters, North African Theater of Operations, called Roosevelt's airbase and told him that he suspected the Germans were moving supplies into Sicily at night. Recon photos taken during the day didn't show any such enemy action but Norstad wanted to know what was happening on the island after dark. He had to know since the Allies were already planning to invade Sicily. Roosevelt took the problem to Humbrecht, who decided that they would need a B-25 to accomplish the mission. Norstad got them the B-25 but there was not enough time to transfer a crew to the 3d Reconnaissance Group to fly the aircraft. Consequently Humbrecht checked himself out in the B-25, loaded the bomb bay with flash bombs for night photography, and the belly of the plane with three K-17 cameras. Roosevelt, the C.O. who had not attended USAAF flight school, went along as co-pilot.

They took off on a pitch-black runway since the Tunisian airfield at La Marsa had no lights, and once the B-25 was airborne Humbrecht headed for Palermo. He maintained an altitude of 12,000 feet, and as he neared the city he motioned for Roosevelt to turn on the cameras. Everything went smoothly until the first flash bomb was dropped. Preset to explode at 5,000 feet and light the target below so that the cameras could record the scene on film, the flash bomb alerted the defenses of Sicily. Within minutes every searchlight in Palermo was centered on the lone B-25. Humbrecht, nearly blinded by the glare, had to resort to his instruments in order to maintain level flight. With flak bursts rocking the B-25 and threatening to ignite the remainder of the dangerous flash bombs inside the bomb bay and blow the aircraft to pieces, Humbrecht jettisoned the flash bombs. Forty flash bombs dropped together, and when they all exploded simultaneously at 5,000 feet the concussion was so great it blew the searchlights out and Humbrecht and Roosevelt slipped away in the darkness. They had obtained only a few frames of photographs but they were enough to prove that the Nazis were moving supplies into the island at night. The bombers began night sorties shortly afterward in an effort to stop the incoming supplies.

The North African campaign provided a testing ground for the Army Air Forces' theories on the use of photo reconnaissance in combat. The findings in that theater singled out two important principles that guided the employment of reconnaissance units in later campaigns. Among the first concepts to be confirmed was the belief that reconnaissance aircraft had to be ranked with the fastest fighters available to the enemy so that escort could be held to a minimum. Combat in North Africa also demonstrated the tactical reasons why reconnaissance planes could not be expected to function properly when attached to ground commands. That system not only led to such wide dispersal of air force units that the small number of aircraft available for each particular mission would accomplish little or nothing, but it also resulted in aircraft being idle when their services were urgently needed on another part of the front.

After the 3d Reconnaissance Group proved that the recon aircraft had to be as fast as any German fighter operating in the theater, modified P-38s, designated F-4 and F-5 (a later version), were used almost exclusively by the unit. The twin engines restricted maneuverability to some extent and since the plane was controlled by a wheel instead of a stick the pilots were hampered to a degree. At its rated altitude of 20,000 feet or higher, however, the stripped-down F-4s and F-5s were more than a match for the Me-109s and FW-190s. The F-4 usually carried three K-17 trimetrogon 6-inch-cone cameras and two K-17 fixed vertical 24-inch-cone cameras or a single fixed vertical K-18 camera with a 24-inch-cone. All the cameras were in the nose. The F-5 had a similar arrangment of cameras although the equipment varied according to the type of mission.

Photo interpreters and technicians were at a premium in North Africa. Colonel Minton W. Kaye, Director of Photography, Army Air Forces, advised Washington that there was an acute shortage of lab technicians and photo interpreters and that the situation was getting worse every day. In addition to the school at Lowry Field, an Army Air Forces Intelligence School was opened at Harrisburg, Pennsylvania. The primary purpose of the school was to train air intelligence officers and one of the most important courses at the school was photo interpretation. Harvey Brown, the captain who had been sent to England to study the RAF reconnaissance methods prior to the entry of the United States into the war, joined the school as an instructor. Yet all this took time and in North Africa Roosevelt and his fliers were providing many more photos than could be processed. The small RAF photographic section at Algiers was swamped with work. The handful of American interpreters who finally arrived were put to work in an old schoolhouse with inadequate equipment, and, with little knowledge of the strange African desert; the Americans at first made errors and overlooked many important items. A tale that went the rounds of the North African bases told about the newly arrived American PIs studying a group of recent aerial photographs and deciding that a convoy of enemy tanks was headed directly toward a British airbase. The British First Army was immediately alerted and had moved nearly a hundred miles toward the reported convoy before a more experienced interpreter studied the pictures and discovered that the "tanks" were camels.

The British and the American technicians and interpreters worked independently of each other with much duplication of activity. Reports to ground commanders were at times delayed as much as forty-eight hours, often with serious consequences.

"I flew reconnaissance for the British First Army," George Humbrecht said, "and every day I photographed the front. I would take the pictures, land, drive the film to the processing lab and wait for it to be developed, and then take the photographs directly to the commanding officer in a big old touring car we had scrounged for that purpose. I even helped them interpret the photos. Yet, even with this service, not nearly all the pictures were used. Once, when I was requested to get some photos of an area which I knew had been covered many times I drove to the British First Army headquarters and began looking around. I not only found those pictures but a barn filled nearly to the haymow with photos which had to be stored to await someone who could interpret them. It was a frustrating situation."

Finally, in February 1943, the Northwest African Photographic Wing became operational. This was an amalgamation of American, British, Italian, and French units, and Roosevelt, promoted to full colonel, was given command of the unit. The wing also merged the interpretation and technical units of the Allies and from that date on the reconnaissance work in the theater was much more efficient—even though one of the "free" Italian reconnaissance pilots did take off on a photographic mission one day in an F-4 and fly straight home to Italy.

At the close of the North African campaign the 3d Reconnaissance Group moved to the outskirts of Tunis, where it remained until it was transferred to Italy in December 1943. Prior to going to Italy, however, the 3d flew a large share of the five hundred missions required of the Northwest African Photographic Wing to map the entire 10,000 square miles of Sicily prior to the invasion of the island. For the naval forces, the 3d and the newly arrived 5th Reconnaissance Group commanded by Major Leon W. Gray daily covered the more important ports from Gibraltar to Corfu and Tripoli and photographed twice daily the ports used by the Italian fleet. Once a week Humbrecht and his companions took aerial snapshots of all enemy airfields in Sicily, Sardinia, Corsica, Italy, and the western Balkans.

On December 8, 1943, the 3d Reconnaissance Group moved to San Severo, Italy, and though it changed bases many times during the next year and a half, it remained in the country until the end of World War II. During the crisis at Salerno shortly after the invasion, the campaign along the Garigliane River, and the Po Valley battles the recon pilots risked great hazards to fulfill Fifth Army requests. Shortly after their arrival in Italy Lieutenant James E. Hill was assigned the mission of photographing an area that extended up the Garigliane River to the Isoletta Dam, an extremely important and well-protected section of enemy-held territory. It was such a dangerous area that Hill was not briefed nor expected to fly over the entire route. The lieutenant, however, had different ideas. Despite an accurate barrage of flak and machine-gun fire, he held his course at the very low altitude of 2,500 feet and covered the entire section. In fact, he kept making runs until four Me-109s attacked him and then he made a successful dash for safety. The prints were of such quality and scale that the army was able to extract highly valuable information.

Roosevelt, meanwhile, was summoned to Washington to aid in planning an expansion of the aerial reconnaissance forces, and to take his place in Italy arrived one of the most flamboyant and inspiring recon pilots that ever turned on an aerial camera. This was Lieutenant Colonel Karl Polifka, who had already gained fame as commanding officer of Flight "A" of the 8th

Photographic Squadron flying out of Australia. Later, as Brigadier General "Pop" Polifka in Korea, he organized the reconnaissance forces for that war and was known as the USAF's ace troubleshooter. Prior to World War II Polifka pioneered mapping and charting work in Alaska and western Canada, testing in the air the many new developments instigated by the technical genius George Goddard.

As the ground forces advanced into Italy Polifka established the main base for photographic reconnaissance near Foggia at San Severo, where he took more than half the buildings in the town for his men and equipment. Flying a modified Lightning, which he had christened *Rosebud*, Polifka traversed Italy from one end to the other, visiting his scattered squadrons, taking photographs on dangerous missions, and encouraging his men during the depressing period when it seemed that everything was going wrong for the Allies. Since he was nearly thirty-four years old at the time, Washington discouraged him from flying combat missions, insinuating that he was too old. Besides, they didn't want anything to happen to the best troubleshooter they had in the reconnaissance field. Pop Polifka had other ideas.

"I'm not going to ask my men to do something I wouldn't do myself," he said over and over again.

Listing himself in the records as "Lieutenant Jones," he continued to take his turn overflying enemy territory for the necessary pictures. This worked well until the day he went to Cassino to try and locate the positions of the Germans' dreaded Nebelwefer weapons, the six-barreled mortar that fired six bombs simultaneously. He flew his beloved *Rosebud* up the valleys on either side of Cassino so low that he was on the same level as the guns when he took his photographs. The pictures were so outstanding that General Mark W. Clark of the U.S. Fifth Army summoned Lieutenant Jones to his headquarters to be congratulated. A sheepish Polifka had to admit that he had taken the photographs. The general enjoyed the joke as much as Pop Polifka although he reminded him that he was too valuable a man to fly such missions. Eight years later in another war Polifka was still flying aerial reconnaissance missions over enemy territory!

The text of the Distinguished Unit Citation awarded to the unit for outstanding performance—War Department General Orders 116, 1945—gave a clear, precise outline of the importance of aerial reconnaissance:

> The 3rd Photographic Group, Reconnaissance, is cited for outstanding performance of duty in action against the enemy on 28 August 1944. This unit distinguished itself in battle by extraordinary heroism, gallantry, and determination in overcoming extremely difficult and hazardous conditions and successfully obtaining photographic intelligence data vitally necessary to the rapid advance of Allied ground forces through the area being photographed. Numerous calls for photographic intelligence made severe demands upon the organization which, in order to comply, necessitated utilization of all personnel on a 24-hour operational basis consisting of the preparation for and actual flights, developing films, producing photographs, rendering interpretations, and rushing the photographs with these interpretative reports to the headquarters requiring them. Results of these efforts proved to be of inestimable value and contributed in a great degree to the rapid advance of our ground forces against a determined enemy. The results have proved tangible evidence of the esprit de corps, leadership, and efficient internal organization of the 3rd Photographic Group, Reconnaissance, and reflect great credit on itself and the armed forces of the United States.

Meanwhile, several hundred miles to the north, Elliott Roosevelt was busy with the greatest aerial reconnaissance task ever attempted—the photographing of France and Germany as the Allied forces moved toward Hitler's homeland.

6

Lens in the Sky Against the European Axis (2)

WHEN the pilots of the 3d Reconnaissance Group went to North Africa in 1942 to provide the necessary aerial photography for the Twelfth Air Force, the 13th Squadron of the 7th Reconnaissance Group headed for England. The squadron, commanded by Major James G. Hall, arrived in the United Kingdom late in 1942 and began an intensive training program under the guidance of the experienced British reconnaissance experts. Hall, later promoted to full colonel and given command of the entire 7th Reconnaissance Group when it was reorganized in July 1943, was one of the oldest fliers in combat. He listed his age as forty-seven years although several officers who knew him well vowed that he was six or eight years older. Jim Hall was half Indian, a handsome, well-to-do broker in civilian life who owned a seat on the New York Stock Exchange but never permitted membership in such a staid organization to interfere with his fun. He had been a pilot in World War I and when he returned to civilian life after the armistice Hall continued his flying. In the thirties he broke several flying records while publicizing an anti-Prohibition group and thus earned the nickname of the "flying broker." When the Japanese bombed Pearl

Harbor, Hall immediately applied for active duty and with the help of Elliott Roosevelt he finally got back into the service. It didn't take long for his superiors to discover that he still had the flying ability and daring that he had displayed in World War I and when the 13th Photo Reconnaissance Squadron was activated at Colorado Springs in 1942 he assumed command. On March 28, 1943, Hall became the first pilot of the United States Army Air Forces to fly a photographic reconaissance mission in Europe over Nazi-occupied territory. This was the forerunner of 1,367 missions flown by the 13th Squadron from its base at Mount Farm, near Oxford.

When the 7th Reconnaissance Group was reorganized in England in July 1943, it was assigned a twofold mission for the Eighth Air Force: mapping European targets to enable air elements and ground forces to spot troop concentrations, ammunition and supply dumps, and gun emplacements; and photographing areas already bombed to assess the damage inflicted. The 7th began mapping operations on a small scale as soon as it was reorganized. Photographic sweeps from the Cherbourg peninsula to the Maupertus and Querqueville airfields, and reconnaissance flights along the Normandy coast in the vicinity of Le Havre added to the store of intelligence that the Eighth Air Force was gathering. In early August 1943, as the Eighth Air Force stepped up the air counteroffensive against the Germans, the 7th was ordered to halt all mapping operations and prepare to photograph targets that had been bombed. Flying the F-5, the 7th, now composed of the 13th, 14th, 22d, and 27th Squadrons, daily crisscrossed the Continent to take strike pictures as soon as the smoke of the bombs had cleared away.

It was difficult, tiresome, and dangerous flying for the pilots of the 7th Reconnaissance Group. Over Europe the Luftwaffe was well organized and its best pilots were assigned the task of defending the homeland from all intruders, in the air or on the ground. The modified P-38 was a good aircraft but even with all its heavy equipment removed it was no match for the FW-190 and the 7th paid dearly in both men and planes for the photographs they obtained. On one of the first bomb-assessment missions over Europe the pilot failed to return, an omen of the trouble that was to follow in the weeks and months ahead. As he droned over the enemy-held coast at 30,000 feet, radio-location equipment in England spotted a patrol of German fighters in that area. A warning was flashed to the American flier but there was no answer. As the air executive officer, James Wright, explained later, "You can get away from one Focke-Wulf fairly easy, from two with a little effort. But six—well, you need guns to fight yourself out of a jam like that and our pilots don't carry guns."

First Lieutenant George F. Owen learned the hard way that the Germans would try every trick to trap a high-flying recon plane. A cheerful, black-haired pilot who never lacked for courage but constantly told everyone that he finally got his promotion from second lieutenant to first lieutenant because he opened doors for his commanding officer and bought him drinks at the officers' club bar, Owen flew some of the most rugged reconnaissance missions in the theater.

On one operation when he was assigned the job of bringing home aerial photographs of a target area in Occupied France, Owen discovered four enemy fighters chasing him:

"Every time I made a turn those bandits banked so that they could stay between my plane and my flight path home. The weather was lousy with a heavy cloud cover over most of France so I kept ducking in and out of the overcast hoping to lose the FWs. I didn't, however, because they always guessed that I was going to turn west towards England.

"Finally I decided to fool them. Instead of turning west after I went into the clouds I banked south and kept going. That lost them but by this time I was in southern France with half-empty gasoline tanks. Since the German fighters were nowhere to be seen, however, I decided to go back to northern France and try and get the target photos which I hadn't been able to get earlier.

I found a break in the cloud cover near the target, dropped down and took the pictures and headed for England. The weather was so bad at this time and my gas supply so low that I decided to try and get home on the deck. I think I was so low that my prop wash blew a couple of thatched roofs off farmers' homes. When I got to the Channel I radioed for help and an RAF squadron came and escorted me to the nearest field in England. Actually, I shouldn't have been sweating so much. I had nearly five minutes' worth of gas left in my tanks."

The slogan of the 7th Reconnaissance Group was "Get 'em, got 'em, gone!" which emphasized the fact that the recon pilot had to go into the target area fast, snap his pictures correctly on the first pass, and head for home at full speed before the defenders knocked him out of the sky. Speed was their chief protection—speed and constant vigilance. Although the Lightnings made a name for themselves in North Africa, the pilots of the 7th weren't satisfied. They removed sections of armor plate that was installed to protect the pilot and even the heavy bulletproof windshield. Some of the pilots spent their spare time on the ground sandpapering the fuselage of the F-5 so as to gain a few miles per hour speed.

The 7th pilots soon learned that they had to guard constantly against relaxing after the pictures were snapped. Most of the losses early in the operations of the group happened on the way home when the weary and busy pilots forgot to keep their heads turning all the time. Handling his own radio communications, solving his own navigation problems, snapping his own pictures, watching his instruments, the recon pilot was constantly on the move. Sometimes in the midst of all this activity he forgot to watch for the deadly specks in the sky that meant trouble.

"Hell," the veteran Wright said, "it's like playing the organ at the Roxy—with the audience shooting at you."

On a mission over the Continent that required Wright to take aerial photographs at Bremen, Wilhelmshaven, and Cuxhaven, he was so busy with his myriad duties that he temporarily neglected to keep his head on a swivel:

"Starting on the run over Cuxhaven at 29,000 feet I suddenly discovered that I had an unwelcome escort of seven FW-190s. I managed to keep ahead of the pack and shoot the pictures I had come after. But while I kept an eye on the FW-190s behind me I neglected to keep a watch on my starboard beam and a Messerschmitt 109 dove on me. I made a tight turn but that put me head-on towards the Focke-Wulf pack. I dove underneath them and then zoomed up behind them—up to 32,000 feet. The FWs gave up but that Me stayed right with me straight out to sea. I dove down to 25,000 feet and managed to get away. Fortunately, I got the bomb-assessment photos home."

The bomb-assessment photographs were invaluable to the men who had to direct the heavy bomber raids against enemy targets. Daylight pinpoint bombing by the American aircraft and night area bombing by the RAF had to be evaluated prior to sending the bombers to the targets for a second or third time. It was a waste of manpower, time, aircraft, and supplies to bomb a target that had been destroyed on the previous mission. Some targets, such as the German underground factory for building jet fighters at Kahla, near Jena, had to be hit periodically. When a photo interpreter at Medmenham spotted some unusual activity near the village and determined from the aerial photos that several tunnels were being dug in the hills, that a camp had been established nearby, and that a railroad spur line was under construction, he immediately forwarded his observations to Walt Rostow, who was working on target analysis for the Eighth Air Force. Rostow, an economist who became better known as Special Assistant to President Lyndon B. Johnson and a staunch advocate of the efficacy of bombing North Vietnam, suggested that a model of the Kahla site be made using the aerial photographs as a guide. The model was then used by the planners to figure out how to attack this new target. From that day until the end of the war the underground factory at Kahla and its supporting complexes were bombed at intervals determined by aerial photographs of the damage caused by previous raids. Whenever it appeared that the Germans had the factory in production again, Rostow would relay the news to Eighth Air Force headquarters at High Wycombe and the bombers would once again go to Kahla.

Another difficult target that was revisited constantly was the U-boat building yard, Deutsche Werke, at Kiel. During the winter of 1943-44 Kiel had to be bombed by radar due to poor weather conditions. Since the bomber crews couldn't even see the U-boat building yard for an approximate evaluation of the bombing results, photorecon pilots were the only source of damage information. The city was one of the most heavily defended areas on the Continent and the antiaircraft gunners were always lying in wait for the reconnaissance planes they knew would come shortly after the heavy bombers turned toward home.

Captain Hershell Parsons was briefed to check bomb damage to the Deutsche Werke after a radar-bombing attempt in late 1943 and the experience he reports was typical of that faced by the pilots who had to take pictures over Kiel:

"I climbed until I hit the vapor-trail level at about 31,000 feet, dropped to just below it, and started on the four-hour flight to Kiel. I had been briefed on the flak areas and possible fighter opposition and I had worked out a course which I hoped would make it as tough as possible for the German radio locators to pick me up. I hoped that I could at least make them think I was going someplace else. After I had been airborne about an hour I suddenly got the 'bends' in my right wrist and the pain was so bad I had to drop down to a lower altitude. Unfortunately, the Germans were still angry about the beating the bombers had given the U-boat yards and they really threw the flak at my plane. I managed to make three runs over the city, getting my photos through a break in the clouds, without getting hit. Since I had some film remaining I decided to take pictures of the German positions at Sylt, Helgoland, and Eckernforde. When I got back to base they told me that I had flown the longest recon mission ever flown by an American pilot."

Parsons' photographs were not good news to Eighth Air Force commander Lieutenant General James H. Doolittle at High Wycombe. Only a few of the combat boxes had dropped their bombs in the assigned target area. Some hard-to-replace machine tools had been damaged by incendiary bombs but most had been well protected by concrete walls constructed to limit blast damage. His aerial photographs showed that the estimate made by Eighth Air Force headquarters of a production loss of a month at Deutsche Werke was much too optimistic.

During the long winter months of 1943–44, aerial photographs revealed that radar bombing was not very accurate. During the period between October 15 and December 15, 1943, on only two missions did bombs fall in the assigned target area. Only six of the total of 150 combat boxes depending upon radar dropped their bombs within one mile of the aiming point; seventeen dropped within two miles; and thirty dropped within five miles. The reconnaissance pilots proved to USAAF planners that radar bombing was not dependable, that its main value was in keeping pressure on the enemy while the weather was too bad for the heavy bombers to drop their bombs visually, using the Norden bombsight.

After Hall was summoned back to the United States, Colonel Homer L. Sanders took command of the 7th Reconnaissance Group. He was not familiar with the modified P-38s the group was using so when he heard complaints that the plane was not as good as the Spitfires being used by the British recon pilots, he decided to find out for himself. Accustomed to the P-51s, none of which were yet available for photography missions, Sanders didn't know that he couldn't use maximum manifold pressure in the P-38 at 30,000 feet. He promptly lost the right engine and caused damage to the left engine. Getting instructions from experienced P-38 pilots in the control tower on how to make a single-engine landing, Sanders nursed the aircraft back to the strip and set it down successfully. His first words after climbing out of the cockpit brought grins to the faces of the group's pilots.

"Boys, we're going to get ourselves some Spitfires!"

After a great deal of arguing and pleading, Sanders managed to get enough Spitfires to equip one of his squadrons. The Mark XI Spitfire could climb to 41,000 feet without trouble and according to Major Robert R. Smith, who commanded the 13th Squadron, it could easily outrun any of the German fighters.

"The Spit could also take a great deal of punishment. The only one we lost while our unit had them was a Spitfire which the Germans gave a wrong steer while the pilot was flying over the clouds. The confused pilot landed in Germany and the Luftwaffe had a new Spitfire," Smith said. "When Roosevelt came back to England from Washington, however, that was the end of the Spits. Roosevelt said that American pilots were going to fly American planes so we went back to the P-38s."

If the pilots needed any proof that the P-38 could also absorb a lot of damage and still fly, a photo mission flown by Captain Charles R. Batson shortly before D-Day gave it to them. Checking the Normandy coast on a "dicing" mission—low-altitude flight using nose oblique camera—Batson flew directly over a German gun position. A fantastic pilot who had shot down three German planes while flying a tour in fighter aircraft, Batson managed to get his battered P-38 back to base where a complete inventory revealed that by all laws of aerodynamics the plane could not fly. There were, by count, 130 holes in the fuselage and wings, and bullets in the camera compartment and camera magazine; the oil radiators on both engines were stuffed full of twigs and leaves; the leading edge of the wing was damaged; the left engine was shot out and the supercharger on the other engine lost. Batson was awarded the Silver Star but unfortunately, the day after D-Day, he was killed on another low-level flight when his recon plane hit some electric wires.

By January 1944 the pilots of the 7th were back at mapping, especially the areas around Blankenberge, Dunkerque, Le Touquet, and St. Vaast la Hougue. Their maps and photographs were an important contribution to the success of Overlord, the invasion of the Continent. During the climax of the preinvasion preparations the campaign against the oil production of the enemy by the heavy bombers began. By the time Germany invaded Poland in 1939 her oil reserves were dwindling and Hitler estimated that he had only six months' supply in reserve. Planned operations by his troops against France, Hungary, Rumania, and other countries and a strict rationing program rebuilt his supplies, however. By 1943 Germany's synthetic oil plants were producing more than 6,180,000 tons of petroleum products and over 2,000,000 tons of oil were being obtained from Rumania and Hungary. Hitler was confident at this time that his oil supply was sufficient to continue operations indefinitely.

In early 1944 the Allied air forces decided to concentrate on a systematic destruction of the German oil facilities, hoping to flush out the Luftwaffe and deplete it prior to the invasion and at the same time cut the enemy oil production to a trickle, thereby hampering German ground forces. Approximately 90 percent of the petroleum output was accounted for by fifty-four crude-oil refineries and synthetic oil plants, and of these, twenty-seven were of great importance. General Carl Spaatz, commander of the Strategic Air Forces in Europe, decided to concentrate his heavy bombers on these twenty-seven centers.

One of the twenty-seven was the plant at Leuna, near Merseburg, Germany. It had been photographed for the first time in 1941 by the British and periodic recon flights by the RAF and American pilots kept close tabs on the facility. Whenever the plant appeared about ready to go back into full operation after the damage from a previous air raid had been repaired, the bombers hit it again. One photographic check on the plant was made early in 1944 by Captain Jacob W. Dixon. Taking off alone in his Lightning, Dixon headed for Leuna, which he knew was one of the most heavily defended targets in all of Germany. Because the Luftwaffe had been making an all-out effort to prevent photography planes from snapping pictures of the oil facilities, a fighter escort was assigned to protect Dixon's aircraft.

When the captain reached Leuna flying at 26,000 feet he discovered the area was covered with clouds and it was impossible to obtain the picture coverage needed.

"I decided that if I had come this far to get the pictures I wasn't going to allow a few clouds to get in my way," Dixon said. "Consequently I told the fighter escort to stay at 26,000 while I dropped to about 15,000 to get under clouds."

At 15,000 feet he still could not see the target. The antiaircraft fire from the German ground positions was extremely heavy at this time but the daring captain refused to quit. He nosed the Lightning down to 10,000 feet, just under the overcast, and tried to make a third pass over the city. He never made it. A flak shell hit his plane and it immediately caught fire. With the flames eating toward the cockpit and the fuel tanks, Dixon still refused to bail out until he had contacted the fighter escort flight leader, who was still circling at 26,000 feet, and relayed a message: "I'm hit but I've seen the target. Tell them that the plant seems to be back to normal operations. I'm sure that it is working again. That's all. I'm bailing out!"

Dixon served the remainder of the war as a prisoner of the Germans. His last radio message was forwarded to Eighth Air Force headquarters and the following day the B-17s and B-24s went to Leuna again and put the plant out of operation once more.

On March 4, 1944, the American bombers attempted to bomb Berlin for the first time in daylight hours. Reichsmarschall Hermann Goering had always bragged that the capital of Nazi Germany could never be bombed in daylight by the Eighth Air Force and it was important to the Allies that they prove it could be done. On March 4 the weather was extremely bad and only one formation—the 95th Bomb Group and a few planes from the 100th Bomb Group—reached the city. They dropped their bombs on the Bosch plant in the Klein Machnow suburb of Berlin, but Goering immediately denied that the American bombs had touched the capital. To disprove his propaganda charges, Major Walter M. Weitner flew the first photoreconnaissance mission to Berlin the next day and brought back pictures that proved beyond a doubt that the Eighth Air Force planes had bombed Berlin. Unfortunately, the pictures also proved that the bombs hadn't seriously damaged the Bosch plant, once again verifying that radar bombing was not accurate.

A few weeks prior to D-Day the reconnaissance forces in England were reorganized along more efficient lines, the aim being to provide all services with the photographs they needed from one central control point. The main interpretation unit remained at Medmenham while an American photoreconnaissance headquarters was established at High Wycombe. A joint committee responsible directly to the Combined Chiefs of Staff was established at Benson to coordinate the requests for aerial photographs and set up the priorities. At High Wycombe a new U.S. reconnaissance wing, the 325th Reconnaissance Wing, was established and Elliott Roosevelt was given command. His photographic intelligence staff officer was the experienced and enthusiastic Harvey Brown. Several other reconnaissance units were active in the ETO by this time, including the 10th Reconnaissance Group commanded by Lieutenant Colonel Russel A. Berg and the 67th (Peck's Bad Boys) commanded by Major George W. Peck.

Flying out of the base at Chalgrove in Oxfordshire, the 10th used a variety of aircraft, including the A-20, P-40, and the P-51. The 67th, using the field at Middle Wallop, Hampshire, flew P-38s and P-51s. The modified P-51, known as the F-6, became an outstanding photoreconnaissance plane, highly valued by the pilots. Its high speed and rate of climb made it a favorite for taking pictures of the invasion coast prior to D-Day. When the 67th first got their P-51s the planes had only one camera and it was mounted in the tail section. The camera could be pointed vertically or tilted to a low-oblique angle but this change of position could only be made on the ground.

Obviously this wasn't an efficient setup. After a great deal of experimenting, the battery and some of the radio gear was moved to a position just behind the pilot and another camera was installed that could take pictures from the high-oblique position. This involved cutting a hole just slightly larger than the camera, reinforcing the cut with another thickness of aluminum skin, and putting a neat deflector flange at the front of the opening. The pilot could then take pictures with either camera at the flick of a switch in the cockpit. The only drawback was that the new camera caught a few inches of the trailing edge of the wing but this was a small price to pay for such an improvement. This same setup was used on the later model P-51s that came to England. The K-12 and, later, the K-17 cameras were the ones most commonly used in the P-51 while the K-18 was used, along with the K-17, in the P-38.

Colonel R. E. ("Doc") Currie, at the time a second lieutenant with the 67th, flew many of the sorties scheduled in May 1944 to obtain the aerial reconnaissance photos needed by the ground forces preparing to invade the Continent. He remembers:

"We had to fly straight-and-level three miles out from the coast at 3,000 feet. We laid it out in small sections, starting at Holland and continuing to Spain. If we got bracketed by enemy fire which we considered too heavy, we'd break off and go somewhere else a goodly distance away. At all ports, cities, or obviously well-defended spots, we fell back on a British camera which the USAAF designated as the K-20. It had a longer focal length and took the same size picture—5 by 4 inches—and same scale from an altitude of 6,000 feet and six miles out. We had only one plane equipped with this camera in our outfit. It was mounted in the high-oblique position just behind the pilot so we would go out on the deck all the way until we got close to the target area and then zoom to 10,000 feet and dive on our target run at full speed."

In March 1944, shortly after its arrival in England, the 10th Reconnaissance Group was given the responsibility of obtaining bomb-assessment photographs for the Ninth Air Force for first-phase interpretation. With the approach of D-Day, however, the 10th was designated to photograph the coastal defenses from Blankenberge to Dunkerque and from Le Touquet to St. Vaast de la Hougue, which the 7th had mapped in January. Between May 6 and May 20 the pilots of the 10th flew 232 operations, many of them hazardous "dicing" missions. In order to provide the assault commanders with extremely detailed information about the proposed invasion beaches and the airborne landing areas immediately behind them, a number of missions were flown at altitudes as low as 15 feet. Of these, eleven were considered outstanding in that the photographs taken on the flights showed the location of shallow-water and beach defenses so clearly that assault forces were able to avoid or remove the obstacles during the initial phase of the invasion. For these missions, flown in the face of some of the strongest antiaircraft emplacements in western Europe, the 10th received a Distinguished Unit Citation.

Immediately after the Allied ground troops landed on the beaches of Normandy on June 6, 1944, a much greater emphasis was placed upon tactical reconnaissance, missions that informed the ground-force commanders just what they could expect from the enemy over the next hill or across the next river. The 155th Night Photo Squadron of the 10th Reconnaissance Group even flew such missions in the darkness during the early hours of D-Day and brought back pictures of roadstrips, crossroads, and artillery emplacements in such towns as Cerisy, Avranches, and Granville. However, night photography continued to be a problem throughout the war. The English had discovered as early as 1940 that only about one-fourth of the photographs taken at night by the reconnaissance crews showed the target area. Navigation was the main difficulty. Either the pilot had to fly at high altitudes because of the intense flak or on the deck to avoid alerting the enemy guns and neither position was good for night navigation. It was almost impossible to spot the rivers, roads, blacked-out villages or other landmarks that were required for visual sighting of the target area, while taking a fix on a star was out of the question due to lack of time. Dead-reckoning navigation and, later, radar were the two main methods used but neither proved to have the necessary pinpoint accuracy. Even with these restrictions, however, the 155th and other night-photo squadrons did an outstanding job.

Usually the K-19 camera was used for night photography in conjunction with either the Edgerton flash system or the M-46 flash bomb. The M-46 flash bomb weighed about 52 pounds, of which 25 pounds was flash powder. It was dropped from the aircraft and detonated by a present-time fuse to set it off at a predetermined altitude. It reached a peak candlepower of about 500 million in times that varied from 13 to 25 milliseconds, with a total duration of about 0.1 second. This time to peak was dependent upon the composition of the flash powder; those containing potassium perchlorate required about 13 milliseconds, while the ones that contained barium nitrate peaked in about 25 milliseconds.

The Edgerton flash principle was a later development adapted to night aerial photography. Discharge of the energy stored in a bank of capacitors through a xenon-filled tube was found to produce a brilliant flash of short duration. Synchronizing the shutter action of an aerial camera with this brilliant flash proved to be much simpler than trying to synchronize the shutter speed with the peak intensity of an M-46 flash bomb. In the Edgerton flash system the shutter was tripped and when it was in the full open position it triggered the flash tube through an auxiliary contact. The D-1 unit was the smallest airborne unit used, weighing only 125 pounds and employing a capacitor bank of 75 μf. It delivered two flashes per second. The main drawback of the D-1, however, was that its maximum useful altitude was only 300 feet and it required a continuous charging current of 100 amperes. The larger D-2 unit weighed 460 pounds, utilized a 600-mf capacitor bank, and was good up to 2,500 feet in altitude. The largest of all the flash units was the D-3. It weighed 3,500 pounds, used two lamps, and had a capacitor bank of 7200 μs. This unit was useful up to 10,000 feet but it required a continuous charging current of 600 amperes.

During the Battle of the Bulge the 155th Night Photo Squadron rendered exceptional service despite the shortcomings of night photography. It won high praise for intelligence work based on night photography carried out in late December and for supplying photographs of the enemy's position to the beleaguered forces at Bastogne, Belgium. General Elwood R. Quesada, commanding general of the 9th Tactical Air Command, which supported the U.S. First Army in its drive into Germany, had triangular radar beams set up for the use of the night recon pilots and this improved the accuracy of their navigation to a great extent. At the same time, however, it was discovered that the regular interval between flashes of the Edgerton flash unit made the reconnaissance planes excellent targets for the Nazi ground gunners, advertising their exact location at all times. Consequently many of the night photo units reverted to the use of the less reliable but safer flash bomb.

As the Allied armies fought eastward toward Berlin, reconnaissance missions became more and more important to the ground commanders. The reconnaissance units moved from airbase to airbase on the Continent as the armies advanced, always staying as close to the front lines as possible. Every day planes would fly photo and visual reconnaissance over an area seventy-five miles from the front lines into enemy territory. It was customary to cover the next seventy-five miles daily by visual reconnaissance alone and anything deeper than 150 miles into enemy territory was checked by aerial photography. All photographs were subjected to three-phase interpretation: the first phase was the immediate delivery of the pictures, sometimes "wet" prints, to the commander who needed them for on-the-spot decisions; second-phase interpretation was done at the various headquarters where the Army or Air Force commander studied them at more leisure; and third-phase interpretation was conducted at the Allied Central Interpretation Unit, where a detailed analysis was made and a complete pictorial dossier of each target maintained.

The continuous coverage of the front lines and enemy territory was murderous duty and losses were high. Lieutenant Currie of the 67th discovered this shortly after D-Day when he was assigned to check a report that there was heavy enemy armor in the Carentan area inland from the beachhead. It was June 9, 1944, and General Courtney H. Hodges of the First Army was desperate for the information.

"I led a flight to have a look-see in the area and made landfall about 8:00 P.M., I was to recce the roads leading south from Cherbourg to the Carentan sector. However, Cherbourg was socked in solid so I turned out over the water to see if I could get in to Carentan that way. I was very carefully skirting the naval prohibited zones, flying at about 250 feet hunting a hole in the clouds to fly through to the target area so that I could get my pictures. I was confident that the Allied ships beneath recognized my plane as friendly because it had the customary wide black and white stripes painted around the wings and fuselage and my electronic signal, the IFF, was turned on.

"I was wrong. Without warning one American vessel let loose with all it had and within less time than it takes to dot an *i* every American ship in the area was firing at my aircraft. The first steel I took set me on fire. I broke left, toward open water where there was a 700-foot ceiling. On my way up all controls were shot out, I took a piece of steel between my left cheek and ear that almost knocked me out, lost a small part of my nose, my chronometer was knocked off my wrist, and a chunk tore through the top of my helmet. At 700 feet I stood up in the cockpit and jumped out. I bounced once on the leading edge of the stabilizer, slid over it, and dropped towards the water. My parachute billowed out, I swung once, and hit the cold water."

Currie's Mae West and dinghy both had been riddled by shrapnel so he had to swim in the water for about twenty minutes before a Navy patrol boat picked him up. Unfortunately, he was caught between two rescue boats and both his kneecaps were badly injured. Within a short time, however, he was back flying, helping to provide the photographic intelligence needed by the First Army.

On his last mission before the end of the war, Currie had another unusual experience. He was acting as a reconnaissance tie between the U.S. troops who were meeting the Russians at the Elbe and the other American forces to the rear. It was a delicate, dangerous hookup between the two great armies and no one was certain just what might happen. Currie was taking photographs and relaying radio messages to the rear headquarters when "suddenly the weather turned sour and it was nip and tuck when three 109s appeared from around a cloud. I beat a strategic retreat, ducking into the clouds for a while. When I popped out again because my plane was icing up, I popped right in front of them. One Luftwaffe pilot put a 23-mm cannon shell in my cockpit, giving me a ragged two-inch gash above my right eye, another smaller one to the left, and three assorted shrapnel wounds in my hair. Fortunately I made it back behind friendly lines and crash-landed about two miles from an evac hospital."

The 10th Reconnaissance Group provided aerial photographic and visual reconnaissance for the Third Army. That was a real task since the Third Army commander, General George S. Patton, Jr., was one of the boldest commanders ever to wear an American uniform and wanted information on everything and every place. On January 5, 1945, for instance, Patton wanted to know if there were any Saar River bridges still standing over which Panzer troops could cross. Captain Robert J. Holbury, assistant operations officer of the group, volunteered to try and get the pictures that would tell the story. There was a 10/10 overcast and the clouds were a mere 600 feet above the ground but Holbury covered the entire Saar River sector from Lettlach to Kanzem at low level. He dodged flak, high tension wires, and trees and brought back 212 photographs for the general, proving that only one pontoon bridge across the river still stood. It was soon destroyed. Holbury also brought back a P-38 that was a complete wreck. The right engine was shot out, the right boom dragged on the runway when he landed, and the wings and fuselage were ripped in a hundred places. The maintenance crew took one look at the Lightning and pushed it into the junk pile.

General Russel A. Berg was stationed in the Pentagon in 1968 as director of the Office of Space Systems, but twenty-four years earlier he was a lieutenant colonel commanding the 10th Reconnaissance Group in England. After D-Day the 10th moved to France and Germany following the Third Army. Berg, a large, rugged pilot who looked as though he should be flying bombers but handled the controls of a P-38 with a gentle, sure touch, personally covered large sectors of enemy territory day and night for Patton. As the war neared its end most of the fighter escort for the bombers was flown by P-51s and P-47s, so that the Luftwaffe pilots soon became aware that any time a P-38 appeared over Germany it was a recon plane. Consequently the recon planes became favorite targets of the German fighter pilots, who not only knew that they were snapping valuable photographs but also that they were easy picking since they were unarmed. Berg, aware of this fact, finally convinced headquarters that the recon P-38s should be armed so that they could protect themselves, promising that his pilots would not use the guns except in an emergency. They would always keep in mind their primary mission: bring back the photographs.

"I still think it was a wise decision," Berg said later, "but it certainly caused me a lot of trouble. For a bunch of pilots who were supposed to shoot only in self-defense, my boys had too many victories. I spent a lot of my time traveling to headquarters explaining why my pilots were becoming aces. One flier, Clyde East, shot down six enemy planes in one day!"

Berg himself had an unusual experience near the end of the war while on a reconnaissance mission near Thuringer Wald. As he was taking photographs he spotted a group of German soldiers in a wooded area and quickly notified a flight of P-47 fighters cruising nearby. The Thunderbolts roared in to attack but the American pilots were amazed to see that the Germans were signaling that they wanted to surrender. Notifying the Third Army units close to the scene, the pilots circled the Germans until the American soldiers arrived. Nine thousand enemy troops surrendered because one lone recon pilot spotted them hiding in the woods. Patton, in a gesture of gratitude, sent a case of French wine to Berg.

As the ground forces pushed across Europe, the Eighth Air Force continued to pound away at the enemy from the air. Oil refineries were still important targets and photographs, before and after the strikes, were a vital necessity. On August 14, 1944, Major Robert Smith of the 7th Reconnaissance Group was asked to fly a photography mission to Dresden, to obtain pictures of a secret synthetic oil refinery the Nazis had recently established. Smith had completed the required number of combat reconnaissance missions but had decided to stay with the group for a while longer. When the request came for the Dresden pictures, he and Lieutenant Waldo Bruns, the operations officer, were the only two pilots available. It was late, about 4:30 in the afternoon, and Smith was well aware that if they didn't leave immediately there would be no photographs that day because it would soon be dark.

Smith and Bruns took off, climbed to 30,000 feet, and headed east at near-top speed in their P-38s. The weather was good and the briefing officer had assured the pair that he had routed them through a relatively flak-free area. Near the secret oil refinery on the outskirts of Dresden, however, the sky was suddenly black with bursting antiaircraft shells. Smith's right engine was badly damaged and he feathered the propeller. He maneuvered out of the flak barrage and took a position on Waldo's wing and the pair continued toward the target.

"Break!"

Bruns's warning came just in time. Two FW-190s were diving out of the sun toward them.

"I immediately dove into the clouds and tried to stay in them in hopes that the FW-190s would give up the attack," Smith said. "Unfortunately, the clouds ran out and I flew into a perfectly clear sky. At that moment I saw four more FWs coming at me so I radioed Waldo to get the hell out of the area and I broke for the deck. I never made it."

Cannon shells ripped Smith's Lightning from both sides and the wing caught fire. When the smoke filled the cockpit after another shell smashed into the instrument panel, Smith bailed out. He broke his ankle on landing but he still tried to hobble into a nearby woods and hide. Within minutes he was caught and the war was over for him. He spent the remainder of the fight in a German prisoner-of-war camp.

"At that, I was luckier than Waldo. He was shot down and killed. The German doctor that fixed my ankle after I bailed out told me that Waldo's body had been found in the wreckage of his plane," Smith said.

Major General Klegler of the German Reichswehr once stated: "Without reconnaissance, command and troops are blind. Reconnaissance without aerial reconnaissance—like aerial reconnaissance without photography—is inconceivable."

There was no reason for U.S. commanders of troops to be blind in the ETO during World War II. The 10th Reconnaissance Group alone, for example, flew a total of 8,830 missions comprising 27,206.15 hours of operational flying. During its nearly twenty-one months of combat operations the 7th Reconnaissance Group provided the Eighth Air Force with more than three million intelligence photographs while the 67th supplied General Hodges and his staff with over five million pictures, more than any other army had ever received. By the end of hostilities the USAAF had developed a photographic system unmatched by any other nation. Aerial photography had advanced from an art to a science, a science that helped greatly to defeat the Nazi war machine.

7

Watching the Rising Sun (1)

IT WAS obvious from the beginning that the same standard operating procedure used by aerial reconnaissance units in the European Theater of Operations would not be satisfactory in the wide expanses of the Pacific. Very few of the reconnaissance aircraft flying over Europe were armed. If they located a target, the pilots notified their headquarters and the required attacking force was dispatched to handle the task. In the Pacific, however, the distances were much too great for this and consequently most of the patrolling and reconnaissance aircraft were armed or loaded with bombs. Once they located a target, they did their own bombing or strafing. Of course, there were certain targets that were photographed regularly for planned ground or sea operations and to accomplish these missions either P-38s with extra gasoline tanks attached, B-24s, or B-29s—all modified for aerial photography assignments—were used. They seldom attacked any targets.

For approximately six months after Pearl Harbor the Japanese moved outward from their home islands, always on the offensive, always pushing the weak and unprepared Allied forces back. Finally an Allied defensive perimeter was set up, a huge semicircle that extended from Alaska on the north to the India-Burma area and included Hawaii and Australia. At intervals along this semicircle airfields were constructed on widely spaced islands to provide a line of communications and to help guard the sea lanes to Australia. Eventually, the Japanese outward movement was halted and they set up an offensive arc concentric with the Allied defensive arc: the Kuriles and outer Aleutians; Marcus, Wake, and the mandated islands; the Solomons, New Guinea, Netherlands East Indies; Singapore, Burma, and Occupied China.

In this eyeball-to-eyeball situation in early 1942, the United States had six air force units to use. The Eleventh Air Force operated in the North Pacific; the Seventh Air Force in the Central Pacific; the Thirteenth Air Force in the South Pacific; the Fifth Air Force in the Southwest Pacific; the Tenth Air Force in the India-Burma sector; and the Fourteenth Air Force in China. Unfortunately there was no unified command. It was an everyone-for-himself setup and each of the air forces tried to provide its own aerial reconnaissance the best it could with the planes, pilots, PIs, and photographic equipment available.

It soon became obvious to American military men that the Japanese intended to punch holes in the south end of the Allied defensive arc in the lower Solomons at Guadalcanal and at northern Papua in hopes of crossing the Owen Stanley Mountains and capturing Port Moresby, from where northern Australia could be hit with bombers. The loss of Australia would be a tragedy to the Allies' hopes of maintaining their defensive position in the Pacific until forces and supplies could be built up to permit their own offensive actions. It was decided that Port Moresby had to be saved from the Japanese at all costs and to accomplish this it was absolutely necessary that the Allies know where the Japanese fleet was and in which direction it was moving at all times. This near-impossible aerial reconnaissance assignment was handed to the small number of recon pilots in the Pacific, both U.S. Navy and USAAF.

Army Air Forces headquarters had been prompt to recognize the need for properly equipped photographic units in the Pacific but a shortage of equipment plus the fact that the European Theater of Operations had priority made for an acute scarcity. One of the first units ready for operation was the "A" Flight of the 8th Photographic Squadron commanded by Karl Polifka, who later was to take over the reconnaissance organizations in Italy from Elliott Roosevelt. Polifka arrived in Australia on April 7, 1942, with a grand total of four F-4s, which were P-38Es modified by the installation of cameras and two additional 75-gallon tanks, and very little else except the pilots to fly them.

Clark Sykes, a flyer who joined Polifka's unit later in 1942 and became one of the outstanding reconnaissance pilots in the USAAF, was deeply impressed with the man when he first arrived in Australia:

"I was a second lieutenant, new to recon and new to combat when I reached Darwin in 1942. Several of us pilots were sitting in operations waiting for an assignment, all eager to join the fighter pilots who were out hunting the Zeros day after day. Any suggestion of flying photography missions would have been laughed off as ridiculous. We were there to fight, not go "click-click" with a camera from five miles high. About that time, however, this character walked into operations and stared at us. He had a long, British-type mustache, had part American flying clothes and part RAF flying clothes, wore cowboy boots, and had a wide-brimmed hat that threw a shadow on his tanned face. To us new second lieutenants he was the picture of a real, devil-may-care fighting man. When he asked us if we would be interested in getting into action right away, we all volunteered, not bothering to ask what type of action. It wasn't until later that I discovered the missions I would be flying were aerial photography missions and by that time I would do anything 'Pop' wanted me to do."

Later Sykes flew with Polifka in Korea and his admiration for this pioneering expert was even greater. No problem was too tough for him, no mission too dangerous.

Nothing stopped the flamboyant Polifka, who recruited men cut from the same mold as himself. When he needed a car he merely told his supply officer, who was well aware that no staff cars were available from the U.S. Army. The supply officer promptly forged a requisition to the Australian depot and Polifka got his automobile without delay. By the time the authorities discovered what had happened, he and his men had moved to another airbase. Once when Polifka needed train service to deliver supplies to his unit, he discovered that the Australian trainmen were on strike. He and some of his staff went to the station to try to persuade the engineer and conductor to cooperate but they couldn't find anyone around. When he discovered that some of his men had worked on railroads prior to the war, he ordered them to take an engine along with several cars and operate it. They did, and for several days the "Polifka Express" delivered the urgently needed war supplies to the airbase from the docks with no one being the wiser. Finally the Australian authorities discovered who was running the train and halted operations. Months later Polifka received a formal financial statement from the Australian government for the cost of the engine and the railroad cars he had "stolen." He promptly forwarded the bill to Washington and never heard of it again. During the Coral Sea engagement, however, he more than settled the debt.

When the Japanese decided to move against Port Moresby Fleet Admiral Isoroku Yamamoto sent a force of some seventy ships including the aircraft carriers *Shokaku, Zuikaku,* and *Shoho.* Against this huge fleet was Allied Task Force 17, which was about half the size and included only two carriers, the *Lexington* and the *Yorktown.* American cryptanalysts had penetrated the Japanese code well enough to warn that the Nip fleet was on its way but the main problem was to locate the enemy ships at a positive position so that carrier- and land-based planes could attack. On May 7, 1942, Commander James H. Flatley lifted his Wildcat off the deck of the *Yorktown* and started a search for the Japanese ships. At 10:30 A.M. he spotted a Kawanishi four-engined Nip flying boat and immediately realized it was hunting the American fleet. Flatley radioed his sighting, warning that it was evident the Japanese knew that Task Force 17 was in the area, and then shot the big plane down. Despite a search that continued until dark, however, neither Flatley nor any of his fellow pilots spotted even one Japanese ship.

Pilots of the 19th Bombardment Group in B-17s and fliers of the 22d Group (Medium) using B-26s also hunted for the Japanese fleet that day but were unable to locate it. As darkness fell on the 7th the commander of Task Force 17, Rear Admiral Frank J. Fletcher, and his staff were discouraged. They were outnumbered in ships and were well aware that surprise was their main chance for success. There could be no surprise attack, however, if the enemy fleet could not be located. At about that same time a radio message arrived at General Douglas MacArthur's headquarters in Australia from a lone P-38 over the Pacific:

"A hostile fleet of two carriers, five cruisers, and ten destroyers are passing through the northern Solomons, heading south at twenty knots."

The pilot who had made the sighting was Pop Polifka.

Admiral Fletcher made a rapid calculation after the message was relayed to him and decided that if he made a fast run north during the night he could get his ships within air range by dawn. He did and the Battle of the Coral Sea resulted, the first in history in which two naval forces fought without their ships' exchanging a shot. When it was over on May 9, the Allies had stopped a Japanese invasion armada for the first time since the war had begun and Australia was secure for the time being. If an aerial reconnaissance plane had not sighted the Japanese fleet moving through the northern Solomons the outcome of the battle might have been entirely different.

The Battle of the Coral Sea caused a temporary hesitation in the Japanese advance across the Pacific but the Battle of Midway less than a month later was the actual turning point of the war. On May 5, 1942, two days before the Battle of the Coral Sea actually began, Imperial General Headquarters in Japan issued an order that stated: "Commander in Chief Combined Fleet will, in cooperation with the Army, invade and occupy strategic points in the Western Aleutians and Midway Island." The objectives were obvious to U.S. Navy headquarters. The Japanese wanted to use Midway as a base for air raids on Pearl Harbor and Admiral Yamamoto wanted to lure the U.S. Pacific Fleet out into the open while it was still in a weakened condition and destroy it.

Once again the cat-and-mouse reconnaissance by aircraft in the broad expanses of the Pacific Ocean began. The USAAF had a handful of B-26s and a few Flying Fortresses based on the tiny island of Midway and these planes were used for reconnaissance missions day and night in hopes of detecting the approaching Japanese fleet. The commander of the USAAF Task Force Group at Midway was Lieutenant Colonel Walter C. Sweeney, a B-17 pilot who always flew in his stocking feet. Sweeney, who later rose to a full general and commanded the Tactical Air Command, had his Flying Fortresses out on visual patrol every day. At that time the Seventh Air Force used any plane or pilot available for aerial reconnaissance. In addition, Sweeney had four B-26s which were rigged to carry torpedoes but were used for aerial reconnaissance prior to the actual battle. The B-26 outfit was headed by Captain James Collins.

On May 29 more reconnaissance help arrived in the form of U.S. Navy PBYs under the command of colorful, daring Commander Logan Ramsey. His green but enthusiastic pilots, who had no idea why they were at Midway, began their 700-mile daily patrol flights the very next day.

Meanwhile Admiral Yamamoto had gathered his full naval force for the assualt on Midway. His sea armada was divided into the Main Force, the Midway Attack Force, and the Midway Bombardment-Occupation Force, plus units aimed at invading the Aleutians at the same time. This totaled more than 160 warships, not counting the small patrol craft. Fleet Admiral Chester W. Nimitz of the U.S. Navy could collect only seventy-six ships to face the Japanese invading force and part of these belonged to the Northern Pacific Force, which never arrived at the battle scene. The outcome of the impending Battle of Midway depended upon aerial reconnaissance, the hope that either a Navy or Army patrol plane could spot the Japanese fleet before one of their planes spotted the outnumbered American fleet.

Unfortunately the reconnaissance missions were not successful during the first tense days of June. Patrol Squadron 44 led by Lieutenant Commander Robert Brixner flew more than 80 hours a week after its arrival on Midway. Squadron 23, commanded by Commander Massie Hughes, flew just as often. Sweeney's B-17s were in the air thirty hours in two days hunting the Japanese fleet but there were no sightings. The weather was bad, the Pacific Ocean broad, the Nips smart. Several of the lumbering PBYs came under attack from enemy planes based at Wake Island as they searched in that area. Both Ensign J. J. Lyons' and Ensign R. V. Umphrey's planes were badly shot up and they barely made it back to the airstrip at Midway. Yet not a single Japanese ship was spotted. The situation was critical since coded messages intercepted by the U.S. cryptanalysts indicated the enemy was well within range of the planes on Midway.

On Wednesday, June 3, the PBYs took off at 4:30 A.M. to patrol their assigned sectors once again and fifteen minutes later the B-17s were in the air. The pilots of the Catalinas kept sending back position reports to Midway and at the 400-mile mark of their search that morning the pilots had not sighted any enemy vessels. Then, shortly after 9:00 A.M., PBY flier Lieutenant (jg) J. P. O. Lyle broke through a cloud and spotted two small patrol boats directly beneath his aircraft. Not certain as to their identity, he eased his PBY lower and was promptly greeted by antiaircraft fire. This was the initial contact by a reconnaissance plane with the advancing Japanese fleet. Thirty minutes later Ensign Jack Reid in another PBY was taking it easy in the cockpit, his aircraft on automatic pilot, when he suddenly saw numerous black dots on the ocean. He checked the dots through his binoculars and then had his co-pilot do the same. There was no question what they had found. It was the Japanese invasion force.

"Main body!"

For the next hour and a half Reid followed the enemy ships, ducking in and out of the clouds when the flak got too heavy. He counted eleven vessels and also spotted other ships converging toward the force in an apparent linkup. From that moment on the Midway task force of Admiral Yamamoto was under constant harassment by the reconnaissance pilots. While the B-17s, B-26s, and torpedo-carrying PBYs plus the carrier planes attacked the force Reid had spotted, more search planes were hunting for Yamamoto's other units. Lieutenant Howard Ady of Squadron 23, searching a sector 315 degrees out of Midway, suddenly was amazed to see an enemy seaplane fly past him heading directly toward the island. He immediately radioed a warning and then began looking for the ship the seaplane had obviously come from. It didn't take him long to spot two aircraft carriers. Further south, Lieutenant William Chase in another PBY saw a huge formation of fighters and bombers heading for Midway. He didn't even take time to encode his message: "Many planes heading Midway. Bearing 320, distance 150."

Ady stuck with the Japanese fleet long enough to relay its course and speed, both absolute necessities for the American carrier planes. That was all that was needed. The attacking aircraft took over and the U.S. Navy was on its way to its first decisive victory in World War II. The cost in United States ships and men was high: the carrier *Yorktown*, 500 men, 150 planes. It would have been much higher, however, if it had not been for the reconnaissance accomplishments of the PBYs based on Midway. Admiral Yamamoto lost four of his carriers and their air groups, one cruiser, and one destroyer and had several other ships badly damaged. There was no wonder that he cursed the lumbering PBY reconnaissance planes.

Some of the reconnaissance load was taken from the carrier planes and land-based Catalinas and heavy bombers by the SOC-3 seaplanes aboard the cruisers. Appropriately named the Seagulls, these planes cruised at less than 100 knots and could reach 135 knots in a near-vertical dive. They could stay in the air five hours and, as was customary in nearly all reconnaissance planes in the Pacific Theater of Operations, carried guns —two .30-caliber machine guns and also a depth charge. Despite these limitations and their vulnerability to the faster, more modern Japanese planes, 70 of the Seagulls were still in service as late as 1944.

One Seagull, plane 6-CS-15, which took part in the Coral Sea–Midway operations, had an ordeal that attested to the situations often faced by the little planes and their two-man crews. Piloted by Lieutenant (jg) John A. Thomas accompanied by Radioman 3/c Otis J. Gannon, the pontoon-equipped plane was launched over the Coral Sea from the destroyer *San Francisco* early on the morning of March 7, 1942. Two hours after Thomas was airborne on his reconnaissance flight, a violent rainstorm swept the area and during the storm plane 6-CS-15 became lost. Thomas radioed the code word for "Am lost" to the destroyer and the lost-plane routine was immediately begun.

Unfortunately, when Thomas switched his radio transmitter to a low-frequency range so that the ship could use its radio direction finder and give him a heading for the destroyer he discovered his transmitter would not work. A second procedure was then attempted. The ship transmitted on a high-frequency covered by the plane's radio direction finder and the roles were reversed. This worked fine, but because he was very low on fuel Thomas decided not to fly the suggested ten minutes perpendicular to the bearing he had received to check whether he had the true bearing to the ship or its reciprocal. He thought he knew which side of the ship he was on, but he was mistaken. At 4:30 P.M. Thomas radioed that he was out of fuel and down in the Coral Sea.

A sea-and-air search was immediately instigated but plane 6-CS-15 was not spotted and the search was finally abandoned the following day. Thomas and Gannon were marked off the duty board. Then, on March 13, more than five and one half days later and 385 miles farther west, the little Seagull was spotted floating on the water. Rescued, the two downed airmen were in remarkably good shape and still had more than half of their emergency rations left. It was the longest hop of any reconnaissance plane in World War II.

Although the Catalina had performed an excellent job of reconnaissance during the Battle of Midway, in the Solomons its limitations soon became apparent. The concentration of enemy fighters made their use impossible in the area north of Guadalcanal. The Flying Fortresses and Liberators soon became the workhorses of the aerial reconnaissance units and once these planes were properly modified, photographic reconnaissance made rapid advances in the Pacific Theater of Operations. They had both the range to reach many areas of enemy activity and the firepower needed to operate singly.

Most of the B-24s were modified so that the rear bomb bay was permanently enclosed. This section housed the aerial photographer with the switch panel giving him control of all the cameras. Both the B-17 and the B-24 had a trimetrogon camera installation in the nose. This setup consisted of three cameras, each having a 6-inch equivalent focal length with a relative aperture of f/6.3. They were extremely wide-angle, covering slightly more than 90 degrees full field on a 9-by-9-inch negative, and low distortion. One camera was installed at the vertical while the other two were at the oblique, thus giving a horizon to horizon coverage. Usually there were also a K-17 camera and a K-18 camera installed in the vertical in the belly of the plane and one or more K-20 hand-held cameras on board.

As the number of Allied airbases increased, however, other aircraft were used more and more frequently for aerial reconnaissance, too. The old standby P-38 was in demand, especially after Charles Lindbergh visited the Southwest Pacific and taught the pilots how to increase their operating radius of action nearly 50 percent. It had the same camera configuration that was used so successfully in the European Theater of Operations. The outmoded but sturdy P-40, with a K-17 camera in the belly and its wing-mounted gun cameras, was often pressed into duty. The B-25 was used on shorter-range reconnaissance missions and usually had a trimetrogon built in the belly of the fuselage. The P-39 with a K-25 at fixed vertical and a K-24 at oblique was an efficient photography plane early in the war. Later, the P-51 was made available to reconnaissance units in the Pacific Theater of Operations and proved once again that it was excellent for armed missions.

The U.S. Navy relied heavily upon the B-24 Liberator for reconnaissance although its carrier planes and seaplanes from the cruisers in addition to the land-based Catalinas also flew patrol. During the invasion of the Marianas, for example, Navy Liberators were able to stay airborne long hours without refueling and were assigned to hunt for enemy search planes. In this battle of recon plane against recon plane, the Liberators came out far ahead; many more enemy aircraft than Liberators were shot down. For antishipping reconnaissance at night, the Catalina was more effective than the faster Liberator. In the South and Southwest Pacific areas the enemy frequently attempted to move troops and supplies at night in small vessels and barges, ducking in and out among the numerous islands and hiding in small bays by day. The slow speed of the Catalinas was an asset and the darkness was all the protection they needed. With special black paint and equipped with radar they became Black Cats searching out enemy vessels and barges every night. The pilots even worked out a technique for guiding motor torpedo boats, destroyers, and other light vessels to Japanese convoys.

A month after the Battle of Midway the 4th Reconnaissance Group was activated at Colorado Springs. Even earlier than that, the 71st Reconnaissance Group was activated at Birmingham, Alabama. Other such units were on the planning boards but the sad fact remains that it was 1943 before any of these reconnaissance units became active in the Pacific. Until then the task was left to the scattered reconnaissance squadrons and individual planes attached to the air forces in their area. Polifka's 8th Photo Squadron was one of the units. So was the 435th Bombardment Squadron which had originally been the 40th Reconnaissance Squadron of the 19th Bombardment Group. Despite its name change, the 435th continued to serve for reconnaissance of the New Guinea, New Britain, and Solomons areas. By July 1942, the 11th Group began aiding the 435th in reconnaissance work from the base on Espiritu Santo. Because of the lack of Army photographic equipment and trained personnel, however, the Navy supplied the cameras, the Marines furnished the photographers, and the 11th Group provided the planes in a procedure that remained standard until USAAF photo and mapping units arrived in 1943.

The 435th, however, flew the majority of the reconnaissance missions in this area through the summer and early autumn of 1942. Originally flying two daily missions out from Townsville, Australia, by August this unit moved four aircraft and eight crews up to Port Moresby and doubled its missions to four a day. One outstanding mission flown during this period was the sighting of a Japanese convoy by Lieutenant Don Tower on July 19. This was the first indication that the enemy intended to make a landing at Buna since the convoy was near Rabaul and headed for the city. It gave the Allied troops already near Buna in small numbers time to prepare for the Japanese offensive.

During the battle for New Guinea the B-17 reconnaissance planes flew in all kinds of weather to get the necessary photographs and to spot enemy activities on the sea and land. On August 26 a B-17 piloted by Lieutenant R. E. Holsey was ordered to Rabaul to get photographs of the Japanese installation for bomb-assessment purposes. Holsey obtained the photographs but while he was in a steep, diving turn over the city in and effort to get out of the heavy antiaircraft fire the flak knocked out two of his engines and damaged a third. Within minutes it, too, died. Left with only one engine operating, Holsey headed for a strip of sandy beach on the south coast of New Guinea about fifty miles east of Port Moresby. Since it was near midnight by the time he reached the area, the lieutenant ordered a couple of flares dropped and using the light from them landed the Flying Fortress successfully, wheels down.

All that night the crew worked on the engines and at dawn Holsey decided that they operated well enough for him to risk a takeoff. Throwing everything out of the plane but the photographic equipment and other essential items, the lieutenant and his crew chief managed to lift the battered Flying Fortress off the beach and fly it back to the strip at Seven Mile. The photographs were a little late but in good condition.

On another photographic mission to Rabaul in November Captain Kenneth McCullar of the 63d Bombardment Squadron ran into trouble. When he was at 29,000 feet and only seventy-five miles from the target a turbo-supercharger on his B-17 exploded, knocking out both engines on the left side of the plane. He was unable to maintain his altitude but the captain refused to turn back. Ignoring the fact that the flak over Rabaul was the heaviest of any target in the sector, McCullar kept the B-17 in a power glide and headed over the city. He snapped his pictures at 19,000 feet, still losing altitude, while the antiaircraft bursts bracketed his Flying Fortress and then he turned for home. Two Japanese fighters made one pass at his damaged plane but his gunners scared them off. Fortunately, the air was heavier at 6,000 feet and the captain was able to stabilize his altitude at that height and reach the Seven Mile strip. Later, General George C. Kenny said they were the best aerial photographs of Rabaul that he had ever seen. In April 1943 McCullar was killed when his aircraft hit a kangaroo during an attempted takeoff.

The reconnaissance missions were extremely hazardous during this period. The Japanese were moving their planes and ships around the ocean and the scattered islands in a massive chess game that provided many surprises for the photography pilots. Many times when they least expected it, the recon fliers found themselves under attack and were often lucky to complete their missions. Losses were heavy. Even the generals took their turns at the reconnaissance flights in those early days until higher headquarters stopped them. Brigadier General Kenneth Walker went out one night looking for Japanese barges and brought his B-17 back with three feet of the left wing missing. He had hooked the wing on a tree. Walker was killed later in a low-level bombing attack for which he was posthumously awarded the Medal of Honor. Brigadier General Ennis Whitehead took a B-25 to inspect the Japanese defenses in the Buna area and came back with a shell hole in the wing big enough for a man to crawl through.

In January 1943 the 4th Reconnaissance Group finally arrived in the Pacific and set up operations at Espiritu Santo where it remained for approximately a year and a half. The group's first mission over enemy territory was flown by Captain John E. Murray, the commanding officer of the 17th Photographic Reconnaissance Squadron, on February 5, 1943. Thereafter the 4th Group played an important role in supporting the Allied drive up the Solomons. Prior to the invasion of New Georgia, the 17th, using P-38s, made daily photographs of Munda airfield as well as other points of interest. Meanwhile the Allied advance northward was stepped up, and the 17th moved to Guadalcanal while the remainder of the 4th Group stayed at Espiritu Santo and was inactive. With its headquarters at Guadalcanal the 17th covered many principal targets during the advance northward.

It took pictures of airdromes and ground installations in the New Britain area, especially near Rabaul. This required a round trip of approximately eight hundred miles with an average flying time of four hours. Missions to southern Bougainville were even more frequent, totaling ninety-four in 1943. Photographs were taken of Kahili and Kara airdromes, Buin, Kangu Hill, Tonolei Harbor, and Molis Point. On the average the round trip to southern Bougainville was three hundred miles and the flying time about two hours. The 17th also flew photographic missions to Buka, north Bougainville, Empress Augusta Bay, New Ireland, and to Choiseul Island.

The kind of operation conducted by the 17th during this period in many respects set the pattern that was followed by the other arriving photoreconnaissance groups for the remainder of the war. The 17th scattered various detachments around the area and this became standard practice. A detachment it sent to Torokina airfield, Bougainville, in December 1943, for example, operated the photographic laboratory there and at Piva airfield. Another detachment of six pilots and sixteen enlisted men were located at Munda airfield, New Georgia. Later a unit of one warrant officer and twenty-four enlisted men was sent to Green Island, located on the northern end of the Solomons, where it printed and developed aerial photographs flown in. This use of detachments was one of the many ways in which the 4th Group facilitated the advance of the Allied ground forces up the Solomons.

Meanwhile, the B-17s and B-24s still maintained their long-range reconnaissance of Japanese targets. One of the epic reconnaissance missions of the war was flown by a B-17 crew of the Fifth Air Force. This crew, commanded by Lieutenant Jay Zeamer, Jr., had already been nicknamed the Eager Beavers since they volunteered for every mission that promised a good fight. On June 16, while on a photographic mission to the Solomon Islands they got more action than they wanted as the citation for Zeamer's Medal of Honor indicated:

On 16 June 1943, Major Zeamer (then Captain) volunteered as a pilot of a bomber on an important photographic mapping mission covering the formidably defended area in the vicinity of Buka, Solomon Islands. While photographing the Buka airdrome his crew observed about 20 enemy fighters on the field, many of them taking off. Despite the certainty of a dangerous attack by this strong force, Major Zeamer proceeded with his mapping run, even after the enemy attack began. In the ensuing engagement, Major Zeamer sustained gunshot wounds in both arms and legs, one leg being broken. Despite his injuries, he maneuvered the damaged plane so skillfully that his gunners were able to fight off the enemy during a running fight which lasted 40 minutes. The crew destroyed at least 5 hostile planes, of which Major Zeamer himself shot down one. Although weak from the loss of blood, he refused medical aid until the enemy had broken combat. He then turned over the controls, but continued to exercise command despite lapses into unconsciousness, and directed the flight to a base 580 miles away. . . .

The photographer, Sergeant William Kendrick, received the Distinguished Service Cross for his part in this outstanding reconnaissance mission while Lieutenant Joseph R. Sarnoski, the bombardier, was awarded the Medal of Honor posthumously.

While the new units completed their training and flew their "break-in" reconnaissance missions in the combat area, the veteran 8th Photo Squadron continued its fine photographic work. Polifka had performed the feat of mapping a large portion of the eastern New Guinea and New Britain areas almost single-handed. His "A" Flight, the first U.S. reconnaissance unit to arrive in Australia after the start of the war, was later joined by Flights "B" and "C." A month after their arrival they were operating out of Port Moresby with the 435th although their supply and service base was 675 miles south in Australia. The regular route of Polifka's P-38s was from Port Moresby up to Rabaul, across Lae and Salamaua, and home. The planes often took a severe battering from the weather as they crossed the equatorial front on these missions.

In June 1943 a photographic mission flown by an 8th Photo Squadron pilot, Lieutenant Fred G. Hargesheimer, had far-reaching effects on the development of the island of New Britain after the end of World War II. Hargesheimer was on an assignment to photograph the harbor at Rabaul when he was shot down over the jagged coastline on the east side of the island. He parachuted successfully from his P-38, landing in the jungle with no injuries except a gash in the forehead. His main problem was that New Britain was heavily populated by Japanese troops and he was more than a hundred miles away from his base in New Guinea. For thirty-one days the determined recon pilot walked through the jungle, getting weaker each day. His emergency rations gave out, water was scarce, and he constantly had to hide from enemy patrols. Then, appearing before him from the deep shadows of the undergrowth, were several natives. While Hargesheimer braced himself for the worst, the leader approached him and handed the startled flier a paper. It was a note signed by an Australian officer which explained that the leader's name was Lauo and that he and his tribe were friends of the Allies.

For the next five months Hargesheimer stayed at their village. Part of the time he had malaria and his life was saved by a native mother who fed him cupfuls of her own milk. Finally, he and two Australian pilots who were shot down later and also rescued by Lauo were evacuated to New Guinea by a submarine. In gratitude Hergesheimer started a fund after the war to build a school on New Britain. After many years of speaking before groups, rounding up free building materials, and contacting various organizations, the Airmen's Memorial School opened to eighty-five students in 1964. As a general at the Pentagon said recently, "In regard to international goodwill, Hargesheimer's reconnaissance mission was probably the most important one flown in World War II." Hargesheimer is still active in behalf of the school, hoping to enlarge its facilities in the future.

As the experienced pilots and technicians of the 8th Photo Squadron continued their reconnaissance activities, other new reconnaissance groups destined for action in the Pacific and Asian areas were on their way to help. Throughout the long conflict, however, these veterans and others like them who flew the B-17s, B-25s, B-24s, P-40s, Catalinas, and any other plane that they could get into the air during the first few months of the war, remained the backbone of the reconnaissance effort.

8

Watching the Rising Sun (2)

IN LATE November 1943, the 71st Reconnaissance Group, which had arrived on New Guinea aboard the USAT *General John Pope*, began to conduct operations against the Japanese. Following the example of the earlier 4th Reconnaissance Group, the 71st scattered its units at different bases. The 82d Squadron took part in armed reconnaissance and strafing missions along the coasts of New Guinea and New Britain. The 110th Squadron and the 17th Squadron began to fly long-range sea reconnaissance missions. With the 17th using B-25s and the other units using fighter aircraft, most of the group's missions involved actual combat as well as visual and photographic assignments. In March 1944 the B-25s of the 17th Squadron, while striking repeated blows at enemy barges and other craft, brought back important information that permitted the invasion of Manus Island to be moved forward several months. After the ground forces landed on Manus Island on March 15, they attested to the accuracy of the squadron's reconnaissance reports. In May low oblique photographs taken by the same squadron revealed that the Sarmi area of New Guinea was unsuited for building an airdrome and that it was full of enemy troops. A planned operation by the Allies to capture this area was called off and instead Biak was invaded.

The mission of the "Ramblin' Reccos" of the 71st varied from week to week. Much of their time was spent on actual bombing strikes and fighter sweeps but during the operations around Luzon in 1945 photographic and visual reconnaissance once again took preference. The reconnaissance conducted by the group elicited much information regarding the movement and disposition of the enemy forces, the location of troop concentrations, bivouac areas, and convoys. Information was also obtained as to road conditions, bridge construction, and weather behind enemy lines. The group's missions were often flown in bad weather, always over rough and hazardous terrain, at low altitudes, and in the face of known concentrations of antiaircraft fire.

The combination of guns and cameras on the reconnaissance planes often resulted in serious damage to enemy equipment and men. One of the pilots of the 71st Reconnaissance Group, Major William A. Shomo, was awarded the Medal of Honor for a mission he flew early in 1945. Shomo and Lieutenant Paul M. Lipscomb, both of the 82d Squadron, took off on January 11 to check the enemy airdromes in the northern part of Luzon. Flying P-51s, the pair flew directly into a swarm of enemy planes. According to the citation:

> . . . Major Shomo was lead pilot of a flight of two fighter planes charged with an armed photographic and strafing mission against Aparri and Laoag airdromes. While en route to the objective, he observed an enemy twin-engine bomber, protected by 12 fighters, flying about 2,500 feet above him and in the opposite direction. Although the odds were 13 to 2, Major Shomo immediately ordered an attack. Accompanied by his wingman he closed on the enemy formation in a climbing turn and scored hits on the leading plane of the third element, which exploded in midair. Major Shomo then attacked the second element from the left side of the formation and shot another fighter down in flames. When the enemy formed for counterattack, Major Shomo moved to the other side of the formation and

hit a third fighter which exploded and fell. Diving below the bomber, he put a burst into its under side and it crashed and burned. Pulling up from this pass he encountered a fifth plane firing head on and destroyed it. He next dived upon the first element and shot down the lead plane; then diving 300 feet in pursuit of another fighter he caught it with his initial burst and it crashed in flames. During this action his wingman had shot down three planes, while the three remaining enemy fighters had fled into a cloudbank and escaped. Major Shomo's extraordinary gallantry and intrepidity in attacking such a far superior force and destroying seven enemy aircraft in one action is unparalleled in the Southwest Pacific area.

To make certain there was no error in the scoring, Shomo flew around taking pictures of the wrecked and smoking Japanese planes, then went to his target and obtained the pictures of the airdromes and went home.

The 20th Combat Mapping Squadron of the 6th Reconnaissance Group flew B-24s modified for photography. When the planes on New Guinea first arrived they were painted a light blue, which made them conspicuous targets when flying with the O.D. bombers, so the reconnaissance crews scraped all the paint off their aircraft. As Lieutenant Dave W. Ecoff, a member of the 20th, explained: "After we scraped the blue paint off our planes we started flying three-ship formations to the target. Our average mission was about ten to twelve hours long and the photos were usually taken at 25,000 feet. We were on oxygen an average of four hours. On a successful mission each plane would bring back sixteen rolls of film, two hundred negatives to a roll."

Later the 20th moved to a field on Biak Island off the coast of New Guinea. The pilots would fly their planes from Biak up to Morotai Island in the Halmahera Group and stage out of there the following morning to photograph parts of the Philippines. On October 24, 1944, three ships took off from Morotai to map portions of Luzon in the Philippines. Ecoff was piloting one of the B-24s.

"One plane aborted because of mechanical trouble so the

flight leader, Johnny Wooten, and myself continued on. Our route took us over the Visayan Sea and then over the Sibuyan Sea just east of Mindoro Island. As we started to climb to a higher altitude, Johnny called my attention to a large task force below us. We did not recognize them as 'friendlies' so we started taking pictures. I later found out that Johnny's radio operator was sending out information on the number of ships, approximate types, position, and heading of the task force.

"We flew on to our target only to find that the cloud coverage below was too much to get successful photographs so we turned around and went back to our lower altitude of 10,000 feet. Our return flight took us to the west of Panay and Negros Islands. It was at this point that one of my gunners called on interphone and told me that he had sighted some more ships to the west of us. I called Johnny Wooten and we decided to have a closer look. We challenged them with the Aldis Lamp but this was unnecessary because we were immediately fired upon. Again radio messages were sent giving the details of this new task force of the Japs and we got out of there fast.

"When we arrived back at Morotai the place was buzzing with excitement. All pilots were escorted to Base Operations immediately upon landing and were ordered to ready their planes for a mission in the morning. We could not participate because our photo ship couldn't carry bombs. We learned that we had photographed and flown over the entire Japanese fleet task force prior to the Battle of the Philippine Sea. Johnny Wooten received a letter of commendation for the sighting."

As plans were made for the Allied landing at Cape Gloucester on New Britain to gain control of the Vitiaz Strait, the 8th Photo Reconnaissance Squadron flew daily missions over the area. As D-Day, December 26, 1943, approached, the First Marine Division ground patrols aided in finding targets for air force preinvasion strikes but aerial photography provided most of the data. The pictures brought back by the 8th showed up bridges, clearings, gun positions, supply dumps, new trails and enemy positions on the beach. The amphibious unit scheduled for the invasion, the Seventh Amphibious Force, used aerial photographs for its navigational charts and the First Marine Division selected its landing beaches from the pictures. Gridded mosaics were in great demand by the artillery units to be used as firing charts and the gridded obliques were important in the scheduling of ground-support strikes. In addition to the 8th Photo Reconnaissance Squadron, Fifth Air Force heavy bomber planes equipped for photography flew 192 sorties during this preinvasion period. After the landings at Cape Gloucester, General MacArthur wrote to General Arnold, commanding general of the AAF: "The Air Force here has been magnificent and is the very hub of our success."

Far to the north the Eleventh Air Force was not quite so magnificent. They didn't have enough planes, enough crews, or enough supplies. The only thing they had plenty of was bad weather, some of the worst flying weather in the world. Alaska and the Aleutians undoubtedly had the honor of claiming the globe's most dangerous weather for airborne missions. There was an overcast nearly all the time. Clear areas over any target were the exception. Clouds covered everything and if they didn't, fog did. Strong winds blowing across from Siberia made navigation difficult. An added hazard of the area was the "williwaw," a wind of hurricane velocity that was liable to sweep down from the naked hills along the north fringe of the islands without a moment's warning. High winds and fog, an unusual combination any place else in the world, often persisted for days in the Aleutians to plague the pilots and navigators. It was not a good section of the world for aerial reconnaissance activities. The Eleventh Air Force gave it a fine try, however.

The Japanese, as part of the Midway action, had occupied the two islands in the Aleutian chain farthest to the west, Attu and Kiska. The Eleventh Air Force planes, operating out of Umnak and Cold Bay six hundred miles one way from these islands, immediately started action against the Japanese invaders. Photographic missions were flown in B-17s and B-24s equipped with cameras over Attu and Kiska in search of enemy activities. Heavy bombers out of Nome and Naknek patrolled the long stretches of the Bering Sea in flights that often lasted eight to ten hours in bad weather. The 54th Fighter Squadron flew shorter-range search missions from Umnak in P-38s, also. On one of these missions on August 4, 1942, the pilots of the 54th discovered two Kawa 97s—Japanese four-engine flying boats used for reconnaissance—and shot them down.

Enemy opposition was secondary to the opposition the reconnaissance pilots received from the weather. In January two B-24s disappeared in the fog and were never heard from again and a few days later two B-17s out of Umnak collided in midair because of clouds. One disappeared and the other, badly damaged, was able to land. A P-40 went out of control in the overcast and crashed into Kuluk Bay and on the same day two B-25s tangled in the fog and were lost.

In February, after the Americans landed on the island of Amchitka next to Kiska, the P-40s had the necessary range to fly reconnaissance missions and the 18th Fighter Squadron made regular flights over the Japanese installations. By March plans had been made to invade Attu and the Eleventh Air Force was charged with conducting the photographic reconnaissance required. The pilots got a series of pictures of the Massacre Bay shore line and beaches and brought home the only available intelligence of the Japanese troop strength. D-Day was May 11 and for the ten days preceding the invasion the planes of the Eleventh Air Force were ordered to photograph Attu and Kiska daily and also, as was customary in the Pacific, to bomb and strafe enemy installations after the pictures were obtained. This task was accomplished according to the instructions contained in Field Order 10, dated 25 April, 1943, and the invasion was successfully accomplished despite fierce enemy opposition.

With landing strips at Attu and Shemya available after the

invasion and Attu within striking distance of the northernmost of the Japanese home islands, the Kurils, 750 miles distant, the Eleventh Air Force planned to carry the war to the enemy for the first time since Doolittle's B-25s had roared over Tokyo. Photos were badly needed, however, so on July 18 six Liberators from the 36th, 21st, and 404th Bombardment Squadrons were scheduled for the trip to the Kurils. The bombs they carried did little damage to the Japanese installations but the crews secured a fine set of photographs of the islands. These pictures showed a considerable amount of military activity, two airfields, a seaplane base, and other construction under way. For the remainder of the war the planes from the Aleutians harassed the Kurils, doing considerable damage and forcing the Japanese to keep four hundred badly needed fighters based in the Hokkaido-Kurils area against a possible invasion that never came.

The invasion of the remaining enemy-held island in the Aleutians, Kiska, was set for August 15 and the Eleventh Air Force kept a steady stream of reconnaissance aircraft over this island. A report on these activities from July 27 to August 4 was issued and stated some unusual facts. The enemy on Kiska had made no move to fill bomb craters on the runway of their airfield and several of the buildings on the island were being dismantled. In the submarine base area alone nine buildings had been destroyed, yet the report underlined a strange fact:

> It is significant that most of the buildings destroyed show no evidence of having been bombed or shelled. It is also significant that the photographs of August 2 and August 4 show all the trucks in identical positions and 10 to 12 less barges than usual in the Kiska harbor area.

The aerial photographs indicated that the 7,000-man enemy force on Kiska had fled but no one would believe it. An invasion force of 34,000 ground troops landed on Kiska on the 15th as scheduled and not a single Japanese was encountered. The total force on the island was three yellow dogs left behind by the enemy when they slipped away. Once again aerial photography had revealed an accurate summary of the situation but, as happened so many times before and since, the pictures were ignored.

With Kiska in American control, the battle of the Aleutians came to an end. For a time Washington considered basing some of the B-29 photo planes in the area but before any of the planes became available for the Aleutians the war was over.

Across the Pacific Ocean to the south, China, Burma, and India received very little attention from the Allied Chiefs of Staff during the first part of the war. The Japanese had overrun Burma in 1942, seized the road to the north which was used to supply China, and planned to drive all the way through India. There were no large-scale Allied forces available for the CBI theater, so only stop-gap measures could be taken to block the path of the Japanese across India. British Brigadier General Orde C. Wingate and his Chindits, long-range guerrilla fighters, were assigned the rugged task. Later a similar group under the command of American Brigadier General Frank D. Merrill helped in this behind-the-lines harassment of the enemy in Burma. The American Tenth Air Force also tried to help.

The Tenth Air Force in 1942 and early 1943, while challenging the overwhelming number of Japanese planes every chance it had, depended mostly on the RAF units for aerial reconnaissance. It wasn't until late in 1943 that some P-38s arrived in the theater and the Americans could do some of their own aerial photography. Finally on April 15, 1944, the 8th Reconnaissance Group of the USAAF arrived in India and set up operations at Bally Seaplane Base, six miles up the Hoogly River from Calcutta. The group was assigned to the Tenth Air Force and the Tenth Air Force, in turn, assigned to the group the 10th Combat Camera Unit, the 9th Photo Reconnaissance Squadron, the 20th Tactical Reconnaissance Squadron, the 24th Combat Mapping Squadron, the 7th Photo Technical Squadron, and the 958th Engineer Topographical Company, Aviation. The mission of the group was to organize and coordinate all photographic and mapping activities of the AAF in the CBI theater. The 8th was unusual in being part of a combined AAF–RAF force, the Photo Reconnaissance Force, or just PRF. The commanding officer of PRF was Group Captain S. G. Wise, one of England's pioneer photo pilots, and his deputy was American Colonel C. P. Hollstein.

The weather in India and Burma during the monsoon period hampered the work of the 8th but by October the photo planes were flying over six hundred sorties a month. During this month the laboratories turned out 135,965 negatives and 335,788 prints for photo-interpretation units and other agencies in India, Burma, China, and Washington, D.C. This involved more than thirty-five miles of film. The group at this time was operating aircraft from nine bases—Barrackpore, Alipore, Gushkara, Dinjan, and Chittagong in India; Myitkyina and Tingkawk in Burma; and Chanyi and Penchen in China—and using P-38s, P-40s, P-51s, and B-24s, all modified for aerial photography.

As the Allied drive picked up speed in 1944–45, the 8th Reconnaissance Group moved its units wherever they were needed most. Their duties also varied during this period from taking low obliques of Rangoon in preparation for the invasion to silencing antiaircraft batteries that were giving Allied pilots trouble. The 10th Combat Camera Unit, for instance, stayed with the ground-force units advancing toward Rangoon and with bombardment groups flying missions in support of the final operations of the Central Burma campaign. The Model Unit of the 17th Photographic Interpretation Detachment completed one of its most interesting projects during this final drive in the war zone—a terrain model 4 feet by 10 feet of an objective that was to be taken by an Indian paratroop regiment in the attack on Rangoon. Based on aerial photographs, the model was so accurate that after the paratroopers were finished with it, many AAF and RAF pilots used it to study flight lines and drop zones.

Also in Burma in 1944 was the 1st Air Commando Group under the command of the colorful, daring, and unconventional Colonel Philip G. Cochran. The group, which was activated in India on March 29, 1944, was organized to provide air support for Wingate's Raiders, who were operating far behind enemy lines in Burma. "Flip" Cochran's planes were the eyes for the jungle fighters of General Wingate, who could barely see ten feet ahead in the thick undergrowth. Much of the reconnaissance work accomplished by the 1st Air Commando Group was visual, but one outstanding photo mission was accomplished by a group pilot who disobeyed orders.

Wingate's Raiders were scheduled for an operation that would take them deep into Japanese-controlled territory in Burma. They were to be transported to three landing zones in the jungle—Broadway, Piccadilly, and Chowringhee—by gliders of the 1st Air Commando Group on March 5 in a surprise maneuver which it was hoped would catch the enemy off guard. For several days prior to the glider landings Cochran and his men dropped dummy paratroops all over various sections of the jungle except on the real drop zones, which were carefully avoided. Wingate strictly forbade any flights over the three landing zones, even for photographic reconnaissance. On March 2, however, Captain Charles Russhon, one of Cochran's pilots who had previously photographed the landing zones to be used, asked permission to make another reconnaissance flight over them just as a precautionary measure. The 1st Air Commando leader told him about the restrictions but Russhon was so persistent that Cochran finally gave him permission to make one photo mission if he promised to keep the news of the flight from Wingate.

It wasn't until nearly noon on the actual day of the landings, March 5, that Russhon finally made the flight in a B-25 piloted by Colonel R. T. Smith. The B-25 flew to Broadway and it was clear and undisturbed but when the aircraft reached Picadilly it was obvious that the Japanese had located the landing zone. Hundreds of large logs had been placed in the jungle clearing, making the planned glider landings there suicidal. Russhon took a dozen pictures of the scene and Smith immediately flew him back to Hailikandi, the airstrip where his laboratory was located.

By the time he had the film developed and the prints made it was late afternoon. There was strict radio silence in effect because of the planned invasion for that night and Russhon was unable to get Cochran on the telephone. In desperation, the captain sent the prints ahead with one of the fighter pilots at the airfield, telling him to deliver them to Cochran only. He then followed in a light plane, arriving just as the 1st Air Commando leader showed the pictures to Wingate. The general was furious that his orders had been disobeyed until he examined the picture of Piccadilly closely. He nodded his forgiveness to Russhon and quickly changed the battle plans, sending the gliders originally scheduled for Piccadilly to Broadway.

"It was the finest aerial photography mission of the war," the gruff Wingate said later, realizing the pictures averted a disaster.

Cochran agreed. "I was never sorry that I gave permission for the flight. It saved a great many lives."

The Fourteenth Air Force was activated in China on March 10, 1943, under the command of Major General Claire L. Chennault. Many of the pilots were from Chennault's American Volunteer Group of fliers who had been fighting the Japanese in the theater for many months, the famed Flying Tigers. The Fourteenth Air Force began operations with bad weather, a fuel shortage, poor equipment, and airbases in danger of being overrun by the enemy. P-40s made a few reconnaissance flights to find targets for the other planes but since the Japanese controlled the air, most of the American attacks were minor and caused little damage. In July six P-38s arrived to help but their advantage of greater range was offset by their greater need for fuel, and there was a distinct gasoline shortage in China at the time. However, the modified P-38s made good photographic planes as had been proven many times to Chennault even before the Fourteenth Air Force was formed. In 1942 Frank Schiel, one of his Flying Tiger pilots, had photographed Japanese installations in China and Formosa. Unfortunately, on December 8, 1942, while trying to make an instrument let-down through a violent storm to deliver negatives to Chennault's headquarters at Kunming he hit a mountaintop and was killed, but not before he had proven the value of both the P-38 and aerial photographs in combating the Japanese in China. The Fourteenth Air Force was quick to put the P-38s to use, as well as the faster P-51 photography aircraft, which they received later.

Formosa was constantly the target of American reconnaissance planes. In November 1943 pictures revealed that enemy bombers were usually parked wing to wing on the field at Shinchiku airdrome. Photographic coverage by a P-38 on November 24 showed seventy-five Japanese bombers on the field, so the following day eight P-51s, eight P-38s, and fourteen B-25s led by Colonel David L. "Tex" Hill, a former Flying Tiger, made a low-level attack on Shinchiku and destroyed forty-two enemy planes. Again the value of reconnaissance photos was demonstrated vividly, permitting Chennault to use his limited force where it could wreak the most havoc.

One of the most important changes in the reconnaissance mission during World War II occurred with the introduction of the B-29 Superfortress by the USAAF in the summer of 1944. Until that time the modified long-range B-17s and B-24s, by staging through fields in east China, had been able to photograph enemy airstrips, supply dumps, and troop positions on the Japanese outer defense perimeter but the heart of the Japanese Empire, the homeland itself, was completely out of range. With the arrival of the VLR (Very Long Range) B-29, however, the situation changed. The Superfortress, with a wingspan of over 141 feet, remote-controlled guns, a speed of more than 350 miles per hour at 30,000 feet and a range of up to 5,000 miles, made an excellent bomber for the Pacific theater. It also made a fine reconnaissance plane.

Since no other plane in the USAAF inventory—or the inventory of any other nation, for that matter—had the range to check B-29 targets in Japan for bomb damage, a few Superfortresses were modified in the field to carry cameras. The first such modified B-29 crashed during the initial Superfortress mission against Japan in June 1944, but other camera-equipped B-29s photographed Okinawa for airfield sites and landing beaches prior to the invasion of the island and did an excellent job. While these early, field-modified Superfortresses were getting the necessary damage-assessment pictures, experts at Wright Field were developing a Superfortress extensively modified for aerial-photography missions. Designated the F-13, it was equipped with long-range fuel tanks in the bomb bay and several K-18 and K-22 cameras to obtain oblique, trimetrogon, and vertical coverage of enemy territory.

On October 30, 1944, several of the F-13s landed at Saipan after a thirty-three-hour flight from California to join the 3d Photo Reconnaissance Squadron. At 0550 two days later one of the F-13s, with Captain Ralph D. Steakley at the controls, took off and headed for the city of Tokyo. Arriving over the Japanese city, the first American aircraft to overfly Tokyo since the Doolittle Raiders had paid their surprise visit in 1942, Steakley photographed military targets in clear weather from an altitude of 32,000 feet. These targets had not been photographed during World War II and the photo labs turned out 7,000 prints of Steakley's negatives.

From that date no area in the Japanese homeland was immune to the reconnaissance planes. Before the B-29s went to bomb Tokyo for the first time on November 24, 1944, seventeen of the Superfortress photography planes had been over the Japanese home islands in single-plane missions. Usually the F-13s could fly 1,500 miles to a target, spend about one hour over it while the crew took pictures, and then fly the 1,500 miles back to base. With its remote-controlled guns the fast-flying F-13 had a very good defense. On November 7 more than a hundred Japanese fighters took off to attack a single F-13 over Tokyo but only two of the fighters got close enough or high enough even to fire their guns and they were ineffective. Consequently the F-13s were assigned photographic missions anywhere in the Pacific until the very end of the war but especially over the Japanese home islands, which had been so inaccessible before the new plane's arrival. When General LeMay initiated his low-level, no-guns incendiary raids on Japan, one of the most daring gambles of the entire conflict, the F-13 photographic planes verified the success of the missions by bringing back pictures of the destruction. It was also the F-13 crews that took the pictures of Hiroshima, the first pictures showing the destruction caused by the explosion of an atom bomb.

When Colonel Paul W. Tibbets, Jr., lifted his B-29, the *Enola Gay*, off the runway at Tinian at 0245 on the morning of August 6, 1945, and started for Hiroshima with the atom bomb in the bomb bay, another B-29 loaded with camera equipment followed within two minutes. This aircraft, No. 91, was piloted by Captain George W. Marquardt and it was his plane that brought back the photographic evidence of the initial explosion, the huge ball of fire, the fearful cloud mass, and the rapidly climbing column that mushroomed high in the air. Within three hours an F-13, flown by Captain Omer L. Cox, was over Hiroshima for damage-assessment pictures.

"Even at 30,000 feet we could distinguish fires on the ground," Cox said. "We got within about a hundred yards of the mushroom cloud where we saw debris being churned into almost nothing. And this was three hours after the *Enola Gay* had dropped her load!"

The photographs taken by Cox were used by President Harry S Truman when he made his announcement to the press.

On August 11, after the fires and smoke were gone, F-13s made a photographic survey of the damage at both Hiroshima and Nagasaki, where a second atom bomb had been dropped on the ninth. Because of the significance of the revolutionary new weapon both for the war about to end and for future wars, a detailed assessment was needed and aerial reconnaissance provided the only method available. The photographs obtained indicated that 4.1 square miles of Hiroshima were completely destroyed and .6 square mile badly damaged. After the war ended and a ground survey was possible it was discovered that these figures were nearly exact.

It was ironic that photographs taken by aircraft that dropped no bombs were instrumental not only in showing the Allies that they had a terrible and powerful weapon at their disposal but also in convincing all nations that the atom bomb should never again be used in warfare. It was a fitting climax to the aerial reconnaissance efforts of World War II.

9

Air Reconnaissance in Korea

SUNDAY June 25, 1950, was a hot, humid day both in the United States and in Korea but the weather was no problem to Lieutenant General George E. Stratemeyer, commanding officer of the Far East Air Forces. He was on an Air Force transport plane returning to Tokyo by way of Hawaii and Okinawa after a series of conferences in Washington, D.C. Major General Earle E. Partridge, the acting commander of the FEAF while General Stratemeyer was away, was spending the weekend in Nagoya with his family. There was nothing to suggest that before this Sunday ended it would be a tragic reminder of that Sunday nine years earlier when the Japanese planes attacked Pearl Harbor.

At 0400 hours on the morning of the 25th the North Koreans launched a sudden and all-out attack across the 38th parallel in an open attempt to grab all of South Korea. It was the most flagrant Communist aggression since the end of World War II and within thirty-six hours the United Nations called upon its members to assist South Korea in repelling the invaders. The first forces ordered into action by President Truman were the air forces, including the aerial reconnaissance units available.

Air evacuation of American nationals took first priority, but the reconnaissance mission of the FEAF planes was of equal importance during the early hours of the conflict since the exact purpose and intentions of the North Koreans were not clear at the beginning. Many military experts, well aware of former Communist terror tactics, were reluctant to call the move all-out aggression until they were certain. The North Koreans had sent raiding parties across the 38th parallel before, but they had always withdrawn them again within a few hours. However, once the reconnaissance pilots of the FEAF reported at 0900 hours on the 25th that the South Korean town of Kaesong had fallen it became obvious that the North Koreans were launching a full-scale invasion.

In 1945 it would have been difficult to find one Army, Navy, or Marine officer in the U.S. military establishment who would not have acknowledged the vital importance of aerial reconnaissance. It had been a long, difficult, uphill battle by the proponents of aerial reconnaissance but it appeared they were finally victorious by the end of World War II, that never again would the United States be caught without the skilled manpower and modern equipment necessary to fulfill the aerial reconnaissance mission efficiently. It appeared that way but it wasn't. The severe "economy" programs between 1945 and 1950 took their toll of the established aerial reconnaissance systems and prevented the required research and development programs necessary if aircraft, cameras, and technicians were to keep up with the fast-moving jet age. The FEAF had no established reconnaissance organization when the Korean War began. All it had was a scattered, undermanned, and underequipped group of units that had little or no communication among them. On Okinawa, stationed at the Kadena Air Base, were a few RB-29s (formerly the F-13 designation) of the 31st Strategic Reconnaissance Squadron, while two RB-17s were based at Clark Air Base in the Philippines. The first jet reconnaissance planes ever used by the USAF, the RB-80s of the 8th Tactical Reconnaissance

Squadron, were parked on the airfield at Yakota, Japan. The ground activities for these widely scattered units were handled by the 548th Reconnaissance Technical Squadron, also based at Yakota. This was the extent of the aerial reconnaissance forces available to General Stratemeyer when South Korea was invaded.

It soon became apparent that the United Nations forces fighting in Korea were going to need aerial reconnaissance even more than did the ground units during World War II. This was a new kind of war, a "limited" war where political considerations were as important as military considerations and every move had to be weighed in terms of its diplomatic consequences. Many targets that appeared important to the military were put off limits for political reasons, such as the Manchurian airfields across the Yalu River. Photographic reconnaissance was the only method the United Nations forces had to keep these fields under surveillance. Using oblique cameras, the reconnaissance planes brought back pictures that revealed a great deal of information about the North Korean air force, such as the length of runway required for the Migs, number of planes based at the field ready to fly south to attack U.N. aircraft and installations, and any new equipment that was moved into the off limits area.

Aerial photographs were also needed to provide basic information about North Korea itself. At the time of the Communist invasion the Far East Command had no combat mission toward Korea and, in view of this, it had no contingent plan for such operations. Target dossiers were nonexistent. In fact, during the first few days a young USAF officer, Lieutenant Colonel John McGinn, in order to get target information for the planes based at Suwon, a small airfield twenty miles south of Seoul, drove six miles to a ground command post. At the command post he studied the situation map on the wall, selected likely-looking targets, and wrote the target descriptions himself, which he then relayed to the pilots.

To alleviate this shortage of target photographs the 8th Tactical Reconnaissance Squadron sent a detachment to Itazuke, a southern Japanese airfield, within a few hours after the Communist troops crossed the 38th parallel. Later the entire squadron moved to this base and attempted to supply the aerial reconnaissance requirements of both the Fifth Air Force and the Eighth Army. It was a clumsy, ineffective arrangement. Once the pilots of the 8th obtained the negatives of the objective, the negatives had to be ferried north to Yakota, where the technicians of the 548th Reconnaissance Technical Squadron developed the prints and did the interpretation. This procedure was slow even in good weather but when the weather was bad the photographs sometimes didn't reach their destination for a week.

Washington made an effort to strengthen the aerial reconnaissance forces in August and September when it was discovered that the requirements of the Fifth Air Force and the Eighth Army were not being met. The 162d Tactical Reconnaissance Squadron, specialists in night photography, and the 363d Reconnaissance Technical Squadron arrived at Itazuke to aid the 8th Tactical Reconnaissance Squadron and eliminate ferrying the film to Yakota for processing, thus making the prints available much faster. The Fifth Air Force, in an attempt to organize its scattered reconnaissance units more efficiently, established the 543d Tactical Support Group with headquarters at Itazuke. In October 1950 the group set up a unit at K-2, Taegu, Korea. The 543d Tactical Support Group was not a success. Supply, especially personal equipment, was in a state of chaos, morale was low, and the lines of communication among its own units and outside organizations were confused and slow. The 363d Reconnaissance Technical Squadron, which had been designated to help process the film, was set up in a school compound in Taegu City and often several hours elapsed before the film arrived from the airfield at K-2. A large percentage of the flash bombs used by the 162d Tactical Reconnaissance Squadron, the night photography specialists, were duds and the film was ruined. Cooperation from the headquarters staff of the Eighth Army was very poor.

During this period, however, and despite the handicaps that affected the overall efficiency of Fifth Air Force reconnaissance, much valuable information was gathered by the hard-working pilots. When General MacArthur, Supreme Commander Allied Powers, planned the invasion at the rear of the North Korean forces he selected Inchon as the site. Inchon, the port and harbor serving the city of Seoul, had one serious drawback that had many military experts convinced the invasion was doomed to failure from the start. The port had a fantastic rise and fall of the tides, so extreme that the Navy vessels supporting the landings would be able to beach only a few hours on certain days in late 1950—September 15, October 11, and November 3.

September 15 was selected as D-Day. The U.S. Navy was decidedly not happy with the plan and told General MacArthur so, but he refused to back down. Even General Omar Bradley, chairman of the Joint Chiefs of Staff, and Army Chief of Staff J. Lawton Collins opposed the plan, but Secretary of Defense Louis A. Johnson sided with MacArthur. As the date for D-Day neared, the Navy realized it needed much more precise information about the high and low tides and underwater obstacles than it had in its files. The 8th Tactical Reconnaissance Squadron was assigned the mission of obtaining the required data. Flying at nearly wave-top level in their RB-80s, the pilots of the 8th Tactical Reconnaissance Squadron took photographs of the harbor at various tidal stages. Many of the pictures were taken with a stereo strip camera, designed by pioneer George Goddard during World War II. These stereo photographs made it possible for experienced PIs to determine the height of underwater obstacles within two inches. Another camera used in combat for the first time during the Korean conflict was the panoramic camera. It too was a valuable help in determining the tide heights at Inchon. Using a single lens of long focal length that rotated across the line of flight to expose a long segment of film, the panoramic camera provided a horizon-to-horizon picture without the need of the trimetrogon setup formerly required.

Fortunately three of the best photo interpreters in the world were in Korea at the time of the Inchon landings, one officer and two civilians from Wright Field in Dayton, Ohio. Air Force Colonel Richard W. Philbrick, Donald J. Graves, and Amrom H. Katz studied the pictures brought back by the pilots of the 8th Tactical Reconnaissance Squadron and determined the height of the seawalls at various tidal stages, an important factor for successful amphibious landings. This information was passed along to the still skeptical Navy officers.

All doubt was erased at 1730 hours on the evening of September 15 when twenty-three waves of LVTs, along with eight LSTs, made the beach assault. The 15-foot seawall protecting the beach was easily surmounted by the Marines because, just as the PIs had predicted, the tide was high enough to permit scaling. Later evidence proved that Katz and his companions were correct in their predictions to within a few inches. The Inchon landings were a magnificent success. The North Koreans were taken by surprise and within ten days the North Korean People's Army, which had been near victory, was broken and beaten. Seoul was captured. In all of military history there was no more effective amphibious operation—and the success of the Inchon landings hinged on the aerial photographs of the harbor obtained by the 8th Tactical Reconnaissance Squadron.

Unfortunately, not all aerial reconnaissance missions were so successful. Shortly after the Korean conflict began it became evident to Washington that there was a possibility that Red Chinese troops might become involved in the fighting. With the large number of men available, it was obvious that any such intervention by the Chinese would be a serious matter. Consequently FEAF reconnaissance planes were ordered to photograph the Yalu River area periodically, not only to assess the bomb damage suffered by the bridges spanning the river but to detect any Chinese Communist forces infiltrating into North Korea. The initial error in this assignment was the fact that the Chinese infiltration had taken place by the time the aerial surveillance began in earnest. It was learned later that by the end of Ocotober four corps of Communist General Lin Piao's Chinese Fourth Field Army had already crossed the Yalu and were hiding in the mountains on the right flank of the American Eighth Army in North Korea.

The Chinese troops used excellent camouflaged positions in the heavily wooded mountains of North Korea to conceal themselves from the aerial cameras and they did a very good job. The FEAF reconnaissance planes did their best but with limited equipment they rarely had time to reconnoiter any area other than that adjacent to the main roads leading south from the Yalu River toward the American Eighth Army. The Communists were intelligent enough to avoid these main roads. Several times, however, the reconnaissance reports indicated that unusual activities were in progress by the enemy. On November 7 the photographs indicated that there was much heavier than normal traffic south from Kanggye to the Choshin reservoir area. The tracks of the vehicles could be plainly seen in the snow.

Since this traffic had not been seen during the daylight hours General MacArthur decided, rightly, that the enemy was moving at night under cover of darkness. The specialists in night photography, the 162d Tactical Reconnaissance Squadron, had switched to daylight missions because of a lack of success with their after-dark efforts. On November 8, after the daylight photos indicated that the enemy was moving large forces south at night, the 162d Tactical Reconnaissance Squadron resumed its night missions. Unfortunately, they met with no more success than the earlier ones. The mountainous terrain forced the aircraft to fly at high altitudes, and the haze and fog common to the country at that time of year made night photography very difficult.

The RB-29s of the 31st Strategic Reconnaissance Squadron tried to operate along the Yalu River but the Mig fighters made such missions costly. On November 9, Migs attacked a flak-damaged RB-29 over Sinuiju and Corporal Harry J. LaVene, the tail gunner, blasted one of the Migs out of the sky. The recon plane was so badly damaged, however, that it crash landed at Johnson Air Base, Japan, killing five of the crewmen. After this mission the RB-29s were not permitted to take photographs in the Yalu River area and the RF-80s of the 8th Tactical Reconnaissance Squadron had to accomplish the task alone. The pilots of this unit kept both the FEAF and the American Eighth Army supplied with aerial photographs of the Yalu River area during the month of November. In fact, they furnished more pictures than the limited number of skilled interpreters could handle. Yet, with all these photographs available, the strong counterattack launched by General Lin Piao's Chinese forces on November 26 took the Allies by surprise and resulted in two months of defeat and retreat for the American troops that had been so near victory after the triumph of Inchon. It was a poor showing for the aerial reconnaissance units of the FEAF.

During December, as the American Eighth Army broke contact with the Chinese forces and retreated south, the whereabouts of the Communist armies became of prime importance. General Stratemeyer ordered every reconnaissance plane out to find the enemy forces and for ten days the crews photographed the forty-mile-deep zone beyond the Eighth Army lines daily. At Taegu the 543d Tactical Support Group interpreters studied more than 27,000 pictures sent to them during this period. Yet the Chinese armies and the North Korean forces were not located. Once again, when information was needed the most, it appeared that aerial reconnaissance had failed. An investigation later exonerated the reconnaissance units, however. The Barcus Board Report (Volume I, Book 2, p. 190) stated:

> Photographic interpreters must be kept briefed up to the minute on the status of areas within which they work. They should be used to confirm, deny, or enlarge upon existing intelligence concerning those areas. They cannot be expected to furnish complete intelligence of any area if they are required to discover anew the information which has already been gathered from other sources.

This USAF evaluation board report emphasized that the Fifth Air Force interpreters at Taegu, working in solitary isolation without any other intelligence sources to give them a hint as to the whereabouts of the Chinese troops and enemy activities, could not be expected to discover this information within ten days from a mass of 27,000 photographs.

Nonetheless the reconnaissance situation in Korea was far from satisfactory and needed to be reorganized. General Stratemeyer requested the services of reconnaissance pioneer Colonel Karl L. Polifka. On January 24, 1951, Pop Polifka was assigned to the 543d Tactical Support Group and immediately began his investigation. The result of the colonel's study of the reconnaissance situation was the activation, effective February 1951, of the 67th Tactical Reconnaissance Wing, under Polifka's command.

During the spring of 1951 most of the echelons of the units making up the 67th were concentrated at Taegu (K-2). Under the new organization set up by Pop Polifka, photoreconnaissance improved but it still was far from peak efficiency. Eighth Army Headquarters complained bitterly that it had not been able to obtain adequate intelligence from aerial sources since the start of the Korean War and all three corps headquarters were extremely dissatisfied with the photographic support they were receiving. One division intelligence officer said that he had requested photographic coverage of a forward area on June 1 but he had not received the pictures until June 4. By that time the division had overrun the area.

There was work to be done and Polifka set out to do it just as he had during World War II. Prior to his reorganization of the reconnaissance units there had been no system for handling requests for aerial photographs. Telephone calls came at all hours of the night for coverage of certain areas and it was impossible to plan the missions for the following twenty-four hours because of this constant change of objectives. Polifka stopped that procedure. He insisted that special requests for photo coverage be channeled through Fifth Air Force headquarters and be incorporated in the daily operations order. When the Eighth Army wanted picture coverage of a special area, the requests had to be screened and consolidated in division and corps G-2 Air offices and then forwarded to the Eighth Army G-2 Air in the Joint Operations Center. If the requests were approved there, they were forwarded to the Fifth Air Force and then down to the 67th Tactical Reconnaissance Wing, where Polifka and his pilots would take care of the assignment. By July 1 the 67th Tactical Reconnaissance Wing was beginning to function smoothly as a unit and most of the difficulties that lay in the way of providing adequate aerial intelligence for both air and ground units were gradually being overcome.

On that date the 67th Reconnaissance Group—and the USAF—lost one of the greatest reconnaissance pilots the world ever knew. Polifka, flying an RF-51 with the 45th Tactical Reconnaissance Squadron, went to Kaesong, Korea, to obtain some up-to-date pictures of the area. Antiaircraft fire hit his aircraft and knocked out the cooling system. Within a few seconds the colonel knew that the RF-51 was doomed, that he had to bail out. He managed to get out of the damaged aircraft but his parachute caught on the tail of the plane and the colonel went down with the ship. He died doing what he liked to do best—improving reconnaissance tactics. His contributions to the United Nations' cause and his advancement of tactical reconnaissance will never be forgotten.

Colonel Vincent Howard immediately replaced Polifka and within a few days it was decided that the front lines in Korea finally had stability enough to permit the 67th Tactical Reconnaissance Wing to gather its units together and function as an integral wing at one location. Prior to this the ground situation in Korea had been so fluid after the intervention of the Chinese that only the tactical group with its crews, planes, and other equipment operated out of Taegu, while the supporting units operated out of Tsuike and Komaki air bases in Japan. This was militarily unsound and very inconvenient. When it was deemed safe for the entire wing to operate from one location in July 1951, the 67th Tactical Reconnaissance Wing moved to Kimpo Air Base (K-14), Korea. This increased the efficiency of the unit and the wing was able to provide the necessary coverage for the Eighth Army.

Although the organizational problems were solved, the tactical reconnaissance effort encountered a variety of technical difficulties that created a great deal of controversy and misunderstanding between the air and ground forces. Under an agreement that the Army and the USAF made prior to the Korean War, the Air Force was to obtain the aerial photographs, develop the film, title the pictures, and make five prints of each negative. The Army then did the necessary interpretation, produced the desired quantities, and delivered them to the requesting ground agencies. The Eighth Army couldn't live up to the agreement during the first two years of the conflict because they did not have the technicians available. Since the Air Force had to man the Joint Photo Center at Taegu with its own personnel without help from the Army, the Eighth Army limited its photo requirements to 1,225 negatives and 5,000 prints a day. In July 1952, however, the 98th Engineer Aerial Photo Reproduction Company joined the Eighth Army and was able to handle 5,000 negatives and 25,000 prints a day at its headquarters in Seoul. The Eighth Army then demanded 3,600 photo negatives a day from the Fifth Air Force, nearly three times what it had gotten before, regardless of the weather or length of daylight flying time available. The Fifth Air Force on its own initiative reduced the number of negatives to be delivered to the ground forces to an average of 2,000 negatives a day.

The problem of picture quality was not so easily solved, however. For the first time in actual combat jet aircraft were taking aerial photographs. Unfortunately the RF-80's cameras and magazines had been designed for the speeds of conventional aircraft instead of the much faster speed of the jet and consequently, to get clear pictures, the pilot had to throttle down over the target. This made him an easy mark for enemy fighters and antiaircraft guns, especially in the Mig Alley sector. If he didn't slow down the photographs were marred by motion blur. Efforts to replace the RF-80 with the swept-wing RF-84F failed. Finally the USAF permitted the FEAF to try and modify six F-86s for aerial photography. A K-22 camera with a 24-inch lens was installed, using a two-mirror arrangement to focus the camera on the target. The camera was mounted parallel to the longitudinal axis of the jet but the mirrors permitted vertical coverage. However, blurring was still a problem and the Honey-bucket, as the RF-86 was called, was never very successful.

There was also a problem of scale. Despite the fact that World War II target photography had been at the 1:6000 or 1:7000 scale, the Eighth Army insisted that it wanted 1:3000 scale surveillance photography. This quickly increased the losses of Fifth Air Force planes and Lieutenant General Glenn O. Barcus, who assumed command of the Fifth Air Force in June 1952, refused to permit his pilots to fly at the lower altitudes required for this scale surveillance photography. He ordered the reconnaissance crews to stay at 9,000 feet or above when within 30,000 yards of the front lines and at 12,000 feet or higher over any heavily defended target.

The controversy was never settled to the satisfaction of both the air forces and ground forces but a compromise was finally reached which was followed for the remainder of the war. General Barcus agreed that every fourth week his reconnaissance planes would fly front-line and corps-area cover at a scale of 1:5000 but at all other times the scale would be 1:7000. Requests for low-level obliques or larger image size photos would be reviewed individually and only in an extreme emergency would a scale of larger than 1:4000 be flown over a highly defended area. It was an agreement that both the Fifth Air Force and Eighth Army tried to live with, but neither was very happy.

Most of the daylight reconnaissance missions were flown by the 15th Tactical Reconnaissance Squadron, nicknamed the Cottonpickers. Paul N. Nadashkevich, one of the squadron's pilots at the time, described the missions and their value to the ground forces:

"One of the old heads usually took a new pilot on his first few missions. The new flier would fly wingman in the customary two-plane formation and if the leader was sincere he would squeeze in a sightseeing trip while performing a regular mission. This served a purpose because the oldtimers who only had a few missions to fly flew full speed between targets and if the new man got behind he stayed behind and eventually had to find his own way home. Knowing the landmarks helped a guy get home."

As Nadashkevich pointed out, the briefings for most aerial reconnaissance missions consisted of individual instructions from one of the intelligence officers describing what was wanted and then a conference between the leader and the wingmen. The routes and targets were marked on the maps, takeoff time was set, and all the other flying details were taken care of at this conference. At most of the bases in Korea the runways were too narrow for formation takeoffs so the two RF-80s took off a few seconds apart and joined wing-to-wing in the air. After takeoff the recon pilots switched to Joint Operations Control and reported in, giving their call sign and mission number, and stating whether they were inbound or outbound in reference to enemy territory. These radio calls were received at Radar Hill, which was a few miles from Kimpo. Radar Hill monitored the aerial reconnaissance flights and warned the pilots of approaching enemy aircraft. This station was tied in with the radars at Chodo which were able to pick up Migs taking off at Antung.

A typical message from Radar Hill was: "Redbird Charley Flight, you have 8 Bandit Trains taking off at Big City, heading 140. More bandits following. Maintain alert." (Translated into layman's English, this is: "Flight leader, there are 8 enemy formations taking off from Antung, heading on a course of 140 degrees. More Migs following. Watch for them.")

If the pilots of the 15th Tactical Reconnaissance Squadron were south of Sinanju when they received the radio warning from Radar Hill, or east of the Chongchon River, they just continued about their business of obtaining the desired photographs and kept their eyes open for the enemy planes. Normally the Migs went to about 40,000 feet and the RF-80 pilots stayed down around 19,000 feet. If the recon pilots spotted the Migs first they usually maintained a tight turn down to the deck and roared back across the MLR (main line of resistance). If the Migs saw the RF-80s first, it usually meant one pass, a burst of cannon fire that might or might not be disastrous for the American fliers, and everyone headed in opposite directions. The Migs didn't have the turn radius or the fuel to play around with the RF-80s for long and the Red pilots knew that F-86s were normally in the area. They didn't want to give the Sabre pilots a chance to dive on them while they were at low altitude.

"The most dramatic of the three types of missions we flew in our jets," said Nadashkevich, "were the ones into Mig Alley. This was the region west of the Chongchon River and above Sinanju. In a tour of a hundred missions we might fly no more than half a dozen such missions and once a pilot had over ninety missions to his credit he was exempt from going into Mig Alley. The targets photographed were troop encampments, airfields, bridges, marshaling yards—generally large, well-defined high-value targets. The south bank of the Yalu River was often photographed but if we accidentally, in the midst of our twists and turns, shot some of the north bank everyone got mad, thinking we violated the boundary.

"This type of mission was first briefed with your own intelligence officer and then you went across the field to brief the F-86 escorts and were in turn briefed by them. Only one RF-80 flew this mission at a time and it usually took off first and got a little lead on the faster Sabres which would come along and take up station alongside and overhead. The closer we got to Mig Alley the higher the escort went until only two usually remained around me. After we crossed the MLR and Chodo started calling an infinite number of bandit trains taking off from Big City, the sky would suddenly fill with twinkling little objects floating down, which turned out to be the tip tanks of the F-86s.

"On one of my flights to Mig Alley I started photographing the railroad from Sinanju to Chongju as soon as I crossed Pyongyang. That was the last I saw of my escorts until we were on our way home. Actually I was relieved. The way they'd been wallowing around trying to keep their speed down to mine I'd been afraid of a mid-air collision. The next target after the railroad was at Yangsi, just southeast of the Mig base at Antung. High above I could see the contrails of the F-86s and the Migs as they battled each other and I could hear their radio chatter. Meanwhile I wasn't being ignored. The antiaircraft shells were enough to keep both the Migs and the F-86s away from me. I finished my picture taking, turned to 140 degrees, firewalled the throttle, and radioed my escorts that I was going home. Passing Sinanju I was joined by four F-86s and two Migs. The Migs were shy and stayed about half a mile away and a few hundred feet above at nine o'clock. The leader of my close escort tried to guide someone from our top cover down on the Migs but before anything happened they made a sharp diving turn to the left and disappeared. We all continued a shallow descent until we passed over Kimpo where I broke off after thanking them for their trouble and landed."

Another type of mission flown by the RF-80s was the photographing of targets in the countryside outside of Mig Alley—bends in the rivers, coordinates that seemed meaningless to the pilots but were important to the ground commanders, back sides of ridges, and deep valleys. These missions were usually flown by two pilots, one shooting the pictures while his wingman watched for enemy fighters and ground fire. The wingman was especially helpful in detecting flak that might be creeping up unnoticed on the plane shooting the photographs and warning the other pilot. These missions were usually fifty or more miles behind the enemy front and were called "bread and butter" trips by the recon fliers because they were not nearly so hazardous as the Mig Alley excursions. On rare occasions one of the photo planes would be hit by a Mig in an area where Migs weren't expected but not often.

The third type of mission was known as EUSAK for the Eighth US Army Corps which was the client of the 15th Tactical Reconnaissance Squadron. The Fifth Air Force had agreed to fly front-line cover for the Eighth Army once a week, and corps area cover three times monthly. This was done on a block-scheduling plan. The thirty-mile zone of enemy territory extending from the MLR was subdivided into two tiers of blocks, each about 15,000 meters square. This gave a total of twenty-seven blocks, each of which could be photographed by one RF-80 at a scale of 1:5000 in one mission. The blocks to be covered each day were designated by the Eighth Army representative at Joint Operations Center and passed on to the 15th Tactical Reconnaissance Squadron headquarters. Approximately 30 percent of the Fifth Air Force's photo capability was spent on front-line and corps coverage.

The 12th Tactical Reconnaissance Squadron, nicknamed the Blackbirds, kept a close tab on the enemy when he began wholesale night movements in the early part of 1952. Flying RB-26s, the pilots of the 12th usually flew three-hour night missions during which they photographed prebriefed targets. To say that these crews had trouble is an understatement. The illumination systems left a great deal to be desired as did the navigational aids provided to help the crew find the targets in the blacked-out areas of North Korea over which they operated. Colonel Robert Smith, the C.O. of the 67th Tactical Reconnaissance Group from May until October 1952, was an expert in RB-26 night missions. This was the same Robert Smith who flew

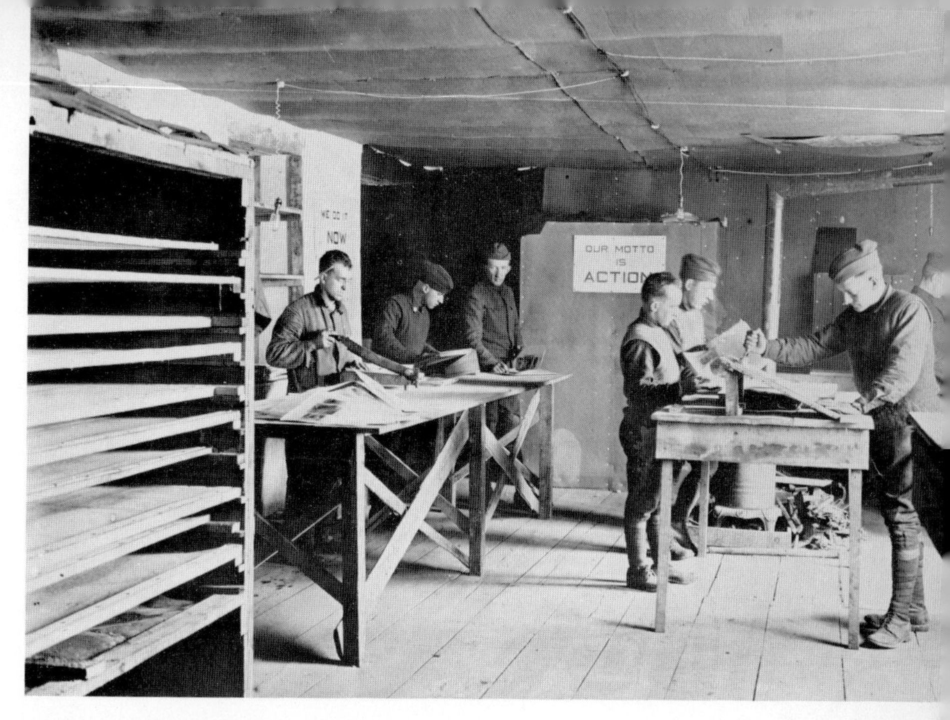

World War I reproduction of aerial photographs brought back by the observation pilots and observers.

A World War I mixing room.

Early Fairchild aerial camera is shown being loaded aboard photo-lane by its designer, Sherman Fairchild (right foreground) in this photograph taken about 1925. A similar model K-3 camera was presented by Fairchild Camera and Instrument Corporation to the Smithsonian Institute for its Hall of Photography in the Museum of History and Technology.

Low altitude reconnaissance photograph of Kothan, Germany. (*U.S. Air Force photo*)

Major Goddard in Boeing B-17B airplane using 60-inch telephoto lens camera. (*U.S. Air Force photo*)

Camouflaged command post—The entrenchment atop this ridge in Korea makes an almost complete circle. It's a Red Command Post, with firing slits around it. This picture was taken April 16, 1951 by a ground force observer in a T-6 "Mosquito." (*U.S. Air Force photo*)

Ground crewman examine the damaged tail section of an RF-80 during the Korean War.

A photograph of a North Korean Headquarters building taken by a reconnaissance pilot in a low-flying RF-80 during the Korean War.

Colonel Victor N. Cabas commanded the USAF 432nd Tactical Reconnaissance Wing stationed at Udorn RTAFB, Thailand during the Vietnam War. His unit, using RF-4 aircraft, flew day and night over North Vietnam obtaining intelligence data.

U.S. AIR FORCE
U.S. AIR FORCE
S. AIR

Film is unloaded from an RF-4 of the 432nd Tactical Reconnaissance Wing seconds after it is parked after returning from a mission over North Vietnam.

At left: Clyde B. East, skilled reconnaissance pilot of three wars—WW II, Korea, and Vietnam.

U.S. Air Force Major William L. Kirk, Tuscon, Ariz. (8th Tactical Fighter Wing) explains to crew members of an EC-121 Warning Star how he shot down a MIG-21 over North Vietnam after the crew had alerted him to the MIG's presence. The EC-121 contacted Kirk's F-4 Phantom flight when an enemy interceptor threatened an Air Force strike force. The Warning Star crew is assigned to the College Eye Task Force, a unit of the 552nd Airborne Early Warning and Control Wing. (*U.S. Air Force photo*)

EB-66 DESTROYER—A recent addition to the Tactical Reconnaissance Force, it has been in the US Air Force inventory since February, 1956. First utilized as a bomber, it now is an electronics warfare aircraft. Utilizing a maze of electronic gear and counter systems, the aircraft greatly aids in pinpointing targets and enemy aircraft in the area.

It has a span of 72 feet 6 inches, length of 75 feet 2 inches, and a height of 23 feet 7 inches. With a speed of 700 miles per hour it can travel beyond 1,500 miles without aerial refueling. Its ceiling is above 45,000 feet.

SAGE AIR ARM—Extending NORAD's radar surveillance far off shore is this EC-121H Super Constellation of USAF Air Defense Command. It carries the latest in target-tracking and communications equipment which enables it to maintain constant automatic contact with shore-based air defense control centers. The system, named ALRI (Airborne Long Range Imput), provides a seaward extension of the SAGE (Semi-Automatic Ground Environment) system. It instantaneously relays early-warning information by data link directly to a ground communications site that speeds it on to the nearest SAGE direction center and NORAD's combat operations center. Time lag between target detection and readout at the SAGE center is less than 1½ seconds. The SAGE center then follows the intercept operation while relaying data link radio guidance to the interceptor through the ALRI aircraft. (*Official NORAD photo*)

RF-4C PHANTOM II—The McDonnell RF-4C Phantom II, a reconnaissance version of the fighter type is one of the US Air Force's newest and fastest tactical reconnaissance aircraft. The RF-4C incorporates an infrared camera and electronic radar, making it possible to perform reconnaissance missions day or night in any kind of weather. The plane's optical system includes automatic in-flight processing.

Carrying a crew of two, the aircraft is capable of traveling more than twice the speed of sound. Its ceiling is above 12 miles, and the Phantom has a range of more than 2,000 miles without refueling. In-flight refueling gives it almost unlimited range. It has a span of 38 feet 5 inches, length of 58 feet 3 inches, and height of 16 feet 3 inches.

The new United States Air Force SR-71 aircraft, assigned to Strategic Air Command, provides SAC with the world's most advanced strategic reconnaissance plane. The SR-71 flies at more than three times the speed of sound and operates at altitudes in excess of 80,000 feet. (*USAF photo*)

RF-101 VOODOO—The McDonnell RF-101 Voodoo was the US Air Force's first supersonic photoreconnaissance plane. This "all-seeing eye" member of Tactical Air Command can photograph an area 217 miles long and 8 miles wide from 45,000 feet, plus an area mosaic equivalent to 20,000 square miles in a single flight.

With a span of 39 feet 9 inches, length of 69 feet, and a height of 18 feet, the Voodoo can obtain speeds of over 1,000 miles an hour. Its range is beyond 1,000 miles without refueling and it has a ceiling of above 50,000 feet.

ASA aircraft attached to reconnaissance attack squadron over naval air station Sanford, Florida.

Air Force technicians adjust KA-56 panoramic reconnaissance camera with in-flight processing cassette in RF-4C aircraft. Fairchild Space and Defense Systems 180-degree scan camera furnishes horizon-to-horizon photos with more than three times the coverage of a conventional frame camera.

Rotating prism of KA-60 panoramic camera peers through V-shaped window in nose of Army Mohawk aircraft. Forward oblique installation of Fairchild Space and Defense Systems 70mm camera is for route surveying, landing field and target selection, damage assessment, and general surveillance.

A tourist's map of Washington, D.C., comes to life in this aerial photograph of the nation's capital taken from a U.S. Navy RA-5C Vigilante jet at high altitude. The area shown enlarged is a small segment from the single Perkin-Elmer reconnaissance camera film strip shown at right (enlarged area boxed). The new camera is one of a highly advanced pair developed to provide height resolution, horizon-to-horizon photographs at both high and low altitudes, even at aircraft speeds of more than twice the speed of sound. Points of interest shown include the Jefferson Memorial (upper left), Washington Monument (upper center), White House (upper right). Smithsonian Institute buildings flank the Mall area (center, vertical) and the Capitol is shown at bottom center.

New York City. This picture was taken by Minipan camera.

BIRD'S SQUAWK—"EAME Bird" was a brainchild of Ground Electronics Engineering Installations Agency (GEEIS), Tinker AFB, Oklahoma. Inside the C-130 aircraft is a maze of equipment including ultrahigh frequency (VHF), local area HF single side band (SSB), long haul HF SSB, continuous wave (CW) communication, teletype, encryption and digitalized teletype equipment and multipurpose long-wire antennas. On the human side of its operation, each "bird" has assigned to it a communications officer, a senior sergeant team chief, four teletype crypto operators, three radio operators, three tech control technicians, three radio maintenance men and one teletype repairman, crypto repairman, ground powerman, and antenna man.

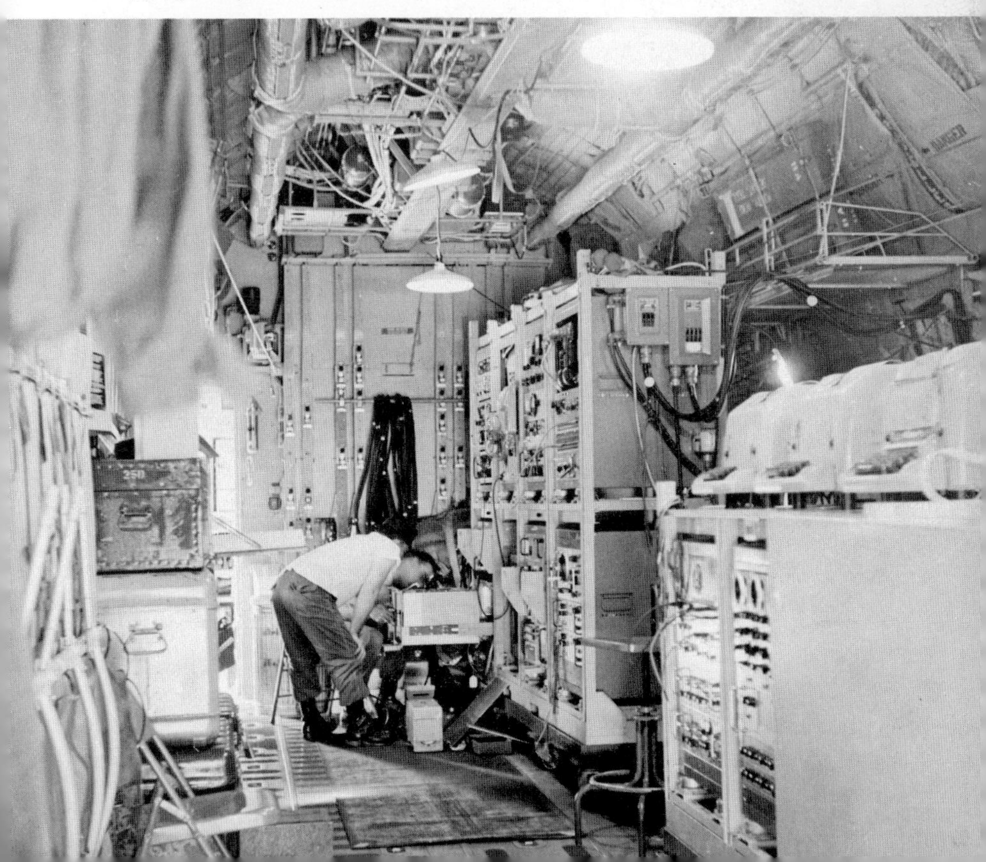

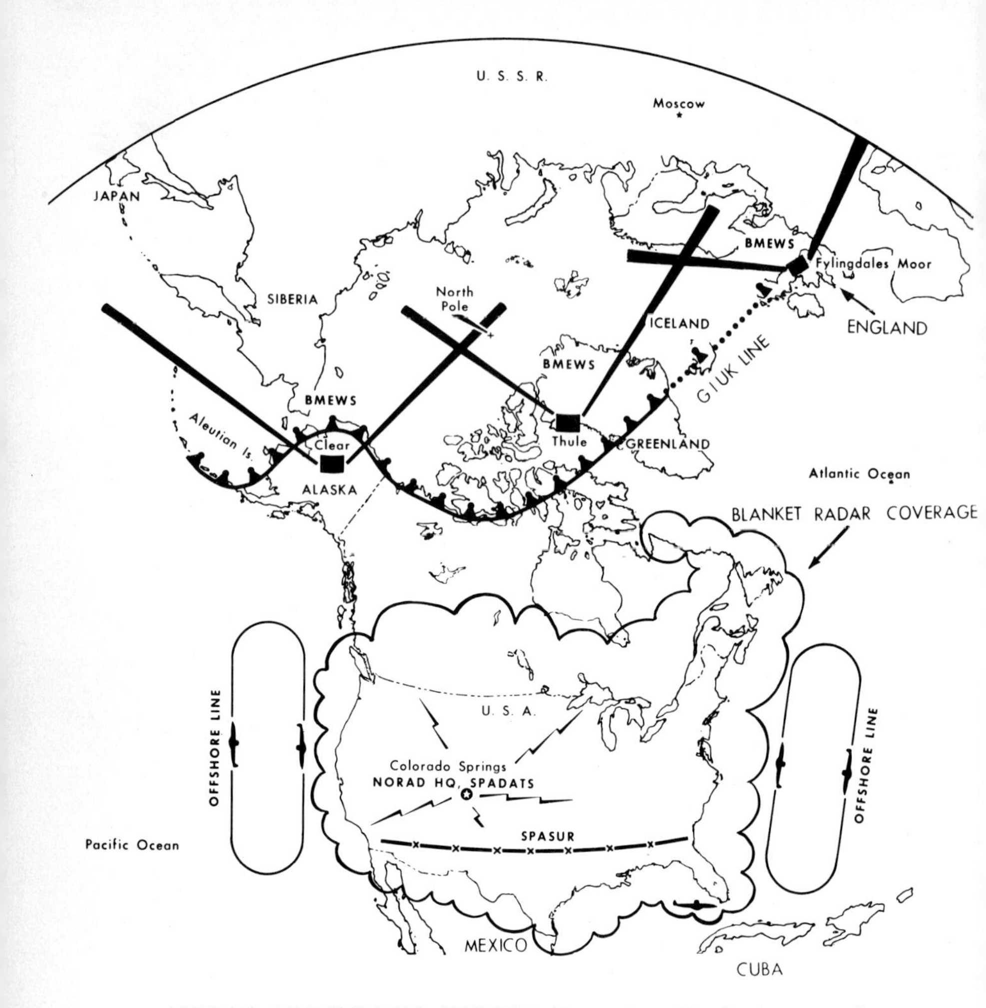

NORAD DETECTION SYSTEM–Protecting North America from surprise attack is an electronic screen stretching from the Arctic to the Mexican border and far off both coasts. At three locations across the top of the world–in Alaska, Greenland, and England–high-powered radar antennas reach out electronically for some 3,000 miles to give warning of an ICBM attack from the Eurasian land mass. Against the manned bomber threat, NORAD employs the Distant Early Warning Line coupled with a system of radars which provides a blanket of radar coverage over the populated area of Canada and the United States. Off both coasts, US Air Force early warning aircraft extend radar coverage seaward. Between Florida and Cuba other USAF aircraft bolster Florida-based ground radars. In space, NORAD's Space Detection and Tracking System keeps watch on man-made space objects. All elements are in instant communication with NORAD headquarters at Colorado Springs. (*Norad photo*)

aerial reconnaissance missions over Germany during World War II and was shot down.

"The pilots of the 12th Tactical Reconnaissance Squadron undoubtedly were the unsung heroes of the Korean conflict," Smith said. "They went out at night in all types of weather, alone, and with very few accurate navigational aids. There was usually an RB-26 covering each of the three zones—west coast, central, and east coast—all night long. The 12th Tactical Reconnaissance Squadron enabled the 67th to round out its twenty-four-hours-a-day reconnaissance mission."

The RB-26 carried a crew of three—a pilot, a navigator who acted as a shoran operator in the rear-gunner position, and a second navigator in the nose, lying on his belly watching the terrain below. For approximately five hours prior to the mission the navigator scheduled to fly the nose position stayed in a dark room conditioning his eyes to the blackness so that when he went aloft over the enemy positions he could see in the night. He would usually wear red goggles when he walked to the aircraft and keep them over his eyes until the RB-26 reached North Korea.

"It was amazing what this man could see visually despite the darkness," Smith said. "He could spot truck convoys, troops marching along the highway, and even count the number of trains in the marshaling yards."

Antiaircraft fire was a hazard but Migs were very seldom encountered at night. An enemy plane attacked Smith's RB-26 over Wonson one dark night. Although it made six passes it did no damage.

The pilots and navigators of the RB-26s did their best but the technical difficulties confronting them were once again overwhelming. When the Squadron first became operational the aircraft had been equipped with the newly developed A-3 cartridge-ejection illumination system. This equipment used A-14 magazines and M-112 flash cartridges and was supposed to be much superior to the M-46 photoflash bombs previously employed. Initially many of the cartridges were defective and didn't provide the necessary illumination for night photographs. After this problem was solved, it was discovered that the magazines malfunctioned because of excessive wear. More serious, however, was the fact that the RB-26 had to stay at a maximum of only 3,000 feet above the ground in order for the M-112 flash cartridges to furnish enough light for the night camera even when the equipment was in good operating condition and this was too low. Finally, in May 1952, the squadron reverted back to the older M-46 photoflash bomb and used it for the duration.

With the illumination problem stabilized, the navigation and camera problems were tackled. The RB-26s used shoran, a radar system for precision position-finding over short ranges. In order to pick up the shoran beams over enemy territory, however, it was necessary for the planes to fly at an altitude of 14,000 feet. The M-46 photoflash bomb provided sufficient illumination for night photography to a maximum of 8,000 feet. A more powerful M-120 photoflash bomb developed at Wright Field, Ohio, was sent to Korea, and proved effective from altitudes of 25,000 feet. Then, much to the frustration of the Blackbirds, the night cameras would not produce a clear, satisfactory picture from higher altitudes than the 8,000 feet formerly used. For a while the squadron attempted to operate at 14,000 feet so they could take advantage of the shoran beams for pinpoint navigation but the photographs were not satisfactory and they had to resume their 8,000-foot flight level. A night camera was not developed during the Korean conflict that would operate successfully at higher altitudes despite constant experimentation.

The flying "Polka Dots" of the 45th Tactical Reconnaissance Squadron flew more than twelve thousand reconnaissance missions in the RF-51 before this aircraft was replaced by the RF-80 jet. Losses were very high during the period the squadron had the RF-51s, one tragic loss being Pop Polifka in July 1951. The modified Mustang fighter was vulnerable to the ground fire and an easy mark for the Migs. At first the squadron's planes operated at 4,000 feet, staying over the enemy front lines for an hour and a half each mission. Eventually this altitude was raised to 6,000 feet and a second RF-51 accompanied the leader to spot ground fire for him. Yet the pilots of the 45th Tactical Reconnaissance Squadron accomplished many valuable tasks for the UN forces.

In March 1951, for example, the squadron became an invaluable part of the "Circle 10" missions. The jet fighter-bombers of the Fifth Air Force had such a limited fuel range that the pilots had no time to hunt for targets. It was imperative that they be able to take off and fly direct to the enemy position or activity. Consequently, a new operating procedure was devised. When the 12th Tactical Reconnaissance Squadron reported night sightings to the Joint Operations Center, these sightings were relayed to the pilots of the 45th Tactical Reconnaissance Squadron. At daylight the RF-51s took off and flew aerial reconnaissance inside a ten-mile circle surrounding the suspected enemy target. When they located the North Koreans they called in the F-80 and F-84 fighter-bombers, who then proceeded to destroy the target. Using this new armed-reconnaissance technique the Fifth Air Force destroyed nearly 2,300 enemy vehicles in the month of March alone. On one mission a month later Captain Gordon S. Bush of the 45th Tactical Reconnaissance Squadron spotted a company of dug-in North Korean troops waiting to ambush an American tank column. He immediately summoned the Thunderjets for a napalm strike. After the first pass by the jets over the enemy position the entire enemy company came out of hiding with their hands in the air and surrendered to the tank column.

During the spring of 1952 it became apparent that the RF-51s of the 45th Tactical Reconnaissance Squadron were outmoded and that emergency measures had to be taken. A few F-80C fighters which had been replaced by F-84s and F-86s were transferred to the squadron. Initially the F-80C planes flew protective cover on the wing of RF-80s but the need for more photography became so critical that the guns were removed from the jets and a vertical camera installed. After the change-over the 45th and 15th Tactical Squadrons each accepted assignments any place in Korea, north or south, and the reconnaissance of the Fifth Air Force was increased greatly.

One of the outstanding developments of aerial photography occurred during the Korean conflict—the introduction of aerial color photography, especially a new type of camouflage-detection color film, a development resulting from research done by George Goddard together with Eastman Kodak Company technicians. The film, known as Aerial Kodacolor, was coated with a special emulsion that was less sensitive to the blue end of the spectrum and eliminated haze. Its speed had to be increased to a Weston rating of 24 so that the jet pilots of the 15th and 45th Tactical Reconnaissance Squadrons could use it while speeding over a target and at the same time a simple process of developing the film once it was exposed had to be devised.

After a great deal of experimentation the film produced excellent results. One layer of the film coating, the infrared, recorded in red all natural vegetation, grass, and leaves of trees containing chlorophyll. The second layer, the panchromatic, recorded the unnatural foliage and spectral-enamel paints used to camouflage netting, tanks, soldiers, and guns. On the developed film natural vegetation was red; unnatural objects were green. The interpreter could easily see military equipment hidden in the woods or under nets. Even when the enemy cut branches of trees and covered their vehicles with them the branches soon turned from red to green and revealed the camouflage. When troops or tanks moved through a field they usually destroyed the grass and left a telltale track on the color film. Once the film was put to use in combat it played a major role in detecting enemy positions and equipment and caused the North Koreans and Chinese heavy losses.

Stereoscopic aerial color photos were also of value during the fighting in Korea and were used for the first time in combat.

These pictures were made with twin-lens, continuous-strip cameras usually positioned in the low oblique. Flight crews could study these three-dimension photographs, using Polaroid glasses, as they were flashed upon a metallic-coated screen and see exactly what they would see later on their mission. The briefing officer could stop the picture on the screen for a detailed study of a particular area without burning the color film as happens when motion picture film is stopped. The 9-inch film, two 4½-inch tracks, was the same as a lantern slide 200 feet long moving through the twin-lens projector at any desired speed and gave those watching the sensation of drifting over the countryside or city in a balloon rather than roaring over the area in a 600-mph jet plane. Paratroop units valued the stereoscopic color films also since the projected three-dimension color pictures showed the exact areas where the paratroopers and their supplies would be dropped. It permitted the men to be thoroughly briefed on the terrain prior to the mission.

Despite the state of unpreparedness and lack of suitable equipment, aerial reconnaissance was of greater importance during the Korean conflict than in any previous war. According to a survey made shortly after the truce, air reconnaissance accounted for about 44 percent of all intelligence used by ground units; in some cases the percentage was as high as 95. Air intelligence was equally important to the United Nations' air forces because it provided a means of determining when to schedule strikes against North Korean airfields about to be put back in service after a previous raid; continuous surveillance permitted the plotting of hostile antiaircraft-artillery movements; aerial photographs provided the basis of information used in compiling air-objective folders and target dossiers; and bomb damage assessment photography afforded air units means for evaluating the successes and failures in their offensive missions.

The proof of the dependency of other units on aerial reconnaissance can be found in a comparison of the performance of the 67th Tactical Reconnaissance Wing in Korea with that of a comparable unit in Europe during World War II. The largest number of missions flown in any month by a single reconnaissance group in the European War was 1,300 in April 1945 while the 67th flew 2,400 such missions in May 1952. During the last year of the war in Europe the average reconnaissance group sortie rate was 604 a month; from April 1952 through March 1953 the 67th averaged 1,792 sorties a month. During the same period the photo reconnaissance group that supported the Third Army made 243,175 negatives, nearly all of them 9 by 9 inches; the 67th produced 736,684, more than 90 percent of which were 9 by 18 inches. Taking the difference in size into consideration, the 67th's accomplishment was six times as great.

While the 67th Tactical Reconnaissance Wing accomplished most of the reconnaissance mission during the Korean conflict other units were also involved on a much smaller scale. The 91st Strategic Reconnaissance Squadron was transferred from Barksdale, Louisiana, to Yakota, Japan, in November 1950 to participate in the Korean War. There its mission was to use its RB-50s, RB-29s, and RB-45s to photograph such targets as airfields, rail lines, troop movements, power plants, and other typical targets. Other missions included daily shipping surveillance over the Sea of Japan near the Siberian coast, photomapping of Japan and Korea, and leaflet drops over North Korea. During the conflict the squadron was credited with the first Mig-15 shot down by a Superfortress. It also flew the last combat sortie of the war on July 27, 1953. For its valor and performance, the 91st was awarded the Distinguished Unit Citation and twice the Air Force Outstanding Unit Award. Altogether the squadron flew 1,995 missions.

The U.S. Navy, while it depended upon the 67th Tactical Reconnaissance Wing for a large percentage of its required photo coverage, also had its own reconnaissance units. Marine Squadron VMJ-1 was stationed at Pohang Airfield, Korea, and did excellent photography work with its ten F2HeP Banshees. Operations by the Navy's patrol squadrons (PatRons) in the

Korean War were routine tasks and their accomplishments more negative or defensive than positive or offensive. The Navy planes kept a constant lookout for enemy ships and a report of "no enemy ships" was as important as a report of an enemy fleet to the naval strategists. The Navy reconnaissance planes kept a close watch over Formosa, permitting the Seventh Fleet to operate in Korean waters although its task was to defend Formosa against an attack by the Chinese. The Navy aircraft made it impossible for the Chinese to attack so quickly or unexpectedly that the Seventh Fleet couldn't return in time to ward off the attack. In addition to the routine antisubmarine reconnaissance patrols, weather and coastal surveillance, the PatRons also flew many unique and unusual missions. They spotted for naval gunfire, directed some bombing strikes from the air, and were very active in the delicate job of aerial mine spotting. The Navy planes also flew weather-reconnaissance missions over the Sea of Japan and the Yellow Sea to estimate and evaluate the following day's weather for carrier operations. The PBM Mariner seaplane was used for these overwater reconnaissance missions and while it had a slow airspeed, its heavy armament and long-range capabilities made it an excellent aircraft for reconnaissance.

Helicopters were also used for reconnaissance sorties during the Korean War, especially for mine spotting. The helicopter pilot was also the long-range eyes of his ship's captain and by providing the commander of the vessel with information about conditions ahead permitted the captain to make his plans more carefully. In September 1950, when the United Nations forces began their rapid counterattack to the north, the fleet was ordered to provide close support and interdiction firing. Helicopter pilots, serving both as spotters for the gunfire and as communication links between ships and land liaison groups, were the eyes and ears of the fleet.

As a result of the helicopters' fine record in the early part of the war, it was recommended that where possible an additional helicopter be assigned to each heavy cruiser for the purpose of reconnaissance. One of the most unusual "dogfights" of the Korean War took place between a reconnaissance helicopter and three Mig-15 jet fighters. While on a surveillance mission, the helicopter spotted some South Korean troops trapped behind enemy lines and dropped down to evacuate them. As he started to take off, the helicopter pilot was surprised to see three Mig-15s diving toward his plane. He made an abrupt turn and the jets swooped past, unable to maneuver fast enough to follow the helicopter. The jets were going so fast that by the time they had turned around and headed back, the helicopter was out of sight.

The Marines used the helicopters for reconnaissance, liaison, visual flank security, and patrol missions. When the First Marine Brigade was ordered to a different location during the heavy fighting of 1952, it was the helicopter pilots who flew protective reconnaissance for the rear and flanks of their columns. As one Marine general stated: "Any military force without helicopters today is back in the days of the Civil War. Even units on the regimental level should have them." It was a prediction of things to come in future wars.

The story of aerial reconnaissance in the Korean War would not be complete without a mention of the Mosquito operation, not only because of its vital importance during this conflict but because it taught military experts a lesson they didn't forget. Visual reconnaissance and fire control from aircraft had been used to a large extent in World War I but during World War II the light spotter plane played only a minor role. The daylight bombing by the B-17s and B-24s using the Norden bombsight didn't require a "seeing-eye" liaison plane. The saturation tactics used at night eliminated the need also. But when the jets were ushered into combat at the beginning of the Korean War, it became obvious that they had neither the fuel, the time, nor the necessary flight characteristics to enable the pilot to hunt his target and then bomb it visually without any help. The F-80s, F-84s, and F-86s flew too fast, used fuel too fast.

Initially, tactical air-control parties operating out of jeeps attempted to control the air strikes but the rough roads of Korea battered the jeeps and put their radios out of commission. The jeeps could seldom get far enough forward to direct the fighter-bombers since they were extremely vulnerable to enemy ground fire. Finally the jeeps were replaced by L-5G and L-17 liaison planes and the concept of airborne tactical air coordinators soon became a standard operating procedure. The L-5 and L-17 were fine aircraft but later they were replaced by the T-6 trainer aircraft, which was faster and more able to avoid enemy aircraft. The concept increased the efficiency of the jet fighter-bombers and more of the T-6 aircraft were requisitioned. When an operations order from Fifth Air Force gave the airborne controllers the radio call signs of "Mosquito Baker," "Mosquito How," and "Mosquito Able" on an early mission the name stayed and from then on the airborne controllers and their planes were "Mosquitos."

In August 1950 the Mosquitos were organized into a formal unit designated the 6147th Tactical Control Squadron, commanded by Major Merrill H. Carlton. Operating out of Taegu airfield, Korea, the pilots of the squadron controlled air strikes and also provided visual reconnaissance for the Joint Operations Center. The T-6s often stayed over the battle area for as long as three hours at a time and continually relayed observations to the Joint Operations Center for its evaluation. When the Mosquitos were flying over an area that was too distant from the Joint Operations Center for the radio messages to be received, the 6147th Tactical Control Squadron kept a plane called "Mosquito Mellow" circling at an intermediate point to relay the messages. Officer observers from the Eighth Army rode in the back seat of the Mosquitos to get a soldier's view of the battle area and the Joint Operations Center was thereby on the receiving end of valuable reconnaissance intelligence that could be acted upon immediately.

There is little question that the T-6 pilots and observers were the unsung heroes of the war. They were the first over the target—often the ones that located the target initially—and the last to leave. Twisting and turning for flak evasion, they placed marking rockets right on the bulls-eye. After the fighter-bombers put their bombs on the spot, the Mosquito always went back for visual bomb assessment. The T-6 wasn't really built to fight in the company of the much-faster jet planes. Loaded with a thousand pounds of extra equipment, its maneuverability was not the best and its effective ceiling was within range of automatic-weapons fire. Losses hit hard among the Mosquito crews, the result of enemy ground fire, bad weather, and Migs and Yaks. The effectiveness of the small planes was outstanding and it soon became apparent to Washington that the mission of the Mosquitos in Korea was a vital necessity. Once awakened to this fact, plans were made for an entirely separate category of planes capable of doing this job and of expanding behind-the-lines visual reconnaissance. It was a fortunate decision because these aircraft were needed when the war started in Southeast Asia a decade later.

The age of jets was born in the skies over Korea during the three-year war. For the first time jet reconnaissance planes were used in combat areas and proved wrong those who scorned the aircraft in the first months of the fighting. While there was no jet plane built purposely for aerial reconnaissance alone, the RF-80 and RF-86 accomplished the task given to them and at the same time pointed up the problems that still needed solution to achieve better reconnaissance aircraft and related equipment. The effort of the 67th Tactical Reconnaissance Group was summed up in citation DAF GO 34, 1953:

The 67th Tactical Reconnaissance Group, Fifth Air Force, distinguished itself by extraordinary heroism in action against an armed enemy of the United Nations from 9 July 1951 to 27 November 1951 in Korea. During that period, the 67th Tactical Reconnaissance Group displayed outstanding combat proficiency in accomplishing around-the-clock photography of enemy activities which provided valuable intelligence for United Nations forces concerning the capabilities and limitations for enemy striking forces. Although the primary mission of the group was the procurement of photographic intelligence, it also provided visual and weather reconnaissance, artillery and naval gun spotting and fire direction. Operating at altitudes from a few hundred feet to twenty thousand feet, the Group flew missions to all parts of enemy territory throughout Korea. The close continual surveillance by the aircrews of the 67th Tactical Reconnaissance Group enabled the United Nations air elements to destroy vast numbers of enemy troops, transportation facilities, and industrial installations. The Group's contribution to the United Nations' Summer-Fall offensive in Korea in 1951 was clearly demonstrated by the outstanding records of 9682 sorties flown, during which 8699 targets were photographed. The heroic manner in which the officers and airmen performed their duties and through their collective professional skill, diligence, and devotion to the best interests of the military service, the personnel of the 67th Tactical Reconnaissance Group reflected great credit upon themselves, the Far East Air Forces, and the United States Air Force.

10

The Need to Know

IN A world where nations show a decided mistrust toward each other, where new developments are jealously guarded secrets, and where even tourist travel is often prohibited, the gathering of intelligence necessary for the security of the United States is a difficult and complex task. When the Iron Curtain was placed between the borders of the free countries of the western world and the Communist countries the obtaining of information became increasingly difficult. While Russian diplomats and attachés can easily learn many facts about the military forces and scientific developments of the United States from written materials, photographs, and radio and television, the Soviet Union volunteers little or nothing in return. Consequently it is necessary to find methods of obtaining this information, covertly if necessary. Among the methods developed during the post-World War II years, aerial reconnaissance was one of the most reliable.

Initially, postwar aerial reconnaissance was accomplished openly and with the full knowledge of the countries being overflown. The 12th Tactical Reconnaissance Squadron, for instance, remained in Europe after the end of World War II to become part of the occupation air force. It remained at Furth, Germany, and continued its photographic missions and flight training, obtaining pictures of Germany for future use should they ever be needed. After its participation in the Korean War it continued to operate from Kimpo Air Base until November 8, 1954, when it moved to Itami Air Base, Japan. After nearly two years of flying over the Demilitarized Zone in Korea, gathering a photo file of that area in case it should be needed later and checking for Communist violations of the truce, the squadron moved to Yokota Air Base, Japan. Here it flew RB-66 Destroyers and continued its functions as a night reconnaissance organization until deactivation on March 8, 1960.

The 91st Strategic Reconnaissance Squadron was sent to British Guiana and Brazil after World War II as part of an overall mapping project of that region of South America. It didn't return to the United States until January 1949, after producing a file of pictures of South America for future reference. Fortunately, the squadron remained in the Far East after the end of the Korean War and continued its aerial reconnaissance missions in that area. An indication of the importance of its work is evident in the citation accompanying the the Air Force Outstanding Unit Award given the squadron:

> The 91st Strategic Reconnaissance Squadron, Medium, Photo, distinguished itself by exceptionally meritorious service of international significance from 28 July 1953 to 1 June 1954, while carrying out the entire strategic reconnaissance effort in the Far East Theatre. During this period, its combat reconnaissance crews participated in numerous flights that provided the Far East Air Force and the United States Air Force Headquarters with vital intelligence data of the utmost importance in planning future operations and in the defense of the United States and the Far East. In most instances, these sorties were flown unescorted and in remote areas, often under adverse weather conditions, with limited chances of survival in the event of extreme emergency. By the superior manner in which it has carried out its mission and its exemplary valor and devotion to duty, the

91st Strategic Reconnaissance Squadron, Medium, Photo, has reflected great credit upon itself and the United States Air Force.

Many of the photographs obtained by the 91st Strategic Reconnaissance Squadron during this period were later used during the early period of the Vietnam conflict.

Later, in 1955, this squadron was involved in the attempt to develop a method of increasing the range of jet reconnaissance planes. This new concept—FICON—was a technique whereby fighter or reconnaissance aircraft would be launched and retrieved by airborne B-36s while in flight. The squadron accomplished its first operational hookups of RBF-84s in December 1955. The recon pilots entered the B-36 after the hookup and subsequently descended through the bomb bay and flew away in their planes. The following month the unit began FICON missions on a regular schedule and although it successfully completed a number of hookups, several near accidents occurred. After further evaluation the program was suspended and finally discontinued. The 91st Strategic Reconnaissance Squadron was deactivated on July 1, 1967.

Other scattered units, with no other duties assigned to them immediately after the end of World War II, flew visual and reconnaissance missions over the countries they had just defeated. One such unit was the 307th Bomb Group (H). Based at Clark Field in the Philippines, the B-24s of the group often covered Vietnam (French Indochina) to observe Japanese activities. Some of the Japanese commanders either didn't know that the war was over or simply refused to quit fighting so the 307th Bomb Group aircraft kept an aerial eye on them.

In 1945, on one of these flights, pilot Don Forke photographed an incident that twenty years later would be meaningful to every citizen of the United States. Forke took off from Clark Field on a direct route to Hue and saw something that made him curious:

"In one of the small villages just north of Hue we saw men in obvious military array drilling, with arms stacked and crude military equipment in the village square. They did not have uniforms and at first appeared to be just ordinary villagers who had managed to collect a lot of weapons. They had a flag—green with a gold ball, as I recall—and were real friendly. They waved and smiled to us as we circled for photos."

Forke had taken pictures of Ho Chi Minh's initial efforts to gain control of Vietnam.

The atom bomb that destroyed Hiroshima changed many concepts regarding the waging of war and the maintenance of security. Atomic energy coupled with rocket propulsion, both developments of World War II, provided the world with the most terrifying weapons ever known. As long as the United States had a monopoly on atomic weapons the nation was certain of its military security. After Russia exploded its first atom bomb in 1949, however, the monopoly ended and it was obvious other measures had to be taken to ensure the security of the United States. There was no hope of reaching an understanding with Russia on the use of atomic weapons or stopping the atomic arms race, so in 1951 President Harry S Truman ordered work begun on the development of a hydrogen bomb. By the early 1950s the U.S.S.R. was a full-fledged nuclear power. Britain tested its first atom bomb in 1952; France and Red China were working hard to develop their own nuclear stockpiles. The United States could no longer sit back and hope that none of these powers were preparing to use their new weapons to start another war or attempt to conquer the world. There was also the nagging concern that even more terrifying weapons might be built without the knowledge of the United States. It was essential to know the facts about the military capabilities of all major nations.

Even after the Soviet Union exploded its own atom bomb in 1949 most of the aerial surveillance accomplished by U.S. aircraft was still done openly. By the end of the Korean War aerial reconnaissance had been accepted as an indispensable part of military tactics but it took a few more years for its strategic importance as a deterrent to future conflicts to be realized. One of the first strategic aerial reconnaissance operations to determine another nation's attack capability occurred approximately a month after the end of the Korean War. The question arose in Washington as to Communist China's ability to attack and destroy the U.S. Seventh Fleet which was patrolling the waters between Nationalist China's Taiwan and the China mainland. A special American naval task force was assembled, including three carriers, to conduct an overflight of the Chinese mainland. The objective of the overflight was to determine how much air power Mao Tse-tung had based within range of the China seas where the U.S. Seventh Fleet was stationed.

The entire fleet was put on general quarters for two days and 300 photo reconnaissance and escorting fighters were launched. The aircraft met no opposition during the overflight and photographed the airfields of Chekiang and Fukien provinces. After studying the pictures, Washington was convinced that there was almost no aircraft of the Red Chinese air force assigned to the area, that there was no threat of an attack on the U.S. Seventh Fleet. This dramatic reconnaissance overflight in force was done openly in actual defiance of another country and was unopposed. But the Iron Curtain that Russia established made it obvious that such reconnaissance flights would not be possible in the future.

In March 1955 President Eisenhower made a careful evaluation of United States policy on disarmament He invited the other four major powers of the world to join in an agreement for the reduction of armaments and on July 21, 1955, at the Geneva summit conference, made his open skies proposal to ensure peace in the world through the use of aerial reconnaissance.

In his plan President Eisenhower suggested that the United States and the Soviet Union exchange complete information about their respective military establishments, their weapons, and weapons-delivery systems. The two countries would also assure each other that no new weapons of significant numbers would be built in secret. Each country, to guarantee that the agreement was being observed, would make available to the other facilities for aerial reconnaissance of its installations. Aerial photographs were essential to detect newly constructed airfields, new ICBM launching installations, secret atomic factories—radiation from which would show plainly on photographic plates—and troop movements.

Eisenhower presented his plan directly to Marshal Nikolai Bulganin and it was given worldwide publicity. On August 4, 1955, Bulganin finally made mention of the proposal in a speech to the Supreme Soviet, saying, "The real effectiveness of such measures would not be great. During unofficial talks with the leaders of the United States government, we straightforwardly declared that aerophotography cannot give the expected results, because both countries stretch over vast territories in which, if one desired, one can conceal anything. One must also take into consideration the fact that the proposed plan touches only the territories belonging to the two countries, leaving out the armed forces and military constructions situated in the territories of other states."

It was a rejection and an expected one. The plan had to be forgotten and other measures devised to obtain the necessary intelligence.

One of these measures resulted in perhaps the most effective operation in intelligence history, the U-2 program. It was a program that started in secrecy and remained one of the world's greatest secrets for four years, during which it yielded for the security of the United States and its allies invaluable results not otherwise obtainable. Even the four years longevity was an added bonus. The U-2 was expected to live as a spy plane for perhaps a year. No longer.

At approximately the same time that it was becoming

obvious to President Eisenhower that the Soviet Union had no desire to cooperate with the United States on disarmament, Lockheed vice-president and chief designer Clarence L. ("Kelly") Johnson designed a completely new aircraft that he was convinced could go any place in the world at any time and bring back the required aerial photographs needed by Washington for the national security. The subcommittee on intelligence for a secret Committee of Surprise Attack headed by Dr. Edwin Land learned of the new design through the efforts of Trevor Gardner, technical advisor to the USAF on research and development. Johnson had submitted his design to the USAF early in 1954 but despite Gardner's arguments in favor of the reconnaissance plane it was rejected. Refusing to give up, Gardner submitted the design to Land's subcommittee and its members agreed that it was a worthwhile project.

Johnson was summoned to Washington where he discussed the plane with the subcommittee members, Land, Edward M. Purcell, and John Tukey. He also met with Harold Talbott, the Secretary of the Air Force, Allen Dulles, Director of the Central Intelligence Agency, and the CIA's famed troubleshooter and idea man, Richard M. Bissell. It was Bissell who convinced Talbott that the new plane was a necessity and finally, in December 1954, the USAF gave its approval to building the U-2 with money provided by Wilfred J. NcNeil, the Pentagon's comptroller. Kelly Johnson, the same man who had turned out America's first jet, the F-80, in 141 days during World War II, went to work.

He had a lot of work to do. He had guaranteed a plane that would fly higher than 70,000 feet when the altitude record at that time was 54,000 feet. He had promised it would have a range great enough to overfly the Soviet Union wherever Washington might desire and if the need arose. Experts said it couldn't be done and they had many arguments to back their theories. A jet engine, they vowed, would have no thrust at 70,000 feet or above. If it did have any thrust, which they doubted, it would consume so much fuel that a range of 2,600 miles or more was ridiculous to consider. What's more, they said, fuel at that altitude would evaporate and cause vapor locks in the engine. Johnson, however, had some ideas that had never been tried before and he incorporated them into the new reconnaissance plane.

The U-2 was basically a glider with a jet engine attached. It had huge glider wings spanning 80 feet which made the plane stable even at extremely high altitudes because of its wing loading. These wings actually supported the entire weight of the U-2 at altitude. The jet engine was used only intermittently, and thus the U-2 could fly great distances without refueling. The unique aircraft also possessed a gust-control system activated by the pilot which, when in operation, automatically deflected the flaps and ailerons when gusts were encountered. This helped reduce loads on the wings and permitted extremely light structures to be used. Johnson further reduced wind resistance by eliminating the conventional landing gear and substituting skids on the wing tips. A 17,000-pound thrust Pratt and Whitney J75 engine later replaced the original J57 jet engine. All of the U-2s were handmade and cost approximately $850,000.

Since the U-2 is still operational and is used on covert aerial reconnaissance missions at present, little information concerning it has yet been declassified. It is known that the first U-2 to take to the air was test flown highly successfully in August 1955. Charles E. Wilson, the Secretary of Defense, was still not convinced such an aircraft was necessary, nor did he think one could be constructed to meet the performance standards listed by Kelly Johnson. In December 1955, while he was in California, Wilson was driven to the Lockheed test area at Watertown Strip and given a demonstration of the prowess of the new plane. After watching the takeoff and talking by radio to the pilot, who stayed in the air for more than eight hours to prove the U-2's endurance capability, the Secretary of Defense became a staunch supporter of the aircraft and the necessary funds to continue the program were quickly allotted.

Dr. Edwin Land, who developed the Polaroid camera and many other photographic innovations, was principally responsible for the sophisticated photographic equipment used on the U-2. His camera could take excellent photographs from 75,000 feet. One picture that was released by the USAF during the early years of the U-2 program was taken at 55,000 feet and clearly showed golf balls on a putting green.

The United States had the plane and the photographic equipment it needed but the question that plagued President Eisenhower was whether to use the U-2 to overfly the Soviet Union. He finally decided that the intelligence information needed was vital to the security of the nation and gave his approval to the spy flights. Since it was obvious that the USAF could not operate such a "black" program because of the consequences possible, the entire operation was given to the CIA. Unfortunately, the CIA had no airfields or other facilities available, so another civilian organization, the National Advisory Committee for Aeronautics was used for cover. The NACA would benefit from the high-altitude research program also planned for the U-2, but its most important task was to conceal the fact that the CIA was really running the operation.

Early in 1956 the NACA distributed a press release that mentioned the U-2 publicly. It stated:

> Tomorrow's jet transports will be flying air routes girdling the earth. This they will do at altitudes far higher than presently used except by a few military aircraft. The availability of a new type of airplane, the Lockheed U-2, makes possible obtaining the needed data on gust-meteorological conditions in an economical and expeditious manner.
>
> The program would not have been possible without the ability of American scientific effort to join forces and the success of the program depends in large degree upon the logistical and technical support which the Air Weather Service of the USAF will be providing. USAF facilities will be used as the program gets under way, to

enable gathering research information necessary to reflect accurately conditions in many parts of the world.

The first data, covering conditions in the Rocky Mountain area, are being obtained from flights made from Watertown Strip, Nevada.

The stage was set for the most intriguing and daring aerial reconnaissance program ever conducted.

No plane is any better than the men who pilot it and as soon as the U-2 was considered operational, the USAF–CIA–NACA combine began the search for qualified fliers. Eight civilian pilots were hired for the proposed spy missions, of whom Francis Gary Powers became the most publicized when he was shot down over the Soviet Union in 1960. Some were USAF pilots transferred to the program secretly. Others were civilians qualified to handle the new and revolutionary aircraft. All, according to the record, were on the payroll of the Lockheed Aircraft Corporation, which in turn had signed a contract with the NACA to provide the necessary pilots for the "upper atmosphere research" supposedly being conducted. The U-2 pilots trained at the Watertown Strip and once they had qualified successfully they were signed to a contract guaranteeing them $2,500 a month.

One former U-2 pilot who made many overflights of the Soviet Union between 1956 and 1960 recently said in Washington that one half of the monthly pay was withheld each month to assure that the pilots adhered strictly to the contract. "This wasn't like some reconnaissance missions that were flown in World War II or Korea where the pilot decided it was too dangerous to try and take pictures over the assigned target so made the excuse the weather was too bad and returned home. Once you started over the Soviet Union in a U-2 you had no place to go but to your destination. Besides, the sophisticated instrumentation and cameras aboard the aircraft were unbelievable. The controllers on the ground knew where we were every minute."

Scientific flights were conducted in the U-2 before and after

President Eisenhower gave the approval to overfly the Soviet Union. During the four years that the spy flights were flown, the civilian pilots also flew over a quarter of a million miles in the interest of upper-atmosphere research and the high-altitude sampling program, gathering enough information for four complete scientific reports that were published later. But plans also went ahead for the important reconnaissance flights across the Iron Curtain barrier. By 1956 the eight civilian pilots, their wives and families, and the American airmen necessary to support the secret operation were established at Incirlik Air Base in Turkey, their home for the next four years. The unit was designated the 10-10 Detachment.

The flights by the U-2 over the Soviet Union began in 1956. The exact date has not been revealed, nor have any of the flight courses been outlined in detail except the one on which Powers was knocked out of the sky. It is known that the U-2s often flew from the airfield at Peshawar, Pakistan, to Bodo, Norway, over the Central Ural Mountains area of Russia, a flight that was long and difficult. A former U-2 pilot no longer affiliated with the CIA recently explained some of the ordeals he faced on such a mission:

"It was rough going right from the start. We had to breathe pure oxygen for nearly two hours before getting into the plane to prepare ourselves for the eight hours we would be at high altitude. Our helmets were airtight and sealed to our body by a cork ring which was so tight it often chafed my neck until it bled. We couldn't take a drink or eat anything during the flight because of the sealed helmet. I got so thirsty at times I thought I wouldn't survive the trip."

Even the takeoff in the U-2 was a hazardous, unusual procedure. Since the long wing was so flexible that it would bend down and touch the ground when the aircraft was taxiing or taking off, Johnson devised a wheel on a stick—a pogo—for each wing tip. As the U-2 pilot began his takeoff run down the runway a ground crewman sat on each wing tip. When the aircraft reached a speed that provided enough lift to keep the wings off the ground, the U-2 pilot signaled the men on the wings. They would then leap off the wings, pull the pins attaching the "pogos" to the wing tips, and the wheels would fall free. The aircraft would then increase speed until it lifted off the runway and started its climb.

The landing was also a tricky, dangerous maneuver. Using only the bicycle landing-gear wheels on the front and rear of the fuselage, the U-2 pilot would make a glider-type touchdown. He would keep the plane balanced on the tandem wheels until his speed slowed and then steer the U-2 off the runway onto the grass where one wing would drop onto a skid and the plane would finally stop.

"When we weren't tired we would bet each other whether we could keep the aircraft balanced long enough on the tandem wheels after we landed for the ground crewmen to put the removable wheels back in place," the ex-U-2 pilot said. "After our missions across Russia, however, we were usually so exhausted that we either had to come in on a radio beam or have another plane lead us into the base at Bodo."

During the long hours in the air over the Soviet Union the U-2 pilot had a checklist of duties to perform at regular intervals. His flight plan and altitudes were carefully plotted in detail long before his takeoff, as well as the times at which he would switch on certain secret electronic equipment and tape recorders, turn on his various cameras, and obtain high-altitude atmosphere samples. At the same time he kept a lookout for Migs trying to reach his height or rockets being launched in his direction. During all these procedures the U-2 pilot could never forget for a single minute that he was over a foreign nation that would use its most sophisticated weapons in an effort to shoot him out of the sky.

The U-2 overflights of the Soviet Union were one of the most closely guarded secrets of the nation during the years the operation was in effect. Yet, as in all such programs, certain incidents at intervals began to penetrate the carefully planned cover for the U-2 flights. Early in 1956 a pilot employed by Lockheed had to bail out of a U-2 when it caught on fire and the plane crashed in Arizona. Many experienced experts in the aviation field saw the wreckage despite the efforts of the military to keep the debris isolated, and their curiosity was aroused. No one had ever seen an aircraft like it before. A year later one of the reconnaissance planes crashed in Nevada and the pilot, Robert L. Sieker, who was also employed by Lockheed, was killed. When the U-2s landed at USAF airbases anyplace in the world they were guarded day and night. Naturally the airmen and officers on the bases were interested in such strict security measures and often went to great effort to see one of the planes. When they were successful they usually told their friends. One interesting fact that emerged during the investigation into the assassination of President John F. Kennedy was that Lee Harvey Oswald might have known a great deal about the U-2 and its espionage flights and have passed this information on to the Russians. Oswald, who served as a U.S. Marine, was stationed in Japan in September 1957 when the U-2 program was in full swing. The reconnaissance planes were flying out of the naval air base at Atsugi, where Oswald was assigned as a radar operator. Since his duties involved ground control of aircraft there is little doubt that he often observed the takeoffs and landings of the secret U-2s. The aircraft were kept under strict security at a remote section of the base but it has even been indicated that Oswald's organization may have performed guard duty for the U-2s.

Later, when Oswald defected to Russia, it is agreed that he undoubtedly gave the Soviets information about the Marine Corps, the radar equipment operated by him while he was in the service, and perhaps vital information about the U-2s. The Russians were well aware by this time that "a dark blue plane" was overflying their country at regular intervals. When a U-2 had to make an emergency landing on a glider-club strip forty miles northwest of Tokyo in September 1959, it was obvious to the Japanese that this was no routine aircraft on a routine training mission. As Eliichiro Sekigawa, editor of a magazine, asked, "Why did the plane have no markings? Why did the pilot have no indentification marks on his clothing? Why was it necessary to threaten Japanese citizens with guns to keep them away from the plane?"

The revealing incidents continued. Two fatal crashes within a twenty-four-hour period once grounded all the U-2s in the United States. In 1957 and 1958 five U-2 pilots were killed and some additional publicity reached the newspapers. In 1960, only a month and a half before Powers' fateful flight, a U-2 made an emergency landing in Canada that was observed by many citizens, yet very few of the individuals connected the strange plane with any covert operation. To them it was just another new plane being tested to get the "bugs" out of it. Meanwhile, the secret reconnaissance program was paying off very well. Thousands of rolls of valuable and detailed photographs of the Soviet Union and its military installations were delivered to the CIA by the U-2 pilots. Through its cameras, tape recorders, and electronic equipment, the U-2 provided intelligence on airfields, aircraft, missile testing and training, atomic-weapon storage, and submarine development and production. There was so much film being brought back for study that U-2 film would often pile up for months and during the life of this blacklog the missions were always suspended. President Eisenhower didn't want to take any chances that were not absolutely necessary, knowing the price the United States might have to pay if one of the U-2 pilots was "caught in the act."

One of the most renowned aerial reconnaissance flights in the history of aviation occurred on May 1, 1960, when Francis Gary Powers attempted to fly a route over the Soviet Union that began at Peshawar, Pakistan, and ended at Bodo, Norway. Takeoff was at 5:30 A.M. on May 1; the target was "something very special." Allen Dulles, head of the CIA, never identified the target for the U-2 that day but some experts believe Powers was ordered to obtain photographs of a satellite launching set for May Day. Others think he was trying to obtain a series of revealing military buildup pictures that President Eisenhower could use to confront Premier Nikita Khrushchev at the summit meeting in Paris on May 16, 1960. Within an hour after taking off, the U-2 crossed the Soviet border, still climbing toward its desired altitude of 70,000 feet.

At that moment Major M. Voronov, Russian commander of an antiaircraft unit, was notified that one of the "dark blue planes" was again violating Russian airspace and heading in his direction. The warning came from a radar station on the Soviet border. The major immediately alerted his gunners and prepared to attack the aircraft as it neared Sverdlovsk.

About thirty miles from Sverdlovsk, which is east of Moscow, Powers made a ninety-degree turn to the left and lined up to fly over the southwestern edge of the city. He saw an airfield there that was not on his map. Making certain that he had the proper cameras and other equipment aboard the aircraft switched on, Powers then began recording, as he had been briefed, things like engine instrument readings, exhaust gas temperature, and the altitude.

The Red major spotted the U-2 just as it entered his firing range and, according to him, only one rocket was fired. Later it was reported by "authoritative sources," according to *The Washington Post*, that the Russians destroyed one and possibly two of their own planes when they shot down Powers' U-2. The Soviet planes had been sent aloft to try and intercept the American pilot and when the gunners on the ground fired the first of the surface-to-air missiles used that day it hit one of the Migs. The second missile, according to this report, struck and disabled Powers' plane. It is thought that the same missile that knocked the U-2 out of the sky also disabled a second Russian fighter plane and caused it to crash.

"I can remember feeling, hearing, and just sensing an explosion," Powers said at a Senate hearing after his return home.

"I immediately looked up from the instrument panel and everywhere I looked it was orange. I don't know whether the whole sky was orange or just the reflection of an orange light in the canopy but I had never seen anything like it before."

The right wing of the U-2 started to drop. When he corrected it, the nose began falling below the horizon.

"I applied back pressure to the control column and felt no resistance," he said. "I immediately assumed at the time that the tail section of the aircraft had come off."

Powers started to throw switches that would, in seventy seconds, blow up the U-2 but since the plane was in such a wild spin he suddenly had doubts that he could eject before the U-2 exploded. Some critics of the entire overflight reconnaissance program insist that the seventy-second delay was not incorporated in the system, that the plane would have blown up the moment Powers hit the switches. It would also have blown up Powers, a convenient arrangement for the CIA, these critics state, since dead U-2 pilots could tell no tales. Whether Powers also doubted the seventy-second-delay story has never been stated.

"I thought that I had better see if I could get out of the cockpit before trying the switch. Then I realized that maybe I could just open the canopy, loosen the seat belt, and climb out."

The altimeter read 35,000 feet when he reached up and opened the canopy. He yanked his emergency belt so that after leaving the U-2 he would have an oxygen supply, but in his hurry to get out he forgot to unfasten the oxygen hose from the cockpit. He opened the seat belt and was immediately thrown forward and halfway out of the aircraft. He lay sprawled over the front of the U-2, still tied to the cockpit by the connected oxygen hose. He tried to get back into the cockpit to throw the destruction switch, as he said he intended to do once he was certain he could get out of the plane before it exploded, but the G-force was so great he couldn't pull himself back inside over the top of the windshield.

"I tried to reach around underneath the windshield but I

couldn't get my hand underneath to activate the switch. When my face plate froze over and blinded me, I gave up. I gave several lunges and finally snapped the oxygen hose free and the next moment I was floating in space."

Powers was immediately captured when he landed and Premier Khrushchev had a fine propaganda subject to use for months. The downing of the U-2 over Russia had international repercussions. The summit meeting was scuttled by Premier Khrushchev and President Eisenhower's invitation to visit Russia in June 1960 was withdrawn by the Communists. For the first time in history the leader of a major country admitted his nation had been involved in espionage. After many controversial statements by different individuals in Washington, President Eisenhower released an announcement that cleared up the situation and also caused an uproar at home and abroad:

> As a result of the inquiry ordered by the President it has been established that insofar as the authorities in Washington are concerned, there was no authorization for any such flight as described by Mr. Khrushchev. Nevertheless it appears that in endeavoring to obtain information now concealed behind the Iron Curtain, a flight over Soviet territory was probably undertaken by an unarmed U-2 plane.

If there ever was any doubt in anyone's mind that aerial reconnaissance had become a factor in international affairs, that doubt was erased with the culmination of the U-2 overflights of the Soviet Union. Were they worth the embarrassment suffered by President Eisenhower, the temporary loss of prestige for the nation, the ordeal suffered by Powers?

The answer is an unequivocal "yes."

President Eisenhower, in a later statement issued to answer his critics, summed it up very clearly:

> Aerial photography has been one of the many methods we have used to keep ourselves and the Free World abreast of major Soviet military developments. The usefulness of this work has been well established through four years of effort. The Soviets were well aware

of it. The plain truth is this: When a nation needs intelligence activity, there is no time when vigilance can be relaxed.

Testifying before the Senate Foreign Relations Committee on June 2, 1960, Secretary of Defense Thomas S. Gates, Jr., stated the U-2 missions had provided just about everything the U.S. needed to know about military matters in the Soviet Union. General Lyman Lemnitzer, who was chairman of the Joint Chiefs of Staff, said that the suspension of the U-2 flights would leave a serious void in the intelligence required for the security of the nation. And the Russian judges who conducted the Powers trial admitted for the record that the photographs taken by the U-2 were of excellent quality and of great importance. When Secretary of State Herter was asked the lesson learned by the U.S. from the U-2 affair his answer was brief: "Not to have accidents."

Powers was sentenced to ten years' confinement in Russia but was later released in a spy swap for Rudolf Abel, the master Soviet undercover agent who had been convicted in the United States in 1957. Today Powers is once again flying in a civilian capacity.

The Soviet Union overflights were canceled after Powers was caught but the U-2s continue to soar at high altitudes in many places. On purely peaceful missions the planes participated in the Smokey Joe Project, High Flight, and HASP. The Smokey Joe Project is conducted at Edwards AFB, California. It is a project "involving the use of infrared devices in connection with rocket launchings." Further information is classified. Every time a satellite or a missile is fired, the U-2s are there at altitudes "over 75,000 feet" to observe and photograph. High Flight missions aid in the study of weather aloft and winds above the jet stream. HASP deals with the gathering of samples of radioactive fallout in the stratosphere.

In addition to these scientific and peaceful missions, however, the U-2s are still gathering intelligence even if they don't fly over the Soviet Union. Information was also needed about military activity inside the Bamboo Curtain of Red China and aerial reconnaissance was the best means of obtaining it. At first, shortly after the end of the Korean War, Lockheed RT-33s, Republic RF-84s, Douglas RB-66s, McDonnell RF-101s, and Martine RB-57s were used in overflights across the mainland of China. These planes were furnished by the United States but usually flown by Nationalist Chinese pilots, who photographed Nanking, Wuhan, Lanchow, Peking, Taiyuan, and other locations. Later, as the Chinese began work on their own nuclear weapons at the Lob Nor complex, this installation was frequently the target of the reconnaissance planes. The People's Liberation Army Air Force of China tried to stop the flights with Mig-15s and Mig-17s but the fighters proved ineffective. In 1959, however, Russia delivered several of the newer Mig-19s to the PLAAF. New ground-to-air missiles were also given to the Chinese by the Soviet Union and a large number of Russian technicians arrived in the country to instruct the Communist Chinese in their use.

These new weapons made the reconnaissance flights over China much more hazardous. In October 1959 an RB-57 was shot down over northern China by a Mig-19. Several months after Powers was knocked out of the sky over Russia, an RF-101 was brought down while taking photographs over Fukien Province. It was about this time that the U-2s also began appearing in the sky over China spying on the nuclear development center at Lob Nor. On September 9, 1961, a U-2 piloted by Colonel Chen Wai-sheng, was shot down over Nanchang, China, and the Nationalist pilot was killed. This was the first U-2 brought down over Red China but not the last. During the following three years three more of the spy planes were brought down, proving beyond doubt that the PLAAF planes and ground gunners had the capability of defending their country against the sophisticated U-2. However, the United States was prepared when the Communist Chinese exploded their first atomic bomb on October 16, 1964. Photographs taken by U-2 pilots at various intervals gave Washington a step-by-step watch on the nuclear construction process and intelligence sources in the capital had a pool on the date of the initial explosion. The winner had the exact day.

While the U-2 was watching Red China, however, Premier Nikita Khrushchev was busy at the other side of the world—Cuba. Once more the U-2 was called upon to prove its value to the security of the United States. It didn't fail.

11

The Fringe War

MAJORS Rudolf Anderson, Jr., of Greenville, South Carolina, and Richard S. Heyser of Battle Creek, Michigan, both spent part of the daylight hours of October 14, 1962, at 78,000 feet altitude over the island of Cuba in the snug cockpits of U-2s. Both USAF majors were pilots assigned to the Strategic Air Command's 4080th Strategic Wing based at Laughlin Air Force Base, Del Rio, Texas, a unit that had the mission of keeping watch on trouble spots all over the globe. On October 14 their task was to determine whether or not the Russians were installing offensive ballistic missiles on the Communist-controlled island of Cuba with which Castro and the Soviet Union could launch an attack against the United States. Both pilots had joined the USAF in 1951, both had served in the Far East—Anderson with the 15th Tactical Reconnaissance Squadron, Heyser in Japan.

This wasn't the first time that the U-2 had been over Cuba. Ever since Fidel Castro had taken control of the island Washington had been well aware of the danger of having a Communist country so close to the shores of the United States and had acted accordingly. On August 29, 1962, a single U-2 had brought back photographic proof for the first time that there were Russian surface-to-air missile (SAM) bases on the island but these short-range weapons didn't particularly worry Washington. They were a defensive not an offensive weapon. As John McCone, director of the Central Intelligence Agency, remarked, "The SAMs have little danger for us except as a means of making possible the introduction of offensive missiles."

Despite the fact that Soviet Ambassador Dobrynin called on President John F. Kennedy on September 4, 1962, on Premier Khrushchev's instructions, to assure him that there were no offensive missiles in Cuba and that Russia promised not to cause any trouble for the United States, Washington was still suspicious. Refugees from the island insisted that they had seen long, round objects shrouded in tarpaulins being hauled into the country from the docks. Others even stated that they had seen huge missiles in firing position. It was because of these unconfirmed reports and the fact that Soviet ships with outsized cargo hatches were docking and unloading at night at the island that the U-2 flights were stepped up. After the discovery of the SAM sites on August 29 the reconnaissance planes were over the island nearly every day instead of just twice a month, which had been their former schedule. These U-2 flights were being flown by USAF pilots who had been transferred to the CIA payroll as Powers had been earlier. By October 7 the pilots had brought back hundreds of photographs of the area east of Havana and while SAM sites, Migs, and torpedo boats were plainly visible there was no evidence of any long-range offensive missiles on the island.

Colonel John Ralph Wright, Jr., of the Defense Intelligence Agency was one of many photo interpreters who had studied the pictures taken by the cameras on board the U-2s and one area aroused his curiosity. Near the town of San Cristobal he noticed that the defensive SAM missiles were installed in a strange trapezoidal pattern, a pattern he had become familiar with during the long hours he studied pictures taken by Powers and other U-2 pilots over the Soviet Union. He suggested that this sector of the island should be photographed in detail as soon as possible. Washington agreed and the mission was set up. Meanwhile, because there was now a possibility of one of the U-2s being shot down by a SAM missile as had happened over Red China on September 9, Secretary of Defense Robert S. McNamara suggested the pilots on the CIA payroll be shifted back to USAF status, not wanting an "aerial Bay of Pigs" disaster that the Communists could use for world propaganda. So, on October 14 when the pair of U-2s took off, Major Anderson and Major Heyser were at the controls as USAF officers.

The two USAF fliers crisscrossed the San Cristobal area without any opposition, their cameras recording the scene more than fifteen miles below them. As soon as they returned to base the film magazines were unloaded and rushed to a waiting jet assigned to take the film to Washington. By noon the following day the resulting long strip of film was cut up and turned over to the supersecret National Photographic Interpretation Center in the nation's capital. The center is manned half by Department of Defense personnel and half by CIA personnel and all photos dealing with the security of the United States, no matter what agency obtains the pictures, are studied by the center. The funds for its operation are provided by the CIA except for the salaries of the Department of Defense personnel. The director of the secret center, Arthur C. Lundahl, was summoned shortly after a three-man PI team had examined the pictures of the area around San Cristobal.

By the time Lundahl arrived the film was on a light table ready for his viewing. The director, a graduate of the University of Chicago, is a veteran in the photo interpretation field. In 1945 after World War II service with the U.S. Navy, Lundahl became associated with the Navy Photographic Interpretation Center at Anacostia. He was chief of the PIC photogrammetry division and assistant chief engineer until 1953 when he moved to the CIA. He studied the pictures from Cuba for a full five minutes. Finally he was satisfied that he hadn't made a mistake, that there was a cylindrical object partially concealed by a tent and several liquid-oxygen tank trucks in the trapezoid area that had looked so suspicious to Wright. Looking up from the photographs to the team that had been studying the pictures earlier, he said, "Let's be clear about what we're looking at. It's a medium-range ballistic missile site."

The team agreed. The Cuban crisis was on.

The CIA was immediately notified about Lundahl's discovery and the remainder of the night was spent by the director and his men studying the other pictures brought back by the U-2s on the fourteenth. At 8:30 A.M. the following day Lundahl carried the pictures to the White House in a locked black bag where they were studied by President Kennedy. Until he had personally viewed the photographs the President had refused to believe that the Soviet Union would install offensive missiles in Cuba. Now, after a minute examination of the film, he looked at Lundahl and asked one question: "Are you sure?"

"I'm sure."

With the evidence that the United States was exposed to nuclear weapons at point-blank range, President Kennedy demanded the fullest possible information on the missiles. How long before they would be operational? How many sites were under construction? What was the total deployment of missiles and technicians in Cuba? The task of obtaining this information fell to the aerial reconnaissance pilots, primarily the fliers of the USAF 363d Tactical Reconnaissance Wing at Shaw AFB, South Carolina, and the 4080th Strategic Wing from Laughlin AFB, Texas. U.S. Navy patrol planes at Lajos in the Azores, meanwhile, tracked Russian submarines and their tenders and Patrol Squadron 56 from Norfolk was deployed to Guantanamo Bay, the U.S. Navy installation on Cuba. To locate and track all Cuba-bound ships and photograph them after finding the vessels required more than 10,000 hours in the air by U.S. Navy planes alone.

The U-2s continued their flights for the Strategic Air Command, making their photographic runs at high altitude while the pilots of the 363d Tactical Reconnaissance Wing went in at low altitude, using their RF-101s. This aircraft was the USAF's first supersonic photoreconnaissance plane. At 45,000 feet it can photograph an area 217 miles long and 8 miles wide plus an area mosaic equivalent to 20,000 square miles in a single flight. It has six cameras in varied combinations plus flare ejectors for night photography. However, when certain targets required more detailed pictures, Lieutenant Colonel Clyde B. East, the veteran recon pilot of both World War II and Korea, and the members of his 29th Tactical Reconnaissance Squadron would roar over the island at treetop level to get them.

On October 21, as the Cuban crisis became more critical and President Kennedy knew that the U.S. had to make a move against Russia, he decided to show the aerial photographs to the heads of states of the countries allied with the nation as proof of the Soviet Union's activity on the island. Sherman Kent of the CIA and three photo-interpretation experts were sent abroad with three sets of the pictures. Former Secretary of State Dean Acheson was asked to show them to French President Charles de Gaulle; Ambassador to West Germany Walter Dowling, to Chancellor Konrad Adenauer; and David K. E. Bruce, Ambassador to the Court of St. James's, to Prime Minister Harold Macmillan of England. Macmillan studied the photographs soberly and nodded that he understood the situation.

"Your government's statements are unchallengeable."

When de Gaulle saw the photographs he was fascinated. He wanted to know from what altitude the pictures were taken and when told fourteen miles he muttered, "*C'est formidable. C'est formidable.*" Using a magnifying glass, he was able to point out four different types of Mig fighters on the Cuban airfields.

It is doubtful if any aerial photographs in history were ever examined by as many high-ranking world leaders as the reconnaissance photographs taken by the American planes during the Cuban crisis.

On October 22, backed by the photographic evidence of the Russian missiles and IL-28 bombers now based in Cuba, President Kennedy announced the blockade of the island. That same day the ambassadors of all the nations friendly to the U.S. and the so-called neutral nations were briefed on the situation by Undersecretary of State George Ball. Roger Hilsman, director of intelligence and research for the State Department, presented the U-2 photographs, pictures that left no doubt in anyone's mind that the weapons were on the island as the U.S. claimed. The following day in the United Nations, when Soviet Ambassador Valerian A. Zorin tried to deny that the offensive missiles and bombers were on the island, Ambassador Adlai Stevenson presented the aerial photographs to the Security Council members and correspondents of more than a hundred nations. The missile installations, supporting equipment, and the bombers were visible to even the least-trained eye.

Meanwhile the reconnaissance pilots continued their overflights of Cuba despite the threats issued by Khrushchev. The U-2s flew as many as eight missions a day while the 363d's Voodoos flashed over the island so low and fast that one pilot nearly hit the ball being used by Russian technicians in a game of volleyball. Some two thousand photo missions were flown the week of October 21, which required the National Photographic Interpretation Center to work twenty-four hours a day. As the pictures were developed the newly discovered missile bases were plotted on a large map of Cuba. President Kennedy inspected the photos each day, learning how to pick out the big crates on the docks that had just been unloaded from the Russian ships, the trucks with rocket fuel, the twin-jet IL-28 bombers sitting on the airfields, and the launching pads for the missiles. One day he was delighted when he counted the holes in a Russian latrine.

At a briefing near the end of the week, as the tension

mounted and the world was on the brink of World War III, President Kennedy told Lundahl: "You photo interpreters are amazing. Even when I see nothing, you fellows detect missile sites."

By Saturday, October 27, the United States and Russia were, as Secretary of State Dean Rusk admitted, "eyeball-to-eyeball" in a nuclear showdown. President Kennedy and his advisers had drafted a letter to Khrushchev stating that it was imperative that the Russian missile bases in Cuba be dismantled. In return the U.S. would lift the blockade around the island and pledge not to invade Cuba. There was absolutely no indication, however, that the Soviets had any intention of removing the bases. In fact, at some instant between ten fifteen and eleven o'clock that morning a tragic incident occurred that made it seem likely that World War III had already started. Major Anderson, the U-2 pilot who had brought back the initial photographic evidence of the Russian missile bases on Cuba, was killed when his reconnaissance plane was hit by a SAM. The U.S. radar controllers had followed the flight of the U-2 from the minute it took off from McCoy AFB, Florida, and had known the moment it was shot down. Cuban citizens later found Anderson's body still strapped in the wreckage of the aircraft.

Shortly after nine o'clock that night President Kennedy approved the call-up of twenty-four troop-carrier squadrons of the Air Force Reserve to reinforce the men, ships, planes, and equipment already crowding southern Florida. At more than eighty bomber bases in the U.S. and overseas, aircraft were loaded with nuclear weapons and made ready to fly at a moment's notice. The reconnaissance pilots continued their aerial surveillance of Cuba but they, too, compounded the tension that Saturday. An Alaskan-based U-2 that had been sent to the North Pole to take air samples of Russia's latest nuclear tests made a navigational error on the return trip. Instead of heading toward Alaska the pilot started straight for Moscow across the Chutotskiy peninsula. The reconnaissance pilot, seeing Soviet fighters below scrambling to intercept him, broke radio silence long enough to ask for a correct heading from the Alaskan ground-control station. Once he received the bearing he turned back toward his base. Such an overflight even during normal conditions was serious. To have such an overflight at the height of the Cuban crisis was tragic. President Kennedy, when notified, could only wonder whether Khrushchev thought the U-2 was taking one final photographic run over Russia prior to a nuclear attack by American bombers.

On Sunday, October 28, it appeared that the Russian Premier had capitulated. Over the radio Khrushchev stated: "The Soviet government has issued orders to dismantle the arms you [President Kennedy] described as offensive and to crate and return them to the Soviet Union." He went on to insist that the weapons had been sent to Cuba only to deter attack but since the United States misunderstood this fact he would have them removed.

The happiness at the apparent backdown of the Soviet Premier was tempered by the realization that the message might be a trick, a stall for more time, a way to throw the massed military might of the U.S. off guard. Was Khrushchev sincere? Was he biding his time in order to get better prepared for the fight? President Kennedy knew that the answers lay with the reconnaissance planes that had already accomplished such valuable intelligence missions. If these planes could bring back photographs verifying the fact that the Russians were, as promised by Khrushchev, dismantling the missile sites, then the blockade could be lifted from around Cuba and the tension of the past few days would be eased.

Lieutenant Colonel Joseph M. O'Grady of the 29th Tactical Reconnaissance Squadron was selected to handle the vital assignment. O'Grady had been flying for the USAF since 1942 and had more than 5,500 hours of flying time to his credit, including seventy-nine missions in Korea. He was considered one of the best pilots in the world for low-level photography. O'Grady chose Captain Jack C. Bowland as his wingman and the mission was set up for the afternoon of the twenty-nineth.

At their briefing shortly before taking off on the mission, O'Grady and Bowland were given a list of EEIs (Essential Elements of Information) and target study folders containing detailed maps, photographs, and drawings of the target area. They were also given a secret radio frequency to use on the flight. In case they were attacked by Migs or their aircraft damaged by SAM missiles they were to relay any information they obtained visually to a secret radio station on the Florida coast before bailing out. O'Grady's code name for radio transmissions was "Dodson Seven One."

The flight down the Florida peninsula from their base at MacDill AFB, Orlando, was made at normal height and was uneventful. The two fliers used normal command hand signals for any communication that was required, maintaining radio silence so as not to alert Castro's listening stations. As they crossed the coastline of Florida, O'Grady nosed his RF-101 downward and within minutes the two supersonic planes were at wave-top level. It was imperative that they stay under the Cuban radar net if the element of surprise was to be maintained. It was tricky, dangerous flying but necessary.

One second the RF-101 Voodoos were over water, the next they were roaring low over the palm trees, roads, and houses of Cuba. O'Grady altered his flight path a few degrees and headed straight for the Russian missile site at San Cristobal. As he approached the installation mechanics and technicians and gunners who had been working in the area scattered in all directions.

"Just as we began our run over the target I noticed a puff of flak aft and above my wingman," O'Grady said later. "It appeared to be 37-mm cannon fire. I have been subject to combat before in World War II and Korea but it is still a strange feeling when you know you are being shot at. The flak appeared to be leading us and way high. Naturally there always is a bit of anxiety on any mission but we had been well briefed and when we had the target in sight we completed our mission. We even had pictures of the flak bursts. After the mission was completed we took the only evasive action to take—we got the hell out of there. There was no damage to our aircraft. We saw Mig-type planes in the air several times but they never made a pass at us."

At 5:10 P.M., exactly two hours and ten minutes after takeoff, the two fliers were back on the runway at MacDill AFB. The photographic evidence that the colonel and his wingman brought back to Florida that day was one of the prime factors in averting World War III. The pictures proved without a doubt that the Russians, true to Khrushchev's promise, had already started to dismantle the missile sites in Cuba. Knowing this, President Kennedy called off the invasion of Cuba by the U.S. military might massed in Florida. The sixteen pilots of the 363d Tactical Reconnaissance Wing of which the 29th Tactical Reconnaissance Squadron was a part were each awarded the Distinguished Flying Cross for the missions they flew during and after the Cuban crisis. President Kennedy also bestowed the Air Force Outstanding Unit Award to the wing stating:

> The 363d Tactical Reconnaissance Wing, Tactical Air Command, distinguished itself by exceptionally meritorious service from 23 October 1962 to 24 November 1962. During this period the 363d Tactical Reconnaissance Wing planned and executed low-level aerial surveillance of offensive weapons in Cuba, thereby contributing invaluable intelligence data which helped our leaders establish the nation's military posture and plan its diplomatic actions. The high degree of professional competence displayed in the execution of both preplanned and immediate reconnaissance sorties is a distinct tribute to pilot skill and to the exactness of the technicians charged with the maintenance of aircraft and accessory equipment. The speed and precision with which the reconnaissance film was processed, interpreted, and delivered was an accomplishment of exceptional magnitude. The fact that the peace has been maintained enhances the vital importance of the unit's contribution to the nation. The individual aggressiveness, leadership, and selfless devotion to duty

demonstrated by the members of the 363d Tactical Reconnaissance Wing during the period of national crisis reflect great credit upon themselves and the United States Air Force.

Major Anderson was posthumously awarded the Distinguished Service Medal, the highest decoration the nation can bestow except in time of war. His body was returned to the United States after an appeal to Fidel Castro by U.N. Secretary-General U Thant and was interred in Woodlawn Memorial Park, Greenville, South Carolina.

Later, as President Kennedy once again examined some of the photographs taken by Anderson and the other reconnaissance pilots, he said, "The camera, I think, is going to be our best inspector."

Cuba has been under the all-seeing eye of the aerial camera ever since. Every time a U.S.S.R. ship refuels it is observed and photographed. Soviet-built radar stations and the fleet of Russian spy ships based on the island are constantly under surveillance. Washington knows that missiles can be hidden in caves and Cuba has more than its share of caves. The reconnaissance photographs are studied closely for roads leading to the mouths of caves or tracks of heavy vehicles leading to a mountainside. If such clues are visible to the PIs, then more detailed pictures are obtained and the area is photographed daily until Washington has determined whether there is any activity that will once again threaten the security of the nation.

If any one single event in the sixties accelerated the development of aerial reconnaissance it was the Cuban episode. This was an important crisis that was "played out" almost entirely by air-reconnaissance missions. Yet it wasn't the first role undertaken by the recon pilot during the fringe-war years of the early sixties. Nor was aerial photographic reconnaissance the only type of aerial spying accomplished during this turbulent, tense period when it was imperative to know about the military preparations being carried out by the Soviet Union. Electronic reconnaissance was also very effective.

Most of the electronic reconnaissance undertaken by the U.S. was accomplished by aircraft. The planes, known as ferret planes, and the electronic specialists who operate the sophisticated equipment on board, known as ravens, operate on the edges of the Communist world recording and analyzing enemy radar signals. The ferrets carry many different types of receivers so that they can pick up signals from new radar stations, measure the pulse rate of the radar and its frequency, and accurately locate the source. The ravens try to pinpoint the location of any new radar station behind the Iron Curtain so that it can be logged for future reference. A dangerous game which might be called international chicken is sometimes resorted to in an effort to get an enemy country to switch on its most secret radar equipment. Since it is known that this equipment will be used only in a dire emergency, a ferret plane may make a headlong dash toward an Iron Curtain country border and sometimes cross the border in a mock attack. The enemy often fires antiaircraft missiles at these intruders and launches Migs to intercept them. They will also use their most secret radar installations which are immediately monitored by the ferret. Usually the electronic reconnaissance plane will get back to friendly territory without incident after recording the information desired, but not always. The RB-47 ferret flown by Major Willard G. Palm over the Barents Sea was one that didn't return.

Palm and his crew were members of the 55th Reconnaissance Wing of the Strategic Air Command. In the early summer of 1960 they were sent on temporary duty to England to fly ferret flights along the borders of the Soviet Union. Their aircraft was a B-47 altered for electronic reconnaissance missions. Instead of bombs its insides were packed with "black boxes" and antennas which were operated by the electronic specialists on Palm's crew—Major Eugene E. Posa, Captain Dean B. Phillips, and Captain Oscar L. Goforth. Palm's co-pilot on the July 1, 1960, mission over the Barents Sea was Captain Bruce Olmstead.

While the ferret missions along the Soviet border were legal as long as the aircraft remained over international waters, the flights were exceedingly dangerous because the Russians didn't always observe international rules. Despite the fact that Red reconnaissance planes had made hundreds of flights along the borders of Canada and Alaska and had, at times, strayed from international areas, never had the U.S. attempted to shoot one down. On the other hand, the Soviets killed seventy-five American airmen in a period of ten years for allegedly violating their territory. Palm was well aware of this as he piloted his RB-47 across the Barents Sea.

At 2:56 P.M. on July 1 the navigator, Captain John McKone, made a close check on the position of the aircraft. The radarscope indicated that the RB-47 was more than fifty miles off the Soviet coast but to make certain McKone checked the location of the Svatoi Nos (Holy Nose Cape), a prominent landmark along the shore. It, too, verified the plane's position. The captain was writing down the altitude—30,000 feet—and airspeed—425 knots—in preparation to telling Palm it was time to change course to the left when suddenly he heard co-pilot Olmstead calling to Palm over the intercom.

"Check right wing. We got a stranger at three o'clock high."

The pilot checked the Mig on his right which was flying a parallel course to the RB-47. "Keep your eye on him."

After a few minutes, during which McKone again checked the position of his own aircraft in respect to the Soviet border and once again made certain that they were over international waters, the Mig turned away and disappeared. A few moments later Palm started his slow turn to the left according to his flight plan but as he did so he was amazed to see another Mig only 50 feet off his right wingtip. The Russian fighter was so close that Palm was very careful in making his left bank so that the two planes wouldn't accidently collide. He was halfway through the turn when he noticed that the Mig had veered away, circled, and was now coming up on the rear of the RB-47.

"Watch him and . . ."

Suddenly the cannons on the Mig flashed and the crew of the ferret RB-47 realized that the Russian pilot was attacking them. Olmstead immediately tried to return the fire with his two radar-controlled 20-mm cannon but the Mig was so close he had to switch to visual firing. Before he could take aim, however, the RB-47 went into a flat spin and flames appeared under two of the three engines on the left wing.

Palm and Olmstead both tried to pull the RB-47 out of the spin but before they could regain control of the reconnaissance plane the Soviet pilot, later identified as Captain Vasily Ambrosievitch Polyakov, made a second firing pass.

"Standby . . . standby . . ."

Palm's warning was the first indication to his crew that the RB-47 was badly damaged, that he wanted them prepared to jump if necessary. During the next few seconds the two pilots fought desperately to pull the plane out of the spin. They managed to get the aircraft fairly stable but by this time the flames from the engines were reaching back toward the tail of the RB-47. Palm didn't hesitate. He made an immediate decision.

"Bail out! Bail out!"

Olmstead grabbed the D-ring that actuated his ejection seat and when he heard Palm give the bail-out signal the second time he pulled it. The 75-mm shell blew him and his seat out of the doomed plane with such force that he was knocked unconscious. The navigator, ejected downward, was also knocked unconscious. Fortunately for both men their parachutes opened automatically at 14,000 feet. Both men managed to unfasten their parachutes after they hit the ice-cold water and climb onto their survival rafts. Several hours later they were picked up by a Russian trawler and turned over to Russian authorities.

Later investigation indicated that Palm remained with the stricken RB-47 for twenty more minutes, making a wide, erratic turn far out over the Barents Sea. The aircraft was monitored by means of secret devices, the precise nature of which have never been revealed for reasons of military security. As U.S. Ambassador to the U.N. Henry Cabot Lodge stated later before the U.N. Security Council:

"The truth is that, at the time the Soviet Union claims our airplane was brought down in Soviet waters, it was actually fifty miles off the Soviet coast. It was still in the air twenty minutes later, over the high seas, two hundred miles from the point alleged by the Soviet Union and flying in a northeasterly direction. United States personnel monitored this flight."

It appears likely that Palm stayed with the RB-47 to give all three ravens a chance to bail out and then landed the plane at sea. Why he didn't bail out was never learned. Of the crew, only Olmstead and McKone survived. Palm's body was recovered by the Russians and buried at Arlington National Cemetery. The bodies of the three electronic specialists were never found. The two survivors were accused by the Soviet Union of invading Russian territory for reasons of espionage and kept in prison for seven months. Finally, as a friendly gesture to the new U.S. President, John F. Kennedy, they were released on January 24, 1961, four days after his inauguration.

Mrs. Nadine Palm, widow of the pilot of the RB-47, although grief-stricken over the loss of her husband, said, "My one consolation is that my husband knew what he was doing, knew how important it was, and would have had it no other way."

Fringe-war aerial reconnaissance is an absolute must, ranking equally with combat aerial reconnaissance. Miscalculations and misunderstandings about the intentions of other nations have to be avoided and one way of avoiding them is an accurate knowledge of the military activities in progress in hostile countries. Photographic and electronic reconnaissance is of vital importance, as Major Willard G. Palm knew.

There are many international problems yet to be resolved about what is and what is not an illegal intrusion on another country's borders. In 1944 the United States invited all nations involved in air travel problems to a meeting in Chicago, a meeting that is now known as the Chicago Conference. Nearly every nation that anticipated being active in postwar aviation, military and civilian, sent representatives with the notable exception of the Soviet Union. Three separate agreements and numerous recommendations were produced at this meeting, some of which now have a direct bearing on aerial reconnaissance flights. The doctrine of sovereignty over air space by each nation was discussed and generally speaking it was recognized that the air space over a country was directly under its jurisdiction and was an integral part of its territory. In later years, with the advent of aircraft that can fly at altitudes seldom considered possible in the past and with the development of satellites, the question has arisen as to whether or not there is an altitude limitation involved in the air-sovereignty concept that was accepted earlier. Where does air space cease to be considered controlled by the country below and international air space begin?

During the yearly meeting of the American Society of International Law in 1956, Dr. John Cobb Cooper stated that while the Chicago Conference in no way precluded the possibility of a state extending its sovereignty beyond the area in which an airplane or balloon can fly, there is no existing international law to act as a basis for such an extension. Other experts believe that the question hinges on a precise definition of the upper limits of "air space" and where, if at all, international "air space" begins. Since the United States did not claim that Powers' U-2 was in international air, it is evident that Washington must consider the altitude boundary higher than the estimated 70,000–100,000 feet reportedly reached by the spy plane on that overflight in 1960.

The sovereignty of air space adjacent to the high seas is also an unresolved problem among nations of the world today. In recent years incidents such as the RB-47 conducting electronic reconnaissance over the Barents Sea have focused attention on the legal status of this air space. As early as September 4, 1954,

Russian fighter planes shot down a U.S. P2V Neptune aircraft flying off the Soviet Pacific coast. The United States at that time insisted that the aircraft was never closer than thirty miles to the shoreline. This placed the plane in the international air space over the Sea of Japan. In order to try and obtain a definition of international air space over the high seas, the United States wanted to submit the controversy to the International Court of Justice for consideration but this action was vetoed by Russia. Later such "intrusion" incidents only magnified the problem.

It is agreed that the legal status of this air space is directly related to the legal status of the high seas beneath it and unfortunately there is no absolute definition between nations on these water boundaries either. International law recognizes that interior maritime waters of a nation are under its jurisdiction. The doctrine pertaining to territorial sea originally stated that a nation's sovereignty extended "as far out to sea as a shot of a cannon would reach." However, this decision was reached in 1702 and today a modern cannon can shoot much farther. The three-mile limit is outdated and gradually nations began to extend this boundary and the air space above it. The United States and England still maintain the three-mile limit but other countries have increased it as far as twelve miles and this variance is a constant source of trouble. The area of the high seas adjacent to the territorial sea is called the contiguous zone, an area that came into being because some nations did extend their territorial-sea sovereignty. The United States itself helped to recognize this zone when in 1945 a Truman proclamation concerning the conservation of fisheries over the continental shelf made the boundary of the territorial sea indefinite. The Geneva Conference of 1958 was held to try and settle the problem.

Prior to the conference twenty-one countries had decided on the three-mile limit as a legal status of territorial waters; seventeen nations used a four-to-six mile limit; thirteen countries based their claims on a nine-to-twelve mile boundary; and an additional nine nations claimed exclusive rights in the waters of the continental shelf. All countries considered the air space above these water limits to be included. The Geneva Conference representatives agreed in Article 24 that a state may exercise the control necessary to prevent and punish any infringement of its customs, fiscal, immigration, or sanitary regulations within its territorial waters and declared that this zone may not extend beyond the twelve-mile limit. Thus it appeared that the twelve-mile limit had resolved the problem —but it hadn't.

The same Geneva Conference stated that all nations had the freedom of the high seas and defined freedom of the sea as freedom of navigation; freedom of fishing; freedom to lay submarine cables and pipelines; and freedom to fly over the high seas. But in addition, the conference stressed that these freedoms existed only so far as they didn't interfere with the freedom of other states. It appeared that reconnaissance aircraft could, if they didn't pose a military threat to another nation, fly within twelve miles of that nation's border and still be in international air. However, due to the potential of high-speed military aircraft and the consideration of security to a country bordering on the sea, international law permitted certain measures to be established. One of the best examples of such measures are those established by the United States. Air Defense Identification Zones were set up in order to prevent unidentified aircraft from approaching the shores of the nation. Any aircraft entering or flying within an ADIZ zone is required to file a flight plan prior to the flight and make a position report to the appropriate ground station when it is estimated to be not less than one hour's cruising distance from the coast of the United States. This means that a military plane of another nation that cruises at 600 mph must report its position while it is still that distance out to sea.

The question is really not so much whether a reconnaissance

plane is violating international law when it flies along the coast of another country outside the normal limits of territorial waters as whether the nation being observed has the right to shoot the reconnaissance aircraft down for the supposed violation. Even the American ADIZ zone regulations state that they apply only to planes entering the United States and it is obvious that an enemy reconnaissance plane would not go that far customarily. The United States does not attempt to shoot down the Russian aircraft that periodically penetrate its territory on reconnaissance missions but the Russians have no hesitation in doing so. Until the boundary between outer space and air space over a nation is defined or, as some experts suggest, a United Nations Reconnaissance Agency is formed to control international reconnaissance activities by aircraft, incidents will occur. Whether any of the "intrusions" will lead indirectly to another world war is problematical.

On March 10, 1964, three American airmen in an RB-66 Destroyer reconnaissance aircraft were flying along the border of East Germany in extremely bad weather. Captain David Holland was at the controls while Captain Melvin J. Kessler and Lieutenant Harold W. Welch, his two crewmen, handled the navigation and camera problems. It has never been stated officially just exactly what their assigned mission was that gloomy day but it is known that the RB-66 can accomplish photo, weather, and electronic reconnaissance. Built by the Douglas Aircraft Company, it has a range of more than 1,500 miles without refueling, a wing span of 72 feet, and a speed of 700 mph. It carries a full range of camera equipment and the most modern electronic reconnaissance equipment available.

As the RB-66 neared the border of East Germany after a "training" flight from a French base, ground controllers monitoring the plane's course suddenly became alarmed. Instead of making a turn as it was scheduled to do, the RB-66 kept on flying straight east. They immediately tried to contact Holland by radio, using coded signals, but were unsuccessful. The reconnaissance plane maintained a heading for the border of East Germany. In desperation, the order was given by the officer in charge to transmit a message "in the clear" warning Holland that his aircraft was in danger of violating Communist territory. This, too, failed to gain a response. Later it was stated that the pilot never received the messages. Some believe he ignored it on orders. This has been denied.

Unable to see the ground and thinking that he was still over West Germany, Holland continued on his course and penetrated East Germany. Approximately sixteen miles inside Red Germany a Soviet fighter appeared and began firing at the American reconnaissance plane. Before the crewmen recovered from their shock, the RB-66 was damaged severely and Holland gave the order to bail out. A British pilot, flying along the border in West Germany, reported seeing three parachutes as Holland, Kessler, and Welch jumped from the doomed reconnaissance plane. The ground controllers immediately relayed the information about the parachutes to USAF headquarters and the effort to get the American pilots back to friendly territory was begun.

Unfortunately, earlier in the year another American aircraft had been shot down in the same area after an alleged intrusion of Communist territory. Since the Soviet Union had already protested that USAF planes were constantly making quick sorties over the border to check opposition radar defenses and since Holland's RB-66 was the second plane within a short period to have been shot down over East Germany, the situation was tense. Washington immediately went to great lengths to assure the Russians that the plane had not been on an intelligence mission and had merely strayed off course. This assurance was given not only by U.S. military authorities but by the State Department, the U.S. Embassy in Moscow, and high government officials. The Russians, however, weren't convinced. They had heard the same story from spokesmen for the U.S. many times before and, whether it was true or not, the Soviet Union refused to release the airmen. The only concession made by the Russians was to permit a U.S. officer to visit Welch, who had suffered leg and arm fractures when his aircraft was shot down.

On March 19, nine days after the incident occurred, Chargé d'Affaires Walter J. Stoessel delivered a message from the United States government to Mikhail Smirnovsky, chief of the Soviet foreign ministry's American section:

> Further delay in release and return of the crewmen will clearly jeopardize possibilities of expanding areas of friendly relations.

Two days later the Russians turned the injured Welch over to American military representatives at a U.S. checkpoint at Helmstedt on the autobahn to West Berlin. They again refused, however, to disclose the whereabouts of the other two crew members. Washington began to fear that the Russians were preparing a show trial for propaganda purposes similar to the one held when Powers was shot down over the Soviet Union in the U-2. Meanwhile, various cover stories were released in the U.S. to explain the "error" that resulted in the RB-66 intrusion on East German territory. A USAF spokesman, Colonel Mark Gilman, said that the Air Force believed that the reconnaissance plane might have been lured across the border.

"It cannot be ruled out that the plane was led off course by radio jamming and false signals," Gilman said. "As long as we have the capability of doing this—and we do—we must assume the other side can do it, too. We have no concrete evidence at this time but we are not ruling it out."

Another release stated that a faulty electronic compass was probably the chief cause of the incident. This combined with weather conditions at the time, the report said, contributed to the RB-66's penetration of Communist areas.

However, the Russians believed only one story—the reconnaissance plane was on a spying mission and was caught in the act. The United States refused to admit this was the truth and the stalemate continued. The cooperation between the two countries about such arrangements as holding a new consular convention, a direct New York-Moscow air link, and relaxation of curbs on East German cultural and sports missions to Western countries came to a halt. Once again the world learned that international relationships often pivoted on the success or lack of success of reconnaissance aircraft as they flew their assigned missions.

For three more days the world waited while the U.S. and the Soviet Union debated the fate of the crewmen. Then, on March 22, Secretary of State Dean Rusk announced that he had just been informed that Holland and Kessler would be returned to the United States in the near future. Six days later the two fliers were delivered by Soviet authorities to a U.S. military liaison officer at Marienborn on the East German border shortly before 3:00 P.M. They were placed in a military sedan and the small party drove past a Soviet Army detachment standing at attention alongside the autobahn and sped to West German territory. The automobile drove at high speed to Hanover Airport, fifty miles to the west, where Holland and Kessler were put on board a C-54 and flown to Wiesbaden, headquarters of the U.S. Air Force in Europe. There were no interviews granted then or later, no answers given about the incident. Seven months later an Air Force evaluation board announced in Washington that it had cleared the RB-66 crew members for further flying duty, laying the blame for the intrusion incident on a faulty electronic compass. Secretary of State Rusk summed up the U.S. position when he stated, after the return of the fliers:

"I would hope the matter will now be taken off the books."

This incident may eventually be forgotten but one thing is certain—there will be more intrusions, planned or accidental, more overflights by reconnaissance planes, more shadowing of Soviet submarines and surface vessels by U.S. Navy patrol aircraft taking photographic evidence for future reference. There is every reason to believe that one or more of these spy planes will be brought down by enemy action. That is the price that must be paid for national security.

A Lockheed U-2 plane that was shot down over Red China is on permanent display at the Chinese People's Revolutionary Military Museum in Peking. The official Chinese version of the downing of the aircraft states that it was knocked out of the sky by Mao's thought power. Perhaps this is a new weapon the high-flying reconnaissance pilots face in addition to the other sophisticated weapons now available to the Communist world.

12

Light Planes and Whirlybirds Take a Look

AIRPOWER has been highly criticized as being an inherently immoral way to wage war because a bombing or strafing attack kills as many civilians as enemy soldiers. Unlike the bombing of defenseless cities during the Spanish Civil War, the Luftwaffe attacks on Coventry and other English cities, or even the Allied bombing raids on Hamburg or Cologne, however, air action in South Vietnam is the most closely controlled in history. In South Vietnam there is a system of check and doublecheck that depends largely upon the visual reconnaissance of pilots and observers in light planes and helicopters.

According to the Department of the Army Field Manual FM1-80 titled *Aerial Observer Training*, helicopters are used for visual observation and reconnaissance missions of short duration requiring frequent landings in restricted areas and slow airspeeds. The manual defines such missions as surveillance, reconnaissance, or special. All three can be accomplished in one flight. In addition, adjustment of fire or target acquisition is inherent in all missions involving aerial observation. The helicopter pilot in Vietnam who is assigned a surveillance mission is expected to maintain a systematic and continuous observation of a specific area. On a reconnaissance mission he has the task of gathering specific information of military value. It is in the special mission category that the helicopter has its greatest value, however.

Special missions, according to FM1-80, are varied. Column-control missions mean that the helicopter pilot must provide security for troops or vehicles on the move by visual reconnoitering of the area on all sides of the movement. He must help the troops or vehicles maintain rapid movement over unfamiliar and unmapped terrain and at the same time minimize the danger of surprise attack by the enemy. At other times, the pilot flies contact-reconnaissance missions, flights to locate friendly troops that are isolated or cut off from the main force. Helicopters are also very good for observing friendly units from the air to determine the condition and effectiveness of their camouflage. There are so many special missions that can be assigned a helicopter pilot by a commanding officer that a new field manual could be written every few months. In the age of the superjet there is still a very important place in aerial reconnaissance for the slow-moving but maneuverable helicopter.

Armed reconnaissance missions in helicopters, during which the aircrews provide both visual observation and security, are the most common. The organizational makeup of the 1st Squadron, 9th Cavalry Regiment of the First Cavalry Division, is an excellent example of a unit performing armed reconnaissance by helicopter. The squadron is composed of the headquarters and headquarters troop, one ground troop, and three air cavalry troops. Each air cavalry troop usually has an aerial scout platoon in addition to a headquarters platoon, an aerial weapons platoon, and an infantry platoon with lift aircraft. The aerial scout platoon handles the reconnaissance missions and, in the case of the 1st Squadron, uses ten OH-13S helicopters. This small whirlybird, made by Bell, is issued with the M-2 weapon kit, which consists of twin skid-mounted M-60s. The squadron maintenance officer devised a system of eight 2.75-inch folding fin rocket tubes clamped to an M-2 frame. These tubes are fired singly from the cyclic stick trigger switch and a ten-position selector switch on the console.

The 1st Squadron's aerial platoons each have ten officers and nineteen enlisted men. Platoon officers fly in two sections of four aircraft with the platoon leader and one rotary wing pilot forming an extra team. Armed reconnaissance missions are performed by teams of two helicopters working together. A trained observer is assigned to each pilot and it has been found from experience that the most effective teams are those who have worked together the longest. While on missions the pilots frequently switch lead and wing positions since it is much more difficult to fly wing than to fly lead.

The OH-13S helicopter has an O-435 turbocharged engine which can take a lot of hits and still keep going. Unless the aircraft receives hits in the fan or carburetor sections of the engine, the mission can be completed. Loaded with a crew of two plus the weapons system mounted on the skids, the average endurance of the OH-13S is two hours and forty-five minutes. The M-2 weapon kits are satisfactory after the proper bore sighting and field modifications to meet combat conditions are met. The weapons are fired by the use of sights grease-penciled on the bubble and by using sighting bursts to get on target. The 2.75-inch rockets are excellent for the marking of targets with white phosphorous rounds, giving the helicopters the ability to stand off from an area it has marked and immediately order in the supporting ground or air weapons required. With ordinary smoke grenades the pilot would have to drop low to mark the area of the target and then climb to altitude to see where he was prior to directing the fighters or artillery, a procedure that takes a lot of time.

CW3 Frederick J. Carll flew more than 800 hours OH-13S time on armed reconnaissance in Vietnam as a pilot with the 1st Squadron. A mission flown near Plei Me by Carll and another pilot, WO Bruce L. Jackson, typifies the importance of the helicopter in reconnaissance activities:

"Jackson and I were ordered to fly reconnaissance in support of an infantry battalion trying to make contact with the enemy west of Plei Me. We left the landing zone early in the morning," Carll reported, "to screen well south of the committed battalion and north along the Cambodian border to prevent or report any movement in or out of the area of concern. We bored by Plei Me and headed for our sector south of the Chu Pong mountains. As we made the initial sweep across to the border and north of the mountains we spent a lot of our time familiarizing ourselves with the area. On the next sweep we searched hard for any sign of Charlie.

"The ground south of the mountains was not heavily wooded except in some large scattered sectors and along the stream beds where the dense bamboo lines the water about a hundred meters from either bank. As we were crossing one of the stream beds I caught a momentary reflection in the brush and broke left in an effort to keep it in view. Meanwhile Jackson started a big circle around me and began setting up to direct operations. As I started back across the stream bed I spotted several North Vietnamese soldiers in camouflaged holes throughout the dense bamboo lining the stream. I hovered about four hundred meters along the stream while Jackson relayed the spot report to operations by radio. The airborne rocket artillery and the Air Force fighters moved in within minutes after we marked the target area and wiped out the enemy force."

Since the enemy in Vietnam is an expert in camouflage, the helicopter is an efficient vehicle for visual reconnaissance. The reconnaissance helicopter crews can bore in close and look hard. Viet Cong and North Vietnamese soldiers have been discovered by such small things as a weapon stock that wasn't covered, a shadow among many shadows, and following footprints in small stream beds.

"Some finds, however, are really comical in their simplicity," Carll said. "One large enemy unit was found in the jungle northeast of Plei Ku because several Vietcong used banana leaves for cover when there wasn't a banana tree for miles. They have been found sitting on a paddy dike in the midst of miles of rice paddies with a banana or coconut leaf held between them and the helicopters, not really very effective camouflage."

Usually, though, Charlie is clever and hard to locate. For a period of time the Vietcong would join a column of refugees whenever a reconnaissance helicopter appeared, thinking that they would be inconspicuous among the more peaceful natives. It didn't take very long, however, for the airmen to spot the guerrillas. Their seeming nonchalance made them stand out from the others in the column and many confirmed Vietcong were captured in the areas where a helicopter could land and the crew could pick the suspect Vietnamese out of the column. Often the helicopters were sent on reconnaissance "treasure hunts," missions on which the crews looked for Communist targets in a certain area. One U.S. First Cavalry Division (Airmobile) helicopter spotted tire tracks leading into a dense patch of jungle. The pilot called in foot soldiers who discovered an immense trove of supplies: six Russian trucks, twenty-five flame-throwers, three hundred rifles, thirty-five mine detectors, a batch of mortar tubes, thousands of rounds of ammunition and a 122-mm field gun.

A very successful tactic involving helicopter reconnaissance in Vietnam is called the Jitterbug. This is a technique devised by Colonel Henry ("Gunfighter") Emerson, former commanding officer of the 1st Brigade, 9th Infantry Division, and used many times by Colonel Ira A. ("Rice Paddy Daddy") Hunt who took over the command after Emerson was injured in a helicopter crash. The Jitterbug is a modification of the earlier Eagle Flights, which were troop-laden helicopters cruising over the countryside looking for the enemy. Once the guerrillas were located the helicopters pounced like an eagle on a hare. It consists of two flights of five Bell Huey helicopters loaded with troops and OH-6 Hughes helicopters flying reconnaissance. When the reconnaissance pilot thinks he has spotted enemy activity in the jungle or a wooded area, a Huey slick with two people-sniffers in its nose and a load of tear gas moves in. The people-sniffer is a device, perfected by the U.S. Army Limited War Laboratory at the Aberdeen Proving Ground, Maryland, that seeks out the concealed enemy by detecting certain chemicals in their perspiration and registering this reaction on an instrument. When the people-sniffer gets a maximum reading, the helicopter dumps tear gas on the suspected position. If the tear gas causes movement in the area, one flight of troop-carrying helicopters deploys its men in a blocking position, then returns to camp to pick up more troops. If everything goes as planned the result is an encirclement of the enemy without heavy contact. When that happens the commander calls in air and artillery to pulverize the enemy position.

The Jitterbug has been very successful. In its first three months of operation in Long An Province, the brigade was credited with 1,453 confirmed enemy kills and 150 prisoners of war. The brigade moved to the Mekong Delta in June 1968, and the new reconnaissance tactic was just as successful there. The people-sniffer is a revolutionary device that is a boon to visual reconnaissance crews.

The helicopter is an excellent aircraft for reconnoitering highways used by American vehicles and troops in Vietnam. Lieutenant Colonel Matthew W. ("The Red Baron") Hoey of San Antonio, Texas, commanding officer of the 26th Engineering Battalion, spent much of his twelve-hour working day in the air conducting aerial reconnaissance of the 135 miles of open road in his area. One of his main duties was to keep Provincial Route 533 between Tam Ky and the Special Forces camp at Tien Phuoc open and repaired.

"Although the enemy seldom attacks engineer work parties," Hoey said, "he often attacks the roads, blowing bridges and culverts under cover of darkness. Every bridge south of Chu Lai all the way to Du Pho was demolished or damaged within a two-month period. One night Route 533 was cut in seven places."

Hoey spots the damage visually while making low-altitude reconnaissance sweeps over the road and then orders his work parties to the scene. Using this method the highway is seldom closed to military traffic.

In critical combat situations where the use of a manned helicopter is too dangerous, unmanned whirlybirds have been tried in Vietnam. These robot helicopters are loaded with information-gathering equipment and have a flight time of about three hours. They can carry television cameras to spot enemy troops and arms, thus eliminating the time lag required for an aircraft equipped with an aerial still camera to bring film back and have it developed before photographs are available to intelligence. The unmanned helicopter is controlled through radio ground stations, usually mounted in a jeep. The plane can be passed from the control of one operator to the control of another operator stationed in another area. It can also be flown on a memory course fed into either an airborne or ground control station, the airborne station being in another aircraft.

Military experts have found many aerial reconnaissance duties for the helicopter in Vietnam. New combat techniques have been developed based on the surveillance abilities of helicopters, especially in the jungle terrain. Reconnaissance helicopters can cover in a few minutes terrain that would require days for ground troops to check. Just as important, once a helicopter reconnaissance pilot or observer does spot the enemy or a supply dump or an encampment he can take immediate action—he can either land troops that he is carrying in his own aircraft or he can call in the slicks with their infantrymen ready to fight. This combination of aerial reconnaissance by helicopter and airmobile troops is a new tactic in Vietnam that constantly harasses the Vietcong and North Vietnamese soldiers who previously enjoyed comparative security in their jungle hideouts.

In addition to the visual reconnaissance chapter being written by the helicopters in Vietnam, the work of the Forward Air

Controllers in their small fixed-wing aircraft will add much to the history of airpower in a brush-fire war. Usually called Bird Dogs because they seek out the enemy and mark his position for the other units to gun down, the FACs perform a crucial function in the Vietnam War. Under the basic FAC plan no target is attacked without the permission of the Vietnamese province chief involved as well as the U.S. and Vietnamese military authorities at corps level, so the pilots who man the small observation planes have an important and dangerous visual reconnaissance mission—to distinguish the "unfriendlies" from the "friendlies." This can be difficult at times.

The FACs are mostly ex-fighter pilots trained in the hot jets of the Century series and accustomed to screaming through the skies at better than 1,000 mph. As forward air controllers they usually fly a small L-19 aircraft, called the O-1 by the USAF, which cruises at 90 mph. They are volunteers who understand the importance of their job, who realize that they are not only pointing out the enemy to the artillery and fighter-bombers but are also protecting the civilians and friendly troops in the area. Before they use their white phosphorous markers to pinpoint a target, the FACs check and doublecheck to make certain it is a legitimate target. Then and only then will they guide the fighters to it. No air war in history has been so closely controlled as that in Vietnam.

The FAC spends about a hundred hours a month in the air and the bulk of this time is devoted to visual reconnaissance. He flies over a designated area, checking on what is going on in the countryside, watching roads, rice paddies, forests, canals, and the jungle. Most of this flight time is spent over contested areas where the enemy is known to be hiding, and sometimes the FAC inspects terrain where no one but the Vietcong has been in ten years. It didn't take the Vietcong long to learn to hide from the silver-colored O-1s, knowing that the "Old Gray Lady," as the VC call the plane, will bring in the strike aircraft. Consequently the FAC has to know the clues on the terrain below that will lead him to the enemy hiding from him. One of the places he learns how to spot these clues is at the Forward Air Controller School at Phan Rang AB, Vietnam. The school, in the spring of 1968, commanded by Lieutenant Colonel Charles J. Servocky, has eighteen instructor pilots and offers courses in the O-1 and the newer O-2 Super Skymaster observation plane.

"The FAC actually controls the entire air war in the south," Servocky said. "Our job is to make him capable both psychologically and academically to do the job. He has to be psychologically capable of handling a wide variety of combat situations and he must learn how to read maps so that he knows exactly where to go. Each student gets practice in firing marking rockets and in locating targets in unfamiliar surroundings. These skills can lead to the survival of friendly forces as the FACs locate enemy targets and tell the fighter pilots from what directions to bomb and strafe these targets."

On his visual reconnaissance missions in Vietnam it is impossible for the FAC to pick out the enemy over a crowded rural area. As one pilot muttered when asked how to tell the VC from the friendly civilians, "Don't ask me. Look for yourself. It's the same as flying over Manhattan Island at a thousand feet and trying to pick out all the Germans." Instead he gathers his information primarily in two ways. One is by people shooting at him. In some sections the O-1s are shot at on nearly every mission, especially in the Mekong Delta region. If it is only one or two shots the FAC doesn't immediately call in an air strike because he knows that the enemy sometimes is trying to get him to do just that. Charlie will sneak into a village friendly to American forces, fire at the observation aircraft, and then leave, hoping that the fighters will come and wipe out the village and the innocent civilians living there. The FAC leaves the back windows of his plane open and at 1,000 feet of altitude or less he can hear shots fired at him from the ground. When the shooting begins he circles the area in an effort to learn where the shots are coming from, usually spotting the snipers by the flashes of the gun muzzles. If the firing continues and it is outside a village he may fire a marker to see if the firing stops. If it does, he reports the matter to the province chief and continues his mission. Rarely will he order an air strike because of rifle fire.

If the firing is done by automatic weapons, however, the danger is greatly increased for the FAC. A machine gunner using a .30-caliber machine gun can often hit the O-1 at 1,000 feet while an enemy soldier firing a .50-caliber machine gun can nearly always bring the plane down if he waits until it is directly overhead. The .50-caliber machine gun can reach to 3,500 feet of altitude and out to a slant range of more than a mile, a distance too great for the small observation plane's speed in case the pilot tries to get out of the area. When the FAC is fired upon by automatic weapons he knows that the enemy is usually around in large numbers and is up to something important. If the initial barrage of gunfire doesn't bring the O-1 down, the pilot clears the immediate area but stays close by using the standard operating procedure for such a situation—never establish a flight pattern. He takes evasive action, never makes the same turn twice, and constantly varies his altitude. The FAC hunts more detailed evidence of enemy positions, the number of soldiers, and other pertinent information. If the situation warrants, he calls in the fighters. The larger the ground weapons and the size of the enemy unit, the larger the air strike.

Lieutenant Alexander Zakrzeski, known as Zac the FAC throughout Vietnam, flew more than five hundred combat missions in the small O-1 and acquired the knack of knowing when and when not to call in the fighters for an air strike. Once as he watched a South Vietnamese Army convoy moving along a stretch of highway running north from Phan Thiet to the district town of Tinh Gia seven miles away he saw and heard a huge blast. Just as the convoy started across a bridge Vietcong ambushers dynamited the structure and opened fire on the trucks. The lieutenant immediately radioed for air support and within minutes four F-100s arrived on the scene. Two pilots strafed along the Song Tran stream bed, raking enemy positions with their 20-mm cannon. When a strong Vietcong force closed on the ambushed Vietnamese soldiers from the rear, Zakrzeski, still circling overhead, directed the fighters to drop antipersonnel weapons among the enemy troops. As the Vietcong scattered, the Vietnamese soldiers from the convoy rushed them.

The lieutenant followed them despite the heavy ground fire and once again his visual reconnaissance paid off. He spotted about eighty-five Vietcong spread out along the banks of the Song Tran waiting to ambush the attacking Vietnamese. Without hesitation he dove through the ground fire and marked the location of the enemy troops and the F-100s moved in to disperse the ambushers. Altogether, 110 Vietcong were killed. It is no wonder the enemy has a price on the head of Zakrzeski.

"They don't want me for questioning," he said. "They want to kill me."

Once an enemy gun or unit is spotted, the FACs disregard ground fire and all other obstacles to mark it for the air strikes. Major Philip J. White went looking for camouflaged enemy field artillery positions that were shelling Allied forces south of the Demilitarized Zone one afternoon. He located four separate guns by flying very low over the rugged terrain which was controlled by the Vietcong. Despite the fact that the ground fire was intense and accurate, White made eleven passes through it to mark the gun positions for the fighters. He was awarded the Silver Star for his courage and determination.

Looking for evidence that the Vietcong are in the area or have been in the area is a major activity for the FACs. One excellent clue is a change in the pattern of the ground traffic. When the Vietcong are in the vicinity, the number of people in the streets is usually cut in half, traffic on the country roads is scarce, and there are very few sampans on the waterways. Even different-from-normal patterns on the scum that forms on small canals and streams indicate to the FACs that the Vietcong have been around. Early every morning the pilots look for new trenches or additions to old trenches which might have been dug during the previous night, knowing that the enemy forces the villagers to dig trenches. Sometimes visual reconnaissance reveals new buildings in Vietcong-controlled area. Another source of value to the FACs is the leads provided by the Army Special Forces and agents on the ground. With these leads the pilot can check a suspected area much more closely than he can check the entire sector for which he is responsible. Often if he stays in the area long enough or doubles back after his first pass over the suspected position, he catches the enemy in the open.

Regardless of how he finds the enemy, the FAC must tell the province chief and the U.S. and Vietnamese military commanders at the district air support center at corps headquarters exactly what he is doing. If he wants to summon artillery, he has to receive permission from the province chief and for air strikes he must get permission from both the province chief and the district air support center. If a village is to be bombed or strafed, no one person can give permission. Approval must be obtained at provincial, corps, and national levels, the villagers are forewarned by leaflets and loudspeakers, and the FAC guides the strike aircraft to the village to make certain the fighter-bombers attack the correct one.

One problem that constantly plagues the FAC is exactly what he should do in emergency situations where U.S. or South Vietnamese forces are in battle with the enemy and in trouble. Nearly 20 percent of all air strikes are ordered for this reason. Such situations require good judgment on his part since there is little time to consult others. Usually he determines first whether an air strike will aid the trapped U.S. or South Vietnamese troops. If in his judgment it will, he asks the friendly forces to mark their lines and tell him from which area they are receiving enemy fire. The FAC then guides the fighter-bombers to that area, making certain that he keeps them away from the friendly troops that have marked their positions.

Captain Burton T. Miller, Jr., discovered how nerve-wracking this can be when he flew his observation aircraft in support of Operation Hawthorne. He was supporting the U.S. Army's 101st Airborne Division during the operation and the first request he received came from U.S. Army Captain William S. Carpenter. His unit, Company "C" of the 502d Battalion of the "Screaming Eagles" 101st Airborne Division, ran into dug-in North Vietnamese regulars as he led his men into a wooded area in the jungle highlands.

"We could hear them talking and moving around as we moved up the hill," he said. "They didn't seem to know we were in the area. Our first platoon hit them first and began cutting them down with machine-gun fire."

The fight alerted other Communist units in the area, however, and soon Carpenter and his men were surrounded.

"More and more of them started coming in on us. They pinned us down. Then they started to get right in with us—right among us. Finally I called air strikes right on top of us."

Miller received the call. "I had run strikes many times to within 50 to 100 yards of friendly troops but Carpenter's request was something I had not met before," he said later. "I was convinced he was serious so I went ahead and directed the fighters as close as I could."

In all, Miller directed nine flights of strike aircraft to support Carpenter and his men. These attacks stopped the Communists long enough for the Americans to set up a defense perimeter and fight off the enemy until Able Company reached them that night. The FAC's visual reconnaissance enabled him to guide the fighter-bombers to within a few feet of the trapped platoon, a feat that would have been impossible otherwise. Carpenter, who won fame earlier as the "Lonesome End" of the 1959 West Point football team, was awarded the Medal of Honor for his actions but he is quick to point out that without the forward air controller and the fighter-bombers he and his men would have been wiped out.

"We had the air with us all the way," he said. "It saved us. They knew exactly where we were."

During search-and-destroy operations by units of brigade or division strength, the gound commander usually is given the authority to call in air support without contacting the province chief. In these situations the FAC has an even greater responsibility for identifying the target as unfriendly. The Vietcong strike suddenly and there is little time for a ground commander to analyze the overall situation, so he depends heavily upon the FAC above his unit to tell him what is in the surrounding area —civilians with guns, villages, trenches, enemy soldiers. Even during heavy fighting the FAC inspects every target in detail to make certain that his advice to the ground commander is correct. Then and only then will the ground commander decide whether to summon an air strike.

The O-1 carries four 2.75-inch white phosphorous rockets which the FAC can use against ground targets. The pilot also takes an M-16 rifle with him in the small aircraft to use if he is shot down. Many times these weapons are useful. Captain Harry J. Pawlak of the 19th Tactical Air Support Squadron at Bien Hoa AB, who flew more than six hundred O-1 visual reconnaissance missions in Vietnam and was forced to crash land twice in enemy territory, saved a government fort by using his rockets. He was flying a routine reconnaissance mission when he spotted suspicious activity near the small government fort about fifteen miles west of Bien Hoa. He descended for a closer look and found himself caught in a barrage of intense ground fire from a force of a hundred Vietcong preparing a surprise attack on the fort. He warned the outpost by radio and immediately requested an air strike by A-1E Skyraiders.

"Each time the VC grouped for an attack," Pawlak said, "I fired a white phosphorous rocket which dispersed them."

Single-handed he held the Vietcong back for nearly thirty minutes by firing his rockets and flares. Fort officials gave the captain credit for saving the government outpost.

Captain Hilliard A. Wilbanks also discovered that he and his observation plane were the only air support available, for a period, to help a trapped South Vietnamese force near Dalat in South Vietnam. Wilbanks was on his 488th combat reconnaissance mission as an FAC on February 24, 1967, when he discovered a large hostile force poised to ambush the advancing South Vietnamese Army Ranger battalion in the Lam Dong Province. Realizing that armed helicopter gunships in the vicinity had used up their ammunition and that it would take considerable time to call in additional air support, Wilbanks flew his own relatively defenseless light plane against the enemy to break up the ambush. His only weapon was an M-16 rifle which he fired through an open cockpit window since he had already expended his rockets. Making several daring attacks on the enemy, he caused some casualties and threw the Vietcong off balance, enabling the friendly forces to withdraw from their exposed positions. During his third sweep he was wounded and his plane went down.

Both South Vietnamese Rangers and rescue helicopters attempted to reach the downed pilot but were driven back by heavy ground fire. On a second attempt Wilbanks was removed from the wreckage but he later died of wounds. On January 25, 1968, at a ceremony at the Pentagon, Captain Wilbanks was awarded the Medal of Honor posthumously. In presenting the medal to his widow, Secretary of the Air Force Harold Brown said, "Captain Wilbanks' selfless act was witnessed by hundreds of men. . . . His comrades and his country will always remember his heroism."

Visual reconnaissance at night by the small observation planes was very limited at the beginning of the Vietnam War but has gradually developed into a valuable source of intelligence to the ground commander. Even the Vietcong like to operate with lights and it isn't unusual for a group of lights in a supposedly uninhabited area to be spotted at night, revealing the presence of an enemy force that otherwise might have gone undetected.

For an Army post that is being attacked at night by the Vietcong or North Vietnamese, the O-1 can provide artillery assistance and relay radio messages from the post to its headquarters. A single flare may be all that is necessary to scare the enemy attackers off but if constant illumination is necessary the FAC can adjust artillery illumination or guide Air Force flare aircraft to the scene.

Captain Skip Robinson of Seattle was one of the first and best of the night reconnaissance pilots in the O-1 aircraft. He learned to know the Cau Mau peninsula area of the Mekong Delta as well as the back yard of his home in Washington State and any change in the daily activity or appearance of the terrain was immediately noticeable to him. After darkness he knew where every river, rice paddy, and wooded area was located. Consequently he felt confident about flying over the delta at night and with a minimum of light from his flares could detect Vietcong units.

"Charlie used to take it for granted that we'd knock off bombing promptly at 6:00 P.M.," Robinson said. "They were really puzzled when we started hitting them after dark."

For effective air control, especially at night, a great many small details must be gathered together and the situation as a whole analyzed. Once, just before dark, Robinson spotted two camouflaged sampans from his plane. It was obvious they were enemy sampans or they would not have been camouflaged, but where were they going? Robinson remembered that for two previous nights a lone friendly outpost at Cai Tai had come under attack and he decided that the two sampans might be loaded with ammunition for another assault. He ordered in the fighter-bombers and the sampans were destroyed. However, when he spotted another sampan at dusk, which at first appeared to be camouflaged, he circled and discovered that it was loaded with rice seedlings. Since the occupants had made no effort to blend the sampan with the scenery when his aircraft arrived overhead, Robinson decided that it was a friendly.

"We have to be very selective," Robinson explained.

With the introduction of the new O-2 Super Skymaster observation plane into the Vietnam War, new techniques in night visual reconnaissance were developed. The O-2 is a high-wing, twin-engine (push-pull) plane which can operate at speeds between 60 and 200 miles per hour. It has four wing pylons for carrying rockets, flares, and other light conventional ordnance including a 7.62 minigun. A reticle gunsight is provided for use with the automatic weapons and rockets. The biggest change between the operation of the O-1 and the O-2, however, is the addition of a forward air navigator—FAN—to fly with the FAC on night visual reconnaissance missions. Prior to the arrival of the navigators, two pilots always flew in the aircraft at night because of the increased efficiency it provided. However, the concept of the FAN was developed when it was determined that the second man in the plane didn't have to be a pilot.

Major James F. Melton was one of the first FANs to fly an actual combat reconnaissance mission. He, like most of the others, was a volunteer from the 460th Tactical Reconnaissance Wing based at Tan Son Nhut AB.

"Our job falls into several categories," Melton explained. "We are navigators, observers, and controllers all at the same time. Actually we do just about everything on the forward air mission except fly the airplane. Since most of us have had experience in the supersonic RF-4C reconnaissance jet, we can use cameras, can make artillery adjustment, are familiar with all navigational aids, and knowledgeable on terrain and intelligence functions."

During the siege of Khe Sanh the FANs flew nightly for forty straight nights in the area, marking truck convoys, supply movements, and gun positions.

"We catch a lot of enemy fire on our missions," Melton added, "but most of the time it hurts the enemy more than it does us because the gun flash gives the enemy's position away. That's when a strike is called in and scratch one gun position."

The FANs also use a device called the "starlight scope" that intensifies the available light and permits the navigator to spot enemy activity on the ground. Other instruments, still secret, are used by the two-man crew of the O-2 on their night reconnaissance missions.

As Lieutenant Colonel G. W. Rutter, air staff project officer for the new plane, said, "All the tools of the trade will be at the FAC's disposal. Victor Charlie's life in the jungle will be far less pleasant, in fact far more dangerous than ever before, now that the O-2s are over Vietnam."

Another reconnaissance aircraft used by the U.S. Army extensively in Vietnam is the OV-1 Mohawk. The Mohawk is a two-place, short-takeoff-and-landing airplane powered by two turboprop engines designed specifically for all-weather reconnaissance and support duty with the U.S. Army. It is one of the few aircraft ever built especially for reconnaissance work. It is also one of the few aircraft in the Vietnam War for which the Vietcong have offered a reward—50,000 piastres to any gunner who can knock one of them out of the sky.

In late 1968 there were five companies in Vietnam using the Mohawk, one of which was the 73d Aviation Company, operating out of Vung Tau. The role of the 73d, as of most of the other Mohawk units, was reconnaissance patrol over the known locations that the Vietcong and North Vietnamese use to infiltrate their forces. To accomplish this mission the Mohawk is equipped with a multitude of sophisticated equipment systems so that the crew is not dependent upon visual reconnaissance alone. Among the systems made public are photographing, radar mapping, and infrared scanning, making the plane a completely integrated battlefield surveillance vehicle which can supply the army field commander with information on strength, disposition, and activity of enemy forces. Another reason it is so adaptable to units such as the 73d Aviation Company is because it is an extremely rugged aircraft that can be maintained in the field and can operate from small unimproved fields and roads. It also has an excellent speed range of between 60 and 390 knots and is exceptionally maneuverable at low speed. Three versions of the Mohawk have been produced: OV-1A, a basic visual, photographic plane; OV-1B, visual, photographic, side-looking radar; and OV-1C, visual, photographic, infrared.

The most sophisticated of the systems aboard the Mohawk is the side-looking radar (SLAR). This system gives the enlisted observer in the aircraft a permanent film record of fixed and moving targets on either or both sides of the plane's flight path. Both fixed and moving targets are recorded on a single 9-inch roll of film, automatically processed within seconds, and immediately displayed on an integral light table for the observer to view. The system can also transmit the same "radar photograph" to ground stations fifty to a hundred miles away. Either the airborne aircraft or the ground station can then call fire in upon the targets scanned.

An additional sensor system available is the infrared system known as Red Haze. This is an airborne scanning device that provides a visual cockpit display and makes a permanent film record of objects on the ground by means of small differences in their visual light emissions. It is so sensitive that it will indicate the spot where an aircraft was sitting earlier because the ground where its shadow was is still not as hot as the surrounding ground. Both the infrared and the SLAR are used primarily at night. Night photographic missions are also made using a new stroboscopic light-flasher system which takes pictures every three seconds. These photographs, which can be made at the rate of three hundred per flight, can be read as wet negatives. This cuts down the time between snapping the photographs and response. A KA-30 camera is installed in the fuselage midsection and is operated by either the pilot or observer aboard the Mohawk.

A few of the planes have a KA-60 camera system for forward oblique panoramic photography, primarily during low-altitude missions. The camera is mounted in the nose of the aircraft at a depression angle of 20 degrees from the horizontal and the film is sized to allow a 60 percent overlap photographic coverage of a flight line sixty miles long from an altitude of approximately 1,000 feet. On the low-level missions, the pilot usually starts his run over the target at from 2,000 to 3,000 feet, dives to a minimum of 200 feet to take his pictures, and then climbs back to altitude.

"We like to come in and get out as fast as possible," said Major Jerry E. Judy, commanding officer of the 73d Aviation Company. "The less time you spend over the target, the less of a target you are."

Many of the missions flown by the Mohawk crews are highly classified. Only recently has it been revealed that electronic sensor devices dropped by aircraft and monitored by aircraft have been keeping track of the North Vietnamese troops infiltrating the south. These sensing devices are also an important part of "McNamara's Fence," the electronic barrier approved for construction a mile below the DMZ in South Vietnam by former Secretary of Defense Robert S. McNamara. Much of this fence—the part that was constructed—is airborne and involves the Mohawk.

The sensors, as small as portable radios, have been strategically placed along the DMZ and across Laos to the Ho Chi Minh trail. Many of these acoustic listening devices were dropped by parachute from aircraft. The USAF alone dropped more than six hundred of them. The sensors pick up enemy movements and transmit them to receivers which then tape the data. Computers analyze the tapes to determine the timing and magnitude of the movements.

The Mohawk with a two-man crew—a pilot and a sensor operator—circles overhead and receives the signals from the black boxes seeded along the ground. Officials say that this procedure was very effective at Khe Sanh where some six thousand Marines and South Vietnamese Rangers were besieged by more than twenty thousand North Vietnamese troops. More than six hundred sensing devices—electronic, acoustic, pressure, and other—reported a total of almost eighteen hundred enemy troop movements in the area and two-thirds of these reports were accurate enough to provide target data for bombing raids. One enemy division at Khe Sanh was so badly battered by American aircraft that it had to be ordered back into Laos for regrouping.

The data gathered by the Mohawks from the black boxes on the ground and the equipment in the aircraft was particularly valuable after the bombing halt in the fall of 1968 and the start of the peace talks in Paris. President Johnson was able to report, for instance, that there was a marked rise in enemy infiltration immediately after the bombing halt, contrary to the agreement made with North Vietnam, and this information was given to the American peace negotiators in Paris to use. It is small wonder that the North Vietnamese gunners, in violation of the terms of the bombing halt agreement, tried to shoot down all U.S. reconnaissance planes that overflew the DMZ to check on infiltration routes. Hanoi is well aware that the Mohawks, the O-1, the O-2, and the whirlybirds may be relatively small aircraft in the American air armada but they have eyes that see everything and electronic ears that hear everything.

13

U.S. Navy Air Intelligence in S.E.A.

ON DECEMBER 3, 1968, Lieutenant Commander Thomas Sullivan, flying a Navy RA5C Vigilante reconnaissance plane from the deck of the carrier *Ranger*, went north to check on enemy infiltration activities. He had no bombs aboard or other armament. His mission was to check on the North Vietnamese compliance with the stipulation contained in the bombing halt agreement approved by President Johnson that there would be no stepped-up infiltration of enemy troops into South Vietnam. Reconnaissance aircraft of the U.S. Navy and Air Force were the only means of verifying the response of the North Vietnamese to the agreement.

As Sullivan and his navigator, Lieutenant (jg) Richard Affeld, crossed the shoreline and headed inland, Affeld spotted a warning on his electronic gear that indicated a Russian-made SAM had been fired at their aircraft. He notified the pilot immediately and Sullivan began evasive action, hoping that he could avoid the telephone-sized missile.

"I heard a muffled noise," Sullivan said later, "and the controls jerked in my hands."

The missile had exploded near the Vigilante reconnaissance

plane and fragments from it slashed fifteen holes in the jet's fuselage. Fortunately, neither crewman was injured and Sullivan was able to fly the damaged aircraft back to the *Ranger* and make a successful landing. The near-fatal incident, occurring during a halt in the air fighting, is clearly indicative of the dangers faced by the U.S. Navy reconnaissance crews on their missions and once again emphasizes the importance the enemy places on aerial reconnaissance.

Sullivan's mission from the deck of the *Ranger* indicates one advantage the U.S. Navy has over the Army and Air Force. The carrier was positioned much closer to the enemy target that was to be photographed and thus the pilot's time over enemy territory and exposure to the ground and air defenses of North Vietnam was reduced. Despite heavy damage, Sullivan was able to fly his plane back to the floating base successfully since the distance was much less than it would have been to return to an airbase in South Vietnam. For limited war in a remote area of the world such as Vietnam the appropriate Navy weapon is the carrier task force, with its ability to deploy a mobile strike force over two thirds of the earth's surface independent of the need for land bases and not hampered by restrictions imposed by local governments on such land bases. Yet, for several reasons, successful use of this force required a new concept in U.S. Navy tactical intelligence support.

A great improvement in force mobility since World War II had been made possible by new developments in aircraft and armament. These new developments, to be successful, required that the tactical commander have accurate intelligence information covering a much larger area of terrain. They also greatly shortened the time available to him for planning his operations. Thus he had to have more information than previously and he had to have it faster. Unfortunately, during the decade after World War II the advances in intelligence technique and hardware development were devoted almost entirely to the support of centralized strategic operations. These developments did not meet the intelligence needs for the tactical operations required in wars such as the Vietnam War.

What was needed was a system integral to the carrier task force—a system capable of frequent collection of detailed information on the enemy forces and their disposition within the entire area of tactical interest, rapid processing and analysis of this information, and a method of so displaying the finished intelligence that effective command decisions and strike planning could be carried out. The need was for a system that could provide "today's intelligence today" on a continuing basis. It also had to be a system that was capable of accepting and utilizing intelligence from sources other than its own collection system.

The concept that was finally developed by the Navy is called the Integrated Operational Intelligence System. Originally this program involved the development of a multisensor reconnaissance system and the modification of the A5A aircraft to carry it, as well as the development of an associated carrier-based intelligence processing center, known officially as the Integrated Operational Intelligence Center (IOIC).

Although other multisensor aircraft can also be used in the system, the RA5C Vigilante is the major modification of the A5A used in the new concept. Built by North American Aviation, the Vigilante has a wingspan of 50 feet, is 70 feet in length, and stands 20 feet high. Using two J-79 turbojet engines, each producing 10,900 pounds of thrust without afterburner and 17,000 pounds with afterburner, the RA5C has a speed of more than twice the speed of sound. Added fuel capacity increases its internal fuel to 24,000 pounds. The Vigilante uses an externally mounted "canoe" to carry its reconnaissance sensors. It is equipped with the AN/ASB-12 Bomb/Nav System that includes an inertial reference platform, and with a digital data system that imprints a code matrix block giving location, time, altitude, and other useful parameters on all image-forming sensors. The crew consists of a pilot and a reconnaissance attack navigator who manages the radar, inertial navigator, television, viewfinder, and all reconnaissance sensors.

The reconnaissance system includes a forward firing camera, an azimuth-stabilized vertical camera, and any of three different modules of 1¾-, 3-, 6-, or 12-inch focal-length serial frame cameras at various angles of obliquity. In addition it can carry 3-inch focal-length or 18-inch focal-length panoramic cameras. Mounted aft in the canoe is the side-looking radar, which can be operated at any altitude with selective ranges of three, six, or twenty miles or extended ranges of twenty to thirty and thirty to forty miles on either side of the plane. All of the Vigilantes are equipped to use passive ECM equipment which mounts in the bomb bay in place of the forward fuel can. Antennas for this system are mounted virtually over the entire fuselage area of the aircraft. This system is a multiband passive electronic detection and recording set. In addition to the electronic fingerprints, navigation data from the autonavigator is recorded on the magnetic tape, providing, after ground processing, accurate emitter locations.

On the inboard wing stations electronic flasher units can be installed, giving the aircraft a night photographic capability. These flasher units are powered by airstream-driven generators. Some of the Vigilantes are also equipped with an infrared mapping sensor.

Almost all of the reconnaissance missions flown over North Vietnam in the Vigilantes are launched from Yankee Station, a rolling, quadrangular expanse of blue-green water that lies mostly north of the 17th parallel, where the South China Sea joins the Gulf of Tonkin. Ships of the U.S. Seventh Fleet's Task Force 77 operate around the clock from this area, the RA5Cs using the decks of the carriers for takeoff and landing. Each mission requires approximately six hours of preflight planning by the crew to optimize the photocoverage while minimizing the exposure. The Vigilante's best defense is speed and luckily it has this in abundance since it is the fastest aircraft in combat configuration being catapulted by the Navy.

During a symposium conducted by the Department of the Navy in Los Angeles, California, the following report was made on combat missions flown in Southeast Asia by RA5C pilots who had just recently returned to the U.S.:

One of the great advantages of the Vigilante over other reconnaissance aircraft in combat is the reconnaissance attack navigator. His ability permits low level, low visibility approaches over the Gulf of Tonkin with accurate land falls. In "backdoor" approaches the wooded mountains that all look similar to the eyeball can easily be identified on the navigator's radar. During the photo run the pilot can keep his head out of the cockpit making last minute corrections and looking for flak and missiles without having to worry about camera switches or altitude and air speed changes on film drive. The navigator, undistracted by the scenery and flak, using his radar, inertial navigator, viewfinder, television, and large scale charts, can call the turns and correct the headings to give good camera coverage on targets which are not identifiable by the pilot. It's always a mistake to make more than one run on a target but it's a great temptation when you've missed it the first pass and you know you're going to have to face your buddies on the ship. With the Vigilante's accurate navigation this temptation is rarely felt.

The reliability, flexibility, versatility and high resolution of the cameras are other combat advantages of the RA5C. This flexibility allows having a "back up" camera on the rare occasions of camera failure. The horizon to horizon coverage afforded by the panoramic cameras can be "backed up" by trimetrogon aerial frame cameras, or vice versa. The high resolution of the cameras, permitting 20 times magnification of the image without appreciable deterioration, allows the pilot substantial stand-off distance from heavily defended areas. Oblique coverage from two or three miles at low altitudes or from longer distances at high altitudes usually gives adequate photo interpretation results.

One of the greatest threats to our airmen in North Vietnam is the mobility of the SA-2 missile sights. On several occasions photographs have been obtained of SAM installations cleverly concealed in an orchard, for example. This picture is of little worth if the location of the orchard cannot be determined. Imprinted on every frame of the RA5C photography is the latitude and longitude to the nearest tenth of a minute. No other operational Navy reconnaissance aircraft before the Vigilante had this feature.

Nearly all Navy pilots are enthusiastic about the RA5C aircraft and its capabilities. It is a large carrier aircraft but it does not require any more wind over the deck than other current swept-wing jets and can be flown aboard safely by an average carrier pilot. It is operated exclusively from its parent carrier in Southeast Asia. Landings are simplified for the pilots by the inclusion of an approach-power compensator, a device that automatically changes power to maintain a constant angle of attack as the aircraft heads for the deck. Since the RA5C went into operation it has flown from the supercarriers *Enterprise, Kitty Hawk, Constellation, Ranger, America, Saratoga,* and *Forrestal.*

Once the Vigilante pilot arrives back on the carrier deck with the sensory records the personnel of the Integrated Operational Intelligence Center take over. This center is divided into four main functional areas: the photo processing area, the electronic data processing area, the storage and retrieval area, and the multisensor interpretation area. In addition to these areas an Air Intelligence Office and Mission Briefing spaces are provided. The inputs to this system consist of intelligence material collected by the RA5C and other reconnaissance aircraft as well as those materials sent to the carrier by the Fleet Intelligence Center and national agencies. The major input is information that updates the present information stored in the system or what is called the Intelligence Data Base.

Upon receipt of the reconnaissance records in the IOIC, the film magazines are passed into the darkroom for development and the airborne tapes containing the passive electronic countermeasure data are loaded on the magnetic tape processors. The electronic countermeasures evaluator (ECM), who is located in the multisensor interpretation area, has several options as to how he can have the airborne tapes processed. Prescribed points or areas may be examined in a specified order, all emitters of a certain type may be examined first, or the tape for the entire mission may be processed without any priorities being established. The output consists of a teletype report listing emitter characteristics and locations along with a map overlay of emitter locations plotted on the digital plotter with symbols indicating the type of emitter at each location. Thus, an update of the electronic order of battle is performed. Any new emitter locations can be given to the photo interpreters and the photocoverage examined to confirm emitter location and determine the site characteristics.

The multisensor interpretation area also contains viewers for the interpretation of roll-film transparencies and film cards. Each viewer provides two channels of rear projection viewing as well as stereoscopic direct viewing. Coded flight data on the film is automatically read and displayed within the viewer. The viewer communicates with a general purpose digital computer for the on-line solution of geographic location and mensuration programs. Multisensor data comparison analysis is performed by one or two operators simultaneously on a single viewer. Each viewing station is supported by a digital plotter for outputting sketch plots, map overlays, and map substitutes. In addition, a teletype is provided for report generation and computer communications.

The storage and retrieval area, while not a direct segment of the multisensor interpretation function, provides the key to what intelligence is held on board and facilitates a comparison of new data with previously collected data of the same area. The basic intelligence files of the ship are placed on electronic accounting machine cards, microfilm, and miniature transparencies, all of which are kept updated. The index file for this information and the order of battle information is also stored on magnetic tape for rapid retrieval of data.

The U.S. aircraft carrier, home base for the majority of Navy reconnaissance aircraft operating over North Vietnam today, is a modern fighting machine without parallel. The carrier *Constellation,* which operated in the South China Sea, has a squadron of RA5C aircraft that uses its 4½-acre flight deck for takeoffs and landings night and day. A night launch is more spectacular—and dangerous. A Vigilante taxies into position in the darkness and is quickly buckled to the waist catapult. The catapult crew checks closely to make certain that the wire-rope bridle connecting the RA5C to the takeoff shoe is tight and that the holdback cable, with its sheerable link, has a high strain on it. The pilot revs up the engines until he is certain he has the proper thrust for takeoff and then, at a signal from the catapult launch officer, the Vigilante is hurled skyward. With its afterburners cut in, the reconnaissance plane leaves the deck in a cloud of steam from the catapult with only the twin tailpipes gleaming in the darkness to mark its course. After that, the reconnaissance pilot and his navigator are on their own.

"It's not like a practice run that takes place a hundred miles out in the desert," a Vigilante pilot on the *Constellation* remarked. "You go out in your plane and you are expected to bring the results home with you in the camera cassette or on the magnetic tape regardless of the flak, SAMs, or fighters. When you get back you lay out the pictures for the entire squadron to see and they had better be good. Our mission is to gather the data and return it to the decision makers."

While the Integrated Operational Intelligence Center on board ship handles the reconnaissance data brought back by the aircraft, many of the decisions concerning the conduct of the Vietnam War are made in Washington. Satellite communications between Vietnam and Washington permit close to real-time contact between individuals in the two countries. It is no secret that before many of the targets photographed by the reconnaissance planes of the Navy can be bombed, high officials in the Pentagon and even the President of the United States must examine the pictures and study the intelligence data. No longer does the overall commander in the combat theater make the important decisions. These are made by the Pentagon and the White House. The organization that provides much of the data to the military and to the President of the United States is the Naval Reconnaissance and Technical Support Center, located along Suitland Road in Washington, D.C.

Much of the work accomplished by this organization is secret but its stated mission is

> . . . to maintain and operate facilities to provide image interpretation support to the Secretary of the Navy, Chief of Naval Operations, and Defense Intelligence Agency; provide image derived information in support of the National Tasking Plan for the exploitation of multisensor imagery; provide miniaturized and automated intelligence data bases and intelligence production support to the operating forces of the Navy; provide targeting intelligence support to the Chief of Naval Operations, Commander, Naval Intelligence Command, Navy planning Staffs, and Fleet Commanders; conduct research, development, test, and evaluation of image exploitation equipment, materials, and techniques.

All master data recorded in the Integrated Operational Intelligence System on board a carrier can be quickly utilized by the equipment at the Naval Reconnaissance and Technical Support Center and distributed to high-level officials within a matter of hours.

The Special Projects Department of the center accomplishes such unusual projects and programs of an intelligence nature as may be assigned it. It has a Special Analysis Division which prepares reports, studies, and briefs from the multisensor reconnaissance collections on foreign naval-weapons components and systems, while the General Analysis Branch prepares photographic intelligence reports and briefs of naval military subjects. One of the most vital units of the Special Projects Department is the Naval Analysis Division, which provides photographic intelligence briefs, detailed reports and studies on items of naval interest to include all missiles and weapons and related support facilities, aircraft, and airfields related to naval operations and capabilities, and on other installations of interest to the U.S. Navy. The Target Division and Target Analysis Branch uses the multisensor data gathered by the RA5C and other reconnaissance aircraft and transfers it into graphic and textual form for further study. The Photographic Branch accomplishes the highly specialized photographic reproduction required, an important factor in the Vietnam War.

Another U.S. Navy organization that is of utmost importance to the efficient conduct of naval reconnaissance in Southeast Asia is the Naval Air Technical Training Unit at the Naval Air Station, Pensacola, Florida, where the highly skilled photographic technicians are schooled. Courses such as applied sensitometry and lab techniques, photographic reconnaissance, camera repair, aerial photography, and color photography develop the personnel needed to man the Integrated Operational Intelligence Systems and the Naval Reconnaissance and Technical Support Center. The four-week photographic reconnaissance course for Navy pilots and navigators trains these officers to take the aerial reconnaissance photographs vital to military intelligence. Using realistic mockup trainers, the crews who will later be flying RA5C planes over North Vietnam plan and fly simulated combat reconnaissance missions. By the time they graduate these naval airmen have a sound background for the tour of duty they will perform in the combat zone.

It isn't easy and all the reconnaissance planes don't return to the decks of the carriers from which they took off. Lieutenant Commander Harvey A. Eikel was one pilot who didn't make it back. Eikel was on a reconnaissance mission near Vinh, North Vietnam, when an accurate barrage of antiaircraft fire turned his aircraft into a fireball and he had to eject. Unfortunately he landed in the midst of the enemy gun positions and within minutes after discarding his parachute, Eikel was surrounded by enemy soldiers. Trapped inside a 100-foot-diameter ring, the pilot set his radio on the emergency frequency and fired a smoke grenade. For the next hour he dodged the North Vietnamese soldiers. Despite a solid wall of flak bursts, a helicopter piloted by Lieutenants (jg) Jeff Wiant and Paskell January hovered over the downed reconnaissance pilot long enough to lower a hoist. Eikel strapped himself into the hoist and was pulled aboard while enemy riflemen, machine gunners, and antiaircraft crews fired at the helicopter as it struggled aloft. The photographs were lost but Lieutenant Commander Eikel was saved to fly another day.

Lieutenant Norman Green, flying off the carrier USS *Franklin D. Roosevelt*, was more fortunate. Green was piloting an RF-8 reconnaissance aircraft when he made a near-fatal error—he decided to get just one more target. The RF-8 is a single-seat aircraft powered by a J-57 turbojet. It has a wingspan of 35 feet, is 54 feet long, nearly 16 feet high, and can reach a maximum speed of 1,300 mph at 40,000 feet. It is not so powerful or well-equipped as the Vigilante for reconnaissance but it was used much earlier in the Vietnam War. There is little doubt about the ruggedness of the RF-8. Green's experience over North Vietnam was proof of the plane's ability to keep flying despite suffering serious damage.

"We had been up by Haiphong looking for shipping," the lieutenant said. "We had swung north and were coming south with the idea of heading toward the sea in case anything should happen. We had drawn some fire but we were pretty much out of range. But down below was one more target which we knew we were going to have to get sooner or later so I swung my jet over it."

Green suddenly felt his plane jolt but it was so slight he couldn't tell whether he had taken a flak hit or not.

"I was doing a little over 600 knots and I thought maybe something had just come off. At that speed this can give you a jolt."

Another pilot eased in close to the lieutenant's plane, however, and radioed an assessment of the damage that had occurred from ground fire.

"You have a piece of the wing missing and there is a hole in your afterburner section."

Green slowed down for a straight-in approach to the deck of the carrier. The plane was unstable but still controllable. He hit the deck, the cables grabbed the crippled plane and yanked it from 150 mph to a dead stop in two seconds. When the lieutenant climbed from the cockpit he saw that the trailing edge of the left wing was a jagged mess with about 10 inches of it missing. The aileron was missing entirely. The hole in the afterburner was not serious but the bullet that made the hole had missed the main part of the engine only by inches. The film, however, was intact.

One of the outstanding escapes of the Vietnam War was accomplished by a Navy reconnaissance pilot of Light Photographic Squadron 63 flying from the carrier *Kitty Hawk*. Lietutenant Charles F. Klusmann was the first Navy pilot to fly a reconnaissance mission over Laos and on that early mission he had encountered heavy flak and his RF-8 Crusader jet had been set afire. Yet he had brought the flaming reconnaissance plane back to the carrier successfully.

"I thought that if I had managed to survive that," Klusmann said, "I could get through anything. I was wrong."

A month later, while on another reconnaissance mission over Laos, the lieutenant encountered scattered clouds and poor visibility so he dropped down to treetop level. Over Muong Soui on the Plaine des Jarres he made a photo run of approximately 1,500 feet at this low level then started a climb to a safer altitude. At that moment enemy gunners on the ground opened fire on his jet.

"I couldn't see any of the usual 37-mm stuff but I could see tracers from the .50-caliber coming by my wind screen. I was not too surprised. After all, I didn't expect them to throw rose petals at me. I figured that with my speed and everything, my chances were pretty good for getting through it okay."

A few minutes later, however, a .50-caliber shell hit the metal skin on the Crusader's wing directly over the fuel tank and peeled it back. He immediately began to lose fuel. Klusmann tried to break right and discovered that his controls were very sluggish. Glancing at the instrument panel he saw that his power-system pressure was dropping fast. At the same time he felt a violent jolt and realized that his left landing gear had fallen into the airstream. With the jet nearly uncontrollable, the lieutenant ejected.

Klusmann landed in a treetop, bounced out of it, and tumbled 20 feet to the ground, twisting his ankle and right knee. After shedding his parachute, he half-crawled, half-walked to the top of a nearby hill and tried to signal other American planes circling overhead. He was still trying to guide a rescue helicopter to his position twenty minutes later when a force of Pathet Lao Communist troops emerged from a clump of bushes and took him prisoner. In the pattern of the Vietnam War, that should have been the last heard from Klusmann except for an occasional letter home from the prison camp.

Reconnaissance pilots, accustomed to being alone and fending for themselves in the air and on the ground, don't give up so easily. Every day for two months the lieutenant paced back and forth across his cell three hundred times, strengthening his injured leg for the escape he planned to make at the first opportunity. His next step was to make friends with the Communist guards. Using sign language and motions, he slowly won them over—so completely that they relaxed their vigilance over him. That was a mistake. Three months after he was captured, the Navy pilot and several Laotians crawled under the wire surrounding the prison camp and disappeared into the jungle. Two days later Klusmann joined a group of anti-Communist Meo tribesmen who inhabit the highland jungles of Laos. Military forces were notified and that same afternoon a light plane landed on a clearing in the jungle and picked up the determined reconnaissance flier. He is one of the few Americans ever to escape from a Red prison camp.

Flying out of Tan Son Nhut airport is another type of Navy reconnaissance plane which keeps a close watch on enemy shipping. This is the P2V, a Lockheed Harpoon which was first delivered to the Navy in 1944. In the desolate wastes of the Pacific during World War II the Harpoon proved that long-range patrol aircraft could extend the ears and eyes of the fleet. Later, a specially modified version of the P2V, the Truculent Turtle, set a world's distance record for straight-line flight in 1946 by flying nonstop from Perth, Australia, to Columbus, Ohio, a distance of more than eleven thousand miles. In Southeast Asia pilots such as Commander Charles M. Walker use the P2V for "rigging" missions, flights during which the patrol plane is flown at altitudes approximately as high as the rigging on old-time schooners. Walker lets down until his aircraft is about 50 feet above the ocean and visually checks and photographs all suspicious-looking ships. The P2V is designed mainly for antisubmarine warfare but has cameras mounted both fore and aft.

The technique is to get down low enough to have the ship's superstructure silhouetted against the horizon for pictures and to check other details visually. These include descriptions of masts, radar antennas, hull shape, waterline indication of cargo, name, nationality, speed, direction, and any cargo visible on the deck. This usually takes several flybys by the patrol plane.

"Eight passes is not unusual," Walker says. "Until we determine the nationality of the ship we must be careful that we are not fired upon. For instance, when we spotted a Communist Chinese ship named *Heping* we gave the vessel a very close scrutiny and took quite a few pictures. It had eighteen or twenty oblong objects on deck and we finally decided that they might be antiaircraft missiles for the 8-inch gun on the ship's bow. You can't be too careful."

The ten-man crew on the P2V carries a reference work on the aircraft with which they can identify nearly any sizable ship in the world belonging to any country. In addition, the data gathered by the crew's visual check of the ship is immediately radioed to the task force authorities where a more detailed check is made on the ship if required. Also, orders from the task force commander to the aircraft in flight often change the mission. Shortly after Walker spotted and checked the *Heping*, he was ordered to look over an island where the Vietcong were reported about to attack a hamlet. The P2V had already been in the air about six hours but its fuel supply of 3,100 gallons at takeoff time permitted the extra reconnaissance of the island. Over Phu Quoc Island, Walker located the fishing village of Ham Ninh and circled it carefully.

"A .50-caliber machine gun can shoot about 15,000 yards," Walker explained. "Our plane carries no armament—only cameras and smoke flares—so we have to try and avoid enemy ground fire if possible."

The commander and his crew patrolled over the island until late afternoon when a U.S. minesweeper arrived in the area. By that time Walker's fuel was getting low and he turned back toward Tan Son Nhut airfield at Saigon, performing normal reconnaissance on the route home. Walker landed the P2V back at base after being in the air eleven and a half hours and having flown the aircraft all that time by "hand" without the help of an automatic pilot. It had been a normal reconnaissance mission for him, one that is repeated day and night by other Navy crews and other P2Vs in Southeast Asia as they keep close watch on shipping in the South China Sea off Vietnam.

Another Navy aircraft used in the reconnaissance role in Southeast Asia is the A4 Skyhawk. This Douglas-built lightweight bomber is the smallest operational plane in the Navy's arsenal and one of the most versatile. Weighing only 8,300 pounds, it has a wingspan of 27½ feet and a length of approximately 43 feet. It is powered by a single J-52 turbojet and can reach a maximum of 685 mph. This relatively slow airspeed makes it a fine aircraft for aerial spotting of shells fired by the destroyers in the Gulf of Tonkin or other areas of the South

China Sea. It is fast enough to take effective evasive action when under fire from the ground yet slow enough to observe where the shells from the offshore ships are hitting in enemy territory. When the destroyer USS *Lofberg* was assigned the task of sealing the Vietcong caves in the Dong Nhut area with its six 5-inch guns, Lieutenant Donald Trimble was the aerial spotter. Dong Nhut Mountain was honeycombed with Vietcong caves and tunnels that the enemy used as storage areas, hiding places for troops, and infiltration routes to the sea. From these caves and tunnels the Vietcong also regularly mortared the village of Phu Loc and shelled a nearby Vietnamese naval junk base.

Although the caves opened out to the sea, they were still a difficult target for the gunners aboard the *Lofberg*.

"Those caves took pinpoint accuracy," Trimble said. "The shells had to be right on the money."

Since it was impossible for gunners on the ship to sight on the target visually, Trimble circled near the target area in his spotter plane and relayed the coordinates of the bursts as they hit the ground and called in the necessary corrections. On board the *Lofberg*, Lieutenant Hal Manicke, received the radio calls from the reconnaissance pilot and translated them into firing data. This data was then fed into a computer which took over from that point.

"There were several direct hits," Trimble explained. "One shell went right into a cave, dead center. The caves and tunnels on the mountain were sealed tight by the time the *Lofberg* quit firing."

When the only U.S. battleship in the combat area, the *New Jersey*, arrived in the South China Sea and began bombarding North Vietnamese targets with her 16-inch guns, the A4 Skyhawk was the aircraft used for aerial spotting for its gunners, too. The *New Jersey* fired twenty-nine rounds from the 16-inch guns, each weighing 2,700 pounds, and forty-five rounds from her 5-inch secondary battery on her first foray on October 1,

1968. The targets were enemy installations—four automatic weapons positions and one artillery emplacement—in the DMZ which formerly would have been attacked by jet aircraft. Spotting throughout this initial operation for the huge battleship were Marine Lieutenant Patrick Orrocco, the observer, and Marine Major John Clark, the pilot. They kept their A4 Skyhawk within visual range of the targets which were twelve miles inland and corrected the fire from the *New Jersey*'s guns.

"After the first five rounds," Orrocco said, "I told them to scratch the target. It just didn't exist any more."

The aerial spotting crew helped the battleship destroy each of the targets in the DMZ in turn during this first operation of the reactivated battleship and helped justify the $50,000,000 experiment. Some critics of the use of the *New Jersey* in the Vietnam War had claimed that her guns were too large and targets too few to justify the cost of maintaining the battleship and its crew of 1,400. They had insisted that the 16-inch guns could not be trained on a target as small as a camouflaged automatic weapons position but Orrocco and Clark in the A4 Skyhawk disproved this theory. With the aerial reconnaissance and spotting technique, the guns of the *New Jersey* can concentrate on any target the jet fighter-bombers can bomb or strafe if the target is within range of the ship's weapons.

Rear Admiral Sam Moore, commander of the surface vessels in the Seventh Fleet, pointed out the advantage of hitting targets in the DMZ and deeper into North Vietnam with the guns of the *New Jersey* directed by aerial reconnaissance aircraft.

"We can reach out and hit them without endangering striking aircraft," said Moore. "We can also use the 16-inch guns against targets that might be invulnerable to Allied bombers. These guns can penetrate 30 feet of reinforced concrete."

It appears that the combination of the Navy's largest ship and smallest operational aircraft is one more potent weapon for use against the enemy in Southeast Asia.

Another technique was developed to help the *New Jersey's*

gunnery at night. A low-light television camera is mounted on a drone (pilotless) helicopter and the drone is flown over the target area by remote control. During the initial weeks of operation a large number of trucks and sampans were destroyed during the night before the North Vietnamese and Vietcong realized that the appearance of the helicopter was the prelude to highly accurate gunfire from the battleship. The television camera carried on the drone can pick up a truck from a distance of three miles under overcast starlight conditions, which is defined in the military as two orders of magnitude less illumination than quarter-moon. Under these conditions, the camera operator at a remote station can positively identify the truck at a range of one mile. The use of the television camera and the pilotless helicopter, both remotely controlled, has increased greatly the effectiveness of the *New Jersey*'s guns at night and is another step forward in the continuing development of unmanned reconnaissance vehicles.

Every day a strange-looking aircraft with what appears to be a huge white pancake over its fuselage takes off from the deck of a carrier in the South China Sea and turns toward enemy territory. This is a Willy Fudd, nicknamed for its old initials W2F1, a carrier early-warning plane. Officially known as the E-1B Tracer, the Willy Fudd is a Grumman-built twin-engine aircraft powered by two 1,525-horsepower engines with a maximum speed of 265 mph. It has a wingspan of 72 feet, a length of 45 feet, and stands nearly 17 feet high on a carrier deck. The E-1B carries radar to detect surface vessels and high- and low-flying aircraft and extensive operational electronic gear for all-weather operation. The pancake extending horizontally above the fuselage is an oval radome 32 feet by 20 feet that houses a 17.5-foot antenna which sweeps at six rpm; two of the four crew members monitor identical 10-inch screens. For airborne early warning operations, the second pilot takes on the job of tactical director.

Even though they carry no weapons themselves, these electronic reconnaissance planes have a great deal of firepower to back them up. Teamed with the F-4B Phantom II or other first-line fighters, the Fudd provides a distant shield for the entire task force. Detection of hostile aircraft by the black boxes on the E-1B and destruction by the fighter's guided missiles is a powerful punch of the Navy's fleet in Southeast Asia. In many cases the fighter-interceptor of the Vietnam War never sees his enemy with the naked eye. The days of colorful "dogfighting" are now left to the pages of history.

Strike control is another mission performed by the Fudd. Controllers on the plane can vector the attack aircraft to any target, regardless of cloud cover or weather conditions and can scan the target area for enemy air resistance. Amazingly accurate results have been amassed in attack operations in Southeast Asia by Fudd controllers. Then when the mission is accomplished, the Fudd controller can guide the strike planes back to the carrier. In addition, by utilizing a system named Bellhop the E-1B can relay its own radar presentation to the ship's radarscope and thus provide a more complete picture for the vessel's CIC. Under a similar system called Autocraft, the Fudd can relay messages automatically between ships of the task force and other aircraft.

Fudds also carry out weather-reconnaissance missions for the task force. By utilizing its radar it can easily pick out storm fronts and vector the surface units to a safer operating place. The crew also carries the KE-28 camera for taking aerial photographs of surface vessels or aircraft operating in the vicinity of the task force. For the first time in the history of aerial warfare, electronic reconnaissance in Southeast Asia is as important as any other type of reconnaissance system in the combat theater.

The modern reconnaissance systems used by the U.S. Navy in Southeast Asia are providing experience for the airmen and technicians that is invaluable. While the U.S. surface vessels are not coming under attack by Red ships or enemy aircraft, the

Seventh Fleet task force must constantly guard against such an eventuality, and the electronic and photographic reconnaissance planes know the minute an unknown aircraft, ship, or submarine turns toward the American fleet and alert the CIC. This mission, too, is sharpening the skills of the reconnaissance pilots, crewmen, and technicians, preparing them for other trouble spots that may later require similar action. The U.S. Navy today has a mobile reconnaissance force that is unequaled by that of any other country in the world.

14

U.S. Air Force Reconnaissance in Vietnam

TWENTY-ONE-year-old A2C Richard Cox stared at a film that two more experienced photo interpreters of the 13th Reconnaissance Technical Squadron had discarded as worthless. Idly picking up the film, the young airman began scanning it under his magnifying glass. He really didn't expect to find anything important on the film which a reconnaissance plane had delivered a few hours earlier but he wanted the practice. Suddenly, however, he stared at six clumps of underbrush. For some reason those clumps appeared different from the rest of the underbrush. They were very similar to one another, all the same shape and height and thickness. Calling to his supervisor, he asked the veteran photo interpreter to take a look. After a few minutes of study the two men agreed that the bushes looked strange and that they should be investigated. The following day American fighter-bombers attacked the "bushes" and knocked out a radar van and five Soviet-built surface-to-air missile launchers.

The camouflaged SAM site that Cox had discovered on the reconnaissance film was less than ten miles from the DMZ, the farthest south these weapons had been located. From that vantage point the missiles were a definite threat to the B-52s that regularly bombed enemy troop concentrations in the area.

Cox's discovery was a rare dramatic payoff for thousands of hours of drudgery spent by the photo interpreters of the 13th Reconnaissance Technical Squadron based at Tan Son Nhut air base, Saigon, South Vietnam. He and the other airmen of the unit study an average of three million feet of film a month furnished them by the RF-4C Phantoms and RF-101 Voodoos of the 460th Tactical Reconnaissance Wing, the aerial workhorses of the USAF in the Vietnam War. In Thailand at the Udorn Royal Thai Air Force Base, the 432d Reconnaissance Technical Squadron technicians process nearly another million feet of film a month. Aerial reconnaissance is vital to the USAF fighter-bombers for various reasons. It tells the commanders where the enemy is and how he is applying his forces. Photos tell whether an air strike has been successful or if a restrike is necessary. Pictures are also given to the strike crews so they will know what the target looks like visually. Without reconnaissance the USAF would be "blind" in Vietnam.

Time is a primary consideration for the photo technicians of the 13th and 432d recce tech squadrons. No mistakes can be made and there are no second chances. Each photo and each frame may contain vital information. Therefore all prints are given high priority status and no film can be in the lab for more than twenty-four hours. All the results must be sent to higher headquarters in high-speed air couriers. This puts a lot of pressure on the processing and printing crews who often work around the clock. Aerial reconnaissance never stops and neither does the job of the processing lab. An average of thirty-seven recon missions are flown daily at Udorn, for instance, and it takes an average of ten hours per mission to complete the entire lab process.

In the case of a top priority mission, however, the results must be reported to higher headquarters in less than six hours. This type of mission demands a well-coordinated team effort if the deadline is to be met. Consequently, when a priority mission comes in, everything else stops. The film is pulled quickly from the plane. Minutes later it is weighed to determine the amount of footage, then rushed through the processing equipment at the rate of 14 to 18 feet per minute. Skilled photo interpreters get the film next. They carefully scan the footage for changes in enemy defenses. These highly trained technicians, such as Cox, working with white gloves, slide rules, and magnifying glasses, can spot an unusual change in the terrain within minutes, small differences that the untrained eye would skip over as unimportant.

The frames, keyed to the aircraft's flight, are then titled to identify the mission and immediate reports are compiled on the targets that were claimed by the reconnaissance pilot. Finally, targets and maps are updated for future missions. Printing the negatives is the next step. Continuous printers speed the film through at 100 feet per minute and where an enlargement of a vital target is required, a technician quickly produces it. Once the prints and film are ready for shipment, distribution by air courier, mail, and communication satellites is started at once.

When U.S. aircraft first bombed the oil-storage facilities near Haiphong and Hanoi in July 1966, President Johnson wanted photographic proof to show the world that the United States planes had not dropped bombs on civilian areas. He wanted it fast. Major Hallett P. Marston was assigned the reconnaissance mission to photograph the target area minutes after the fighter-bombers left the scene and get the film back to base safely. It was a priority mission of the highest level. Marston, a veteran of the low-level reconnaissance missions over Cuba, 101 recon missions during the Korean War, and 78 photo flights earlier over North Vietnam, took his camera-equipped RF-101 Voodoo jet over the Hanoi oil complex before the smoke from the bombing raid had completely cleared. During the initial part of his pass over the target the cockpit cooling system was knocked out by antiaircraft fire. He then decided to climb to high altitude and take the photographs where his lack of a cockpit cooling system would not affect him. As he nosed his Voodoo skyward, however, he discovered that his high-altitude camera had been damaged by the antiaircraft barrage and that it was impossible for him to obtain the necessary photographic proof desired by the White House except at low-level.

Rather than go back to base without the pictures, Marston made a pass over the target area at low level in a cockpit that was nearly as hot as a sauna bath. The Red gunners bracketed his aircraft with ground fire but fortunately the RF-101 didn't receive any additional serious damage and the major was able to get back to friendly territory with his film. The pictures were excellent, so good that once the film was on its way to Washington Marston was flown to Saigon to receive personal congratulations from the then-ambassador, Henry Cabot Lodge. After the photographs were examined by the President and the top military and intelligence officials in the Pentagon, General Earle Wheeler, chairman of the Joint Chiefs of Staff, telephoned Marston in Vietnam and added his thanks. He also awarded the major the Silver Star for the mission. The pictures proved beyond a doubt that the American planes had not bombed civilian areas and once the photographs were shown on television and published in printed media the Communist propaganda efforts to the contrary quieted down considerably.

The RF-101 reconnaissance plane being used in Vietnam is essentially the same aircraft that was used so successfully during the Cuban missile crisis. Flying out of bases in Thailand and South Vietnam, the Voodoos cover all of North Vietnam and any targets designated by 7th Air Force headquarters in South Vietnam, Laos, or Cambodia. Each RF-101 in Vietnam carries six cameras. While the plane is capable of traveling at more than 1,100 mph, most of the picture taking is done at 600 mph or less, thus increasing the effectiveness of enemy ground fire. The majority of the Voodoo pilots agree that the antiaircraft defenses over North Vietnam are heavier than any they encountered during World War II or Korea. One RF-101 pilot, Major James F. Young, a veteran of 18 years of military service, said that the photo run over the Bac Giang railroad and highway bridge twenty-five miles northeast of Hanoi was the roughest reconnaissance mission he had ever flown.

"On one flight over the bridge my plane was hit by antiaircraft," he said. "On another trip I evaded a SAM which had been fired at my plane. The bridge was finally destroyed by the F-105s."

The Voodoo pilots have worked out a number of evasive techniques for use when under heavy antiaircraft fire and when they find themselves in the sights of a SAM or chased by Migs. The Voodoos almost invariably approach their picture targets at altitudes just above the treetops, thus blending with the foliage and becoming difficult for enemy pilots to spot. The antiaircraft gunners don't have the aiming time afforded by high-flying planes, which even at supersonic speeds seem to creep past gunsights. Trees, mountains, and other solid objects at low levels help to confuse the surface-to-air missile radar systems, too. When the pilots spot a Mig on their tail it is their standard procedure to let out the throttle and head for home. Sometimes, however, they will head for the nearest cloud cover and use it for a temporary hiding place.

"Most of us would like to have a gun," Major Jack P. Blomgren said, "but we'd like to have a million dollars, too. That doesn't mean that a gun would really help us, though. We might get involved with the shooting and forget our primary job—taking pictures."

Blomgren was a member of the 460th Reconnaissance Wing during the period when it was commanded by Colonel Edward H. Taylor, known as "Mr. Recce." Under his command this hard-flying wing flew a record of more than thirty thousand sorties over North and South Vietnam in ten months. One of the veteran reconnaissance pilots of World War II, Taylor has served most of his military career since 1942 as a reconnaissance pilot and commander. During the Korean War he served as director of operations for the 67th Tactical Reconnaissance Wing and then was transferred to Headquarters, Far Eastern

Air Force, as director of reconnaissance. While in Vietnam he personally flew the 460th's twenty thousandth reconnaissance mission, one of sixty missions he flew in Southeast Asia. After his return to the U.S. he was appointed director of aerospace vehicles at Headquarters, Air Training Command. During a Southeast Asia Symposium at the Air Force Association Convention in San Francisco in 1967, Taylor was quick to admit that the reconnaissance forces in Vietnam are effective but not perfect.

"The successes," he said, "are due to the men in the cockpit and on the ground who face a job that is costly and gargantuan. The limitations are due mostly to four causes. The first is weather, a real bugaboo. Forward-looking radar is a help but not a perfect one. A second curb is the failure of the equipment. The majority of these are in the 'black boxes.' A third is a requirement for modernization of the equipment. There is a real need for instant intelligence. This calls for a system that can gather the information and transmit it without the aircraft having to return to its home base."

The size of the reconnaissance job was also emphasized by Taylor. He explained that the Seventh Air Force reconnaissance wing had one squadron that produced 4,500,000 feet of "imagery" in one month. He also told of a single Sunday when more than 100,000 square miles were photographed. The results of these missions of the 460th Tactical Reconnaissance Wing are delivered to as many as forty agencies and headquarters, from the Seventh Air Force back to Washington.

"In practice, I tried to have a picture of a pinpoint target, such as a bridge, in the hands of the Seventh Air Force in, basically, forty minutes," he said. "This includes unloading the aircraft, the film processing, interpretation. Dissemination depends on how far you have to deliver. But we need it much faster. We need it when it happens. Instant intelligence."

Taylor also emphasized that the North Vietnam reconnaissance missions were rugged.

"The trips north have been exacting and as our losses and

battle damage indicate, more often than not 'hairy.' After a bombing strike the enemy expects the camera plane and is ready with itchy fingers and beady eyes," he said.

There is no question that flying an unarmed reconnaissance plane over North Vietnam is not the safest thing for a USAF pilot to do. Captain Robert W. Pitts can testify to that fact. He was flying one of two RF-101s on a photo mission over North Vietnam when he received four hits from automatic antiaircraft weapons. He was just 30 miles northeast of Hanoi when his aircraft took the hits from an enemy 85-mm cannon and immediately caught fire.

"I felt the plane get hit," he said, "but I didn't realize how serious it was until my wingman, Major Martin Weissgarber, Jr., radioed and informed me I was on fire. I shut down the left engine and decided to try for the gulf where they would have a better chance of rescuing me.

"Shortly after I shut down my engine, Weissgarber told me the fire was out but my plane was still smoking. I had to recross the valley where I had been hit so I punched my afterburner and headed across the valley at 400 knots. I must have caught them by surprise because they didn't shoot at me on my way back. After I made the Gulf of Tonkin, I noticed my hydraulic system was leaking. This meant that my flaps, gear, and other control surfaces wouldn't work except by manual operation.

"About this time the major rejoined me and made a visual check of the aircraft again. He said the whole underside of the plane and part of the left wing were shot away. After thinking it over I decided to try for Danang anyway. I began a shallow glide and lowered my gear by hand. I lined up with the runway all right but as I touched down on the runway I noticed I had lost directional control. I drifted to the side of the strip and crashed into a radio control shack, leveling it, and continued sliding along on my right wing. I thought the aircraft was going to turn over but it stayed upright, made a 180-degree, gearless ground loop, and stopped."

Pitts suffered several severe sprains but no serious injuries. The film was intact.

Captain Norman P. Huggins took longer to get home from his RF-101 reconnaissance flight near the port city of Haiphong. Just as he began the run, his aircraft was hit by intense automatic-weapons fire. He turned his crippled Voodoo out to sea and ejected, landing in the water about 150 yards from an off-shore island.

"As I hit the water I shed my chute and started swimming for shore. There were several boats in the area," Huggins explained. "Two armed swimmers entered the water and I exchanged shots with them. After I had been in the water about half an hour, a sampan with a machine gun in the bow started for me."

At that moment Captain David P. Westenbarger arrived on the scene with his crew, flying a HU-16 amphibian. Westenbarger had been alerted within minutes after Huggins was shot down. Seven minutes later Westenbarger dropped below the overcast to check the water depth for a possible landing and immediately his plane came under ground fire from the island. The captain spotted the sampan heading for Huggins, and radioed for two A-1E Skyraiders flying cover to attack it. The fighters blew the junk out of the water and Westenbarger set his Hu-16 down in a narrow channel about 500 yards from where Huggins and the two enemy swimmers were still having a pistol duel. Westenbarger taxied his aircraft between Huggins and the swimmers, shielding him from their fire, and A2C James E. Pleiman, a para-rescue specialist, jumped into the water with a rope and swam to Huggins. He helped the weary reconnaissance pilot back to the rescue plane and less than an hour later the Voodoo pilot was at Danang telling his story to intelligence officers.

Another RF-101 reconnaissance pilot, Major Paul P. Curtis, went down over North Vietnam and didn't have time to reach the water before he had to eject. Curtis had been flying above the DMZ on a photo operation when he had a loss of power in his jet engine. As the plane neared the ground he ejected. Curtis, who injured his back during the bail-out, noticed a village in the area and immediately left the crash scene. Hurrying away from the village, he fell 75 feet down a mountainside, snapping off his radio antenna and reducing the range of his emergency signal.

Several rescue planes passed overhead before he was able to make contact with two F-105 pilots returning from a mission. They quickly relayed his position to Detachment 5, 38th Aerospace Rescue and Recovery Squadron, and a rescue helicopter was sent to the scene. Because of the thick foilage in the area, however, the crew of the HH-3 Jolly Green Giant couldn't see Curtis despite the fact that the pilot made numerous wide circles over the scene. Finally, on its final sweep across the area, a crewman spotted an emergency flare fired by the reconnaissance pilot and he was picked up by a hoist cable. Curtis had been on the ground in North Vietnam twenty-seven hours before he was rescued.

Captain Henry ("Bob") Roethle's RF-101 was hit several times by enemy artillery fire as he attempted to obtain bomb-damage photos of a rail complex just outside Hanoi but he refused to turn off the target.

"It was terrifying but I was concentrating so hard to get pictures that I forgot about the flak and everything else," he said. "After the mission was over I had a fantastic sense of job satisfaction. Most of the pilots feel the same way. The more difficult the mission, the better you feel when you return although you don't look forward to going again."

Roethle's mission provided information on dozens of targets not scheduled to be photographed as well as on the bomb damage to the rail complex. It gave strike forces the first real assessment of their results in several days because bad weather had prevented earlier evaluation. The captain was awarded the Silver Star for the reconnaissance mission.

Some of the RF-101 pilots never return to base from North Vietnam. Captain Jack W. Weatherby was one of the reconnaissance pilots who didn't. An account of his last mission, related by his wingman, Major Jerry Lents, gives a crystal-clear picture of the hazards faced by the photo pilots who go north on aerial reconnaissance operations.

"Both Weatherby and myself had flown an early morning 'in country' mission [that is, in South Vietnam] the day Jack was killed. This second mission was ordered by higher headquarters while we were still airborne, an operation to obtain photos to pinpoint the exact location of a surface-to-air missile site northwest of Hanoi. Jack landed from the first mission shortly before I did and immediately volunteered to lead the mission even though he had flown against a SAM site only two days earlier. Naturally, I said I would go with him.

"We planned the flight so as to approach the target at low level, feeling at the time that this was the safest approach. We departed Tan Son Nhut on time and had only flown north a few minutes when Jack lost his UHF radio transmitter. I assumed the lead, made the rendezvous with the tanker, and we both took on a full load of fuel. After departing the tanker, Jack started clicking his microphone button and through a series of questions from me and 'click' answers from him, made it clear that he wished to take over the lead again. He did so and we continued on to the low-level portion of our flight. We had to deviate around a good many thunderstorms en route—typical weather for Vietnam in July—and for a time it seemed doubtful that we would get through. However, we broke out of the clouds and, recognizing our position, descended to the start point of our run roughly forty miles from the target.

"We leveled off at 200 feet and were indicating 600 knots airspeed. I soon saw what looked like a strobe light on the ground and a moment later Jack radioed that he had been hit. These were the first words I had heard from him since his transmitter went out. It was obvious that his radio was operating again. He turned to the left and during the turn I crossed over him to his right wing. I saw a hole on each side of his aircraft in about the midsection of the fuselage. A small amount of fuel was streaming from each side of it. I concluded that the shell had failed to explode on contact and had passed through the airplane. I started to tell him this when I saw small flames come from the hole. I pressed the transmitter button and shouted, 'Jack, you're on fire . . . Get out, get out!'

"Instantly, the aircraft exploded. The entire tail section came off in one piece. The rest of the plane was nothing but a large orange fireball. This tumbled to the ground. The time element from the shell's impact until the explosion was only about fifteen seconds.

"I remained low until I got clear of the hills, then climbed and returned to Saigon, refueling with the tanker en route."

Captain Jack W. Weatherby was posthumously awarded the Air Force Cross for his attempt to photograph the heavily defended SAM site.

Lents, his wingman on the flight, flew more than 250 reconnaissance missions in Vietnam before he returned to the U.S. to a new assigment at the Tactical Air Reconnaissance Center, Shaw AFB, South Carolina.

One of the most outstanding planes to come from the drawing board in many years is the McDonnell Phantom II, which is now being used in Vietnam. The reconnaissance version is the RF-4C. The Phantom is powered by two J79 turbojets and is capable of speeds more than twice the speed of sound. It is approximately 63 feet in length and has a wingspan of 38 feet. Tactical reconnaissance aircraft of the USAF in the past have been limited to a single, usually optical, sensor capability. The RF-4C, in contrast, is more like the Navy's Vigilante in that it incorporates optical, infrared, and electronic sensors necessary to perform reconnaissance missions day or night in any kind of weather. The RF-4C optical system includes cameras of various focal lengths such as the KS-72 in the forward oblique and vertical position; the KA-56A in vertical panoramic position; or combinations of the KS-72 in a three-camera fan, side oblique or split vertical. In addition the Phantom has an integrated sensor control system, automatic in-flight film processing and ejection, and a camera station. The plane also is the first high performance reconnaissance aircraft to have a high frequency (HF) communications system installed. This system extends the communications capabilities of the Phantom beyond the line of sight range limitation normally associated with the ultrahigh frequency (UHF) equipment.

Adding the HF communications transreceiver to the electronics system makes voice communication possible between the aircraft and its home base anywhere within the performance envelope of the Phantom and brings instant intelligence one step closer. Direct reconnaissance sighting can be reported back to base and strike aircraft rapidly deployed, a vital requirement of guerrilla war like that in Vietnam. Other equipment aboard the RF-4C also brings instant intelligence closer: the in-flight film processing capability of all the cameras, a jettisonable cassette for ejection of the film developed in flight, and in-flight data recording on all film frames of such information as date, time, barometric pressure, altitude, latitude, heading, pitch, roll, drift, angle, squadron or detachment number and mission number, all factors that aid the photo interpreter once he gets the film.

The rear cockpit of the RF-4C is filled with the most sophisticated sensors available, including inertial navigation systems, infrared devices, side-looking and forward-looking radar. This equipment is now usually operated by a navigator while earlier in the war a second pilot was used for the job. On the Phantom the side-looking radar is capable of mapping terrain strips on either side of the aircraft ground track with a high degree of resolution under all weather conditions. The forward-looking radar, through its ground mapping modes, provides a checkpoint identification and general radar navigation capability to aid in the penetration to and return from the target area. At high speed the RF-4C must be exactly on target to get usable photographs. There is no room for error. The forward-looking radar also utilizes a terrain following mode which permits operation at very low altitudes over varying terrains at night. The infrared recce system on the Phantom, like the one on the Vigilante, is a scanning mapper used to obtain a thermal map of the area under surveillance in either day or night conditions.

The various optical, infrared, and electronic sensors cross-check each other as the reconnaissance pilots of the 460th and 432d Tactical Reconnaissance Wings watch the enemy around the clock in Vietnam. For example, a Phantom flying an operational reconnaissance mission to check on an enemy factory near Hanoi will bring back photos that show the factory's location and size. The infrared sensor tells the PI whether or not the factory is operating at the present time, while the electronic sensors determine whether the enemy has search, tracking, and guidance radar equipment in the area to protect the factory from air strikes. Once these factors have been determined, the pictures are then distributed to the pilots who are assigned the strike mission.

The RF-4C is used for both high- and low-level reconnaissance missions, day and night. A typical high-altitude reconnaissance flight formula is for the pilot to climb to a cruise altitude of about 34,000 feet, climb to 41,000 feet for the run over the target, allow two minutes for evasive action at normal power settings, climb an additional thousand feet for an eight-minute escape run, and head for home. For low-level reconnaissance he also climbs to the 34,000-foot altitude en route to the target but approximately fifty miles from the target he drops to minimum altitude for the photo run. He then climbs to 42,000 feet on an escape pattern and heads home. Most RF-4C missions into North Vietnam require two tanker refuelings.

For operational purposes North Vietnam has been divided into seven segments by the Military Assistance Command, Vietnam. Each segment is called a Route Package or "Pack." No. 1, also known as Tally Ho, is in the southernmost part of the North Vietnam panhandle and the USAF has the primary responsibility for targets in this area. Packs 2, 3, and 4 going northward are usually covered by the Navy's Crusaders and Vigilantes flying from the carriers based in the Gulf of Tonkin and on Yankee Station. Pack 5 is the bulge of North Vietnam west of Hanoi and USAF reconnaissance planes also keep an aerial watch over this sector. The rough area is Pack 6, which is divided into two parts. Pack 6A includes Hanoi and the surrounding territory and is assigned to the Phantoms and Voodoos of the Air Force. Pack 6B, along the coast from Haiphong to the border of Red China, is under the constant surveillance of the Navy and Marine reconnaissance aircraft.

If a pilot is scheduled for a reconnaissance mission in Pack 6 he is well aware that he will be attempting to penetrate the most threatening area of North Vietnam. When a strike mission is planned for this sector it may consist of up to twenty F-105 jets, eight Phantoms flying escort, several EB-66 radar-jamming planes, and an EC-121 warning plane which reports SAM-site activity and tracks enemy planes for the strike pilots from the moment they take off. The reconnaissance pilot, however, goes to Pack 6 by himself. Originally the Phantom and Voodoo pilots had fighter escort but it was discovered that more escort aircraft were being lost than reconnaissance planes so the escort was withdrawn. Now the RF-4Cs and RF-101 pilots go alone.

Many of the Phantom reconnaissance planes that penetrate North Vietnam and especially the hazardous Pack 6A sector come from the 432d Tactical Reconnaissance Wing based at Udorn Royal Thailand Air Force Base, Thailand. In September 1967 Colonel Victor N. Cabas became the commanding officer of the wing. Cabas is a veteran USAF pilot skilled in the techniques of aerial reconnaissance. He originally enlisted in the Royal Canadian Air Force at the beginning of World War II but transferred to the Army Air Corps after the U.S. entered the conflict. Flying Spitfires and Thunderbolts over North Africa and Europe, he is credited with more than 230 missions and five enemy aircraft shot down. After World War II he became a member of the 363d Tactical Reconnaissance Wing and since that time his chief assignments have been in the aerial reconnaissance field. He is a command pilot with nearly 5,000 hours of military flying time, including more than 1,506 hours of jet time and 368 hours of combat time.

Cabas has two squadrons of RF-4Cs—the 11th and the 14th Tactical Reconnaissance Squadrons—to accomplish the aerial surveillance assignments given to his unit. The pilots assigned to these two squadrons are among the best reconnaissance pilots in the world. They have to be to survive the enemy defenses of Pack 6.

"Where the target might be located determines the amount of anxiety my pilots feel prior to the mission," Cabas said. "If it's deep into the Hanoi sector the butterflies start moving around in a guy's stomach."

RF-4C pilot Major Robert K. Nystrom agrees. "Your mouth gets dry while your'e looking at the mission," he explains, "and all the time you're planning it the tension grows. Once you get into the aircraft the adrenalin starts to flow and you forget about all the anxieties you might have had. Then the last three minutes prior to the target are usually the greatest moments of your life. It's hard to describe."

Lieutenant Colonel Steve Neely, operations officer of the 14th Tactical Reconnaissance Squadron, noted one advantage the reconnaissance pilot has over the strike pilot. "When the fighter-bombers are on their way to the target the North Vietnamese radar is tracking them from the time they make their first tanker rendezvous. The SAM and antiaircraft gun crews are ready and waiting for them. When we go in we keep quiet about it. There is no chatter on the radio and we are either very high or very low which makes the enemy radar have a difficult job to 'paint' us as long as we keep our ECM pods shut off. We're a lot more free-wheeling than the strike pilots.

"The main advantage we have is speed. We aren't loaded down with guns and bombs. We seldom cruise at less than 500 knots and when we leave the target we may get up as high as 900. At that airspeed, if we stay low, no Mig can catch us."

As it has always been, the photo run over the target in Vietnam is the most dangerous time of the mission. The reconnaissance pilot and his navigator are strapped into a hurtling Phantom that must fly a straight line, often for minutes at a time, regardless of the intensity of the ground fire. Fortunately, modern camera and sensor equipment does not need to be level, so the pilots can and do climb and dive in erratic high-G maneuvers to confuse the enemy gunners.

As Neely explained, "A pilot can't do the same thing twice or he is asking for trouble. We're always adding new wrinkles to our tactics in an effort to keep the enemy off balance. But sooner or later the time comes on the mission when we have to line up on the target and those ground gunners can make us real uncomfortable."

During the initial three-year period in which the USAF conducted air operations over North Vietnam the reconnaissance units had a much higher loss percentage than the fighter-bombers. The loss rate for the Voodoos attempting to penetrate Pack 6A became so high that the RF-101 was withdrawn completely from this area. In 1968, with the introduction of new electronic equipment that aided in suppressing the enemy radar-directed guns on the ground, the odds improved to the point where six out of seven reconnaissance crews could expect to survive their hundred-mission tour. About thirty of the hundred trips would be into Pack 6, the toughest of all missions. Because of the heavy defenses in the area, however, a Phantom crew going to this sector is usually assigned only one target or two or three very close ones that can be covered with one photo run.

The chances of making more than one photo run and surviving are very low.

During daylight hours two RF-4Cs fly together on the reconnaissance missions but at night each crew operates alone.

"We use two planes in daylight to improve our coverage," Colonel George Hammond, the 432d Wing operations director, said. "Also, if one should be knocked down or the crew has to eject, the second plane can call for help and direct the rescue. At night, however, there is too much danger of a mid-air collision if two planes operate at high speed in the close formation necessary to get good photo coverage."

Flying alone may have this one advantage of not being subject to mid-air collision with a wingman but there are a great many disadvantages. There are no wingmen to warn of approaching Migs or SAMs. There are no fighters in the area to help if enemy fighters trap the Phantom and no Jolly Green Giant rescue helicopters standing alert in the darkness. Many RF-4C crews have gone out on a night mission and disappeared without a trace. No one knows for certain whether they were shot down over the target, rammed into a mountain, or dove into the sea. Usually they are carried as "missing in action" because their fate can't be officially verified.

Night-flight planning is very critical. During the day the pilot can alter his course if he sees it would be best to do so but at night the navigator is pretty much in charge. The navigator uses radar that allows the Phantom to follow or avoid the terrain. There are really three methods of flying a night mission in Vietnam: One is to plan to be above the highest terrain in the area at all times; two, to watch for the hills by moonlight so they can be avoided; or three, to use Terrain Following Radar (TFR). Much of this sophisticated system is still secret but essentially it consists of radar antennas in the nose sweeping ahead of the Phantom, spotting the height and distance of obstacles in the flight path. A computer figures out what flight course the plane should take to clear the obstructions then instructs the autopilot to fly that course. Just how close to the terrain the TRF can keep the RF-4C is classified information but some experts believe it is reliable at 50 feet above the obstructions. The pilot can choose a "hard ride," following every hill and valley contour, or a gentler undulation. TFR also has a built-in "fail-safe" feature designed to pitch the aircraft upward to a higher and thus safer altitude in case something gets out of kilter with the system.

For pilots, this "hands-off" low-level flying at near supersonic speeds through the darkness only a few feet off the ground is a test of nerves.

"It's pretty terrifying going up a valley in pitch darkness," says Lieutenant Colonel Gabe Bartholomew. "It takes a lot of confidence to use it. But we're getting it and it does work."

Another pilot who has flown many reconnaissance missions in the RF-4C in Vietnam, Major Earl E. McClintock, says, "When I first arrived in Southeast Asia I questioned whether the system could be used safely or not. I found out that it can if the mission is planned and flown properly. However, I learned one important fact. When flying TFR you must be right every time. You can be wrong only once."

The TFR is still not above suspicion since, as several Phantom pilots have said, "Any time there is a rock around higher than your aircraft, there has to be a hazard." Any turn steeper than a 45-degree bank causes an error in the system, an error that can be fatal if not immediately recognized. Rain sometimes disrupts the TFR and throws the Phantom into a steep climb unexpectedly. If this happens at the wrong time or place, as, for instance, over the target, it can make the reconnaissance plane very vulnerable to enemy ground fire. The advantages are great, however. It permits the Phantom to come in so low at night that the enemy radar can't pick up the aircraft's approach and the gunners are usually taken by surprise. It takes some of the burden from the back-seat navigator. Approaching a target on a black night a pilot is hesitant to rely completely on the radar operator to spot obstructions in the path of the plane on his scope. The Guy in Back (GIB) gets very busy at times, especially when things are not going exactly as planned, and it is possible for him to be distracted enough not to notice the large rock-filled shadow ahead. TFR, if it is in good working condition, avoids the obstruction automatically.

The RF-4C carries flash cartridges for night photography but these are seldom used in Pack 6A because they illuminate the plane for the enemy gunners as well as light the target. Instead the Phantom crews use an infrared camera which records the heat given off by the objects on the ground. Detection and mapping by infrared has always been less reliable than conventional aerial photography but in Vietnam it is proving very successful when used in conjunction with other records. A pure infrared record is actually a heat map of the sector being checked. There is very little resemblance to the physical characteristics of the ground. Good results have been obtained by combining the infrared film with color emulsions. This produces false color prints which are easy to interpret and penetrate enemy camouflage. For example, a red dye that is sensitive to near-infrared wavelengths will reveal the foliage in a reddish color instead of green and make interpretation of objects in the area much more accurate. The Phantom also uses the side-looking radar at night, primarily in searching for traffic on roads and railroads. It is also helpful when a reconnaissance crew finds it impossible to fly directly over a target.

It takes skill, experience, and a large measure of luck for a reconnaissance pilot to complete his tour in Vietnam. The RF-4C fliers based at Udorn RTAFB combine all three factors, even adding a fourth sometimes—superstition. One crewman wore white socks on his first mission and since his aircraft returned safely has refused to wear any other color since. A young pilot has a Thai "Yod-thong" Buddhist amulet on a gold chain that he loops around his neck prior to each flight. He vows that he hasn't had an enemy gunner fire at his plane since he started wearing the amulet. A navigator who always insisted on taking a gold-colored pen with him on a reconnaissance mission into Pack 6, even to the extent of delaying a takeoff one day until he retrieved the pen from operations, was teased about his phobia. He was, that is, until the day his plane came home with a hole in the wing big enough for both crew members to stand up in. If the shell had hit an inch to the right or left the RF-4C would never have made it back. No one laughs at the navigator and his gold pen anymore.

Not all the RF-4C pilots and navigators make it home despite having taken all the precautions possible. Major General Robert F. Worley, the 48-year-old deputy commander of the Seventh Air Force, decided 10 days before he was scheduled to leave Vietnam that he wanted one more look at the north. He and Major Robert F. Brodman, a member of the 460th Tactical Reconnaissance Wing, flew across the DMZ toward Hanoi in an RF-4C on July 23, 1968. Approximately sixty-five miles northwest of Danang enemy gunners opened fire on the plane and knocked it out of the sky. Brodman ejected safely but Worley died in the wreckage of the aircraft, the first general to be killed in Vietnam while on an aerial photography mission.

While the Voodoos and the Phantoms accomplish most of the reconnaissance missions for the USAF in Vietnam they are not the only aircraft engaged in such operations. The twin-engine RB-66 Destroyer is used for both night photography and electronic reconnaissance in Southeast Asia. The RB-66 is a USAF version of the shipboard A-3 Skywarrior and has a wingspan of approximately 72 feet, is 75 feet long, and stands 23 feet high. It is powered by two J79 turbojets. The RB-66B three-seat version is used for night photography while the C model is employed for the black-box snooping. The pictures are taken at altitudes varying from 1,500 to 35,000 feet, with cameras positioned in the forward and aft sections of the aircraft. Up to an altitude of 8,000 feet flash cartridges are used for illuminating the target, while between 8,000 feet and 35,000 feet it is necessary to us photoflash bombs. The Destroyer can carry 144 of the from 110 to 265-million-candlepower cartridges and 48 of the 165-pound bombs that produce 4 billion candlepower. Both the photoflash bombs and flash cartridges are ejected automatically.

The RB-66C, used for electronic reconnaissance, carries four electronic warfare officers to monitor and pinpoint enemy radar stations and other electronic devices. Each electronic warfare specialist is assigned a specific radio or radar frequency band to monitor during the flight. When he interprets an enemy signal it is graphically displayed on a pulse analyzer which tells whether it is search or precision radar. By simple triangulation an airborne direction finder locates the exact geographic position and site of the enemy radar. This takes only minutes. Other equipment automatically records the data on tape and film which is processed as soon as the aircraft returns to base. The equipment aboard the RB-66 also can send out a signal that fouls up the screen of the enemy radar.

Detachment 1, 432d Tactical Reconnaissance Wing, flew Destroyer operations from Takhli Royal Thai AB, Thailand, during the summer of 1967. In June of that year the unit had a total of 1,819 hours of flying time on electronic reconnaissance missions with six of the RB-66 aircraft flying better than 100 hours each that month.

Another old-timer plane flying reconnaissance missions in Southeast Asia, mostly in South Vietnam, is the RB-57 Canberra jet. This aircraft was evolved from the B-57 tactical bomber for both electronic and photographic reconnaissance. The D1 model is a single-seater intended primarily for photoreconnaissance with various vertical and oblique cameras, while the D2 has tandem seating for two crew members. The first reconnaissance version of the RB-57 went into operational service with the USAF in 1954. The Canberra is outdated for modern-day aerial spying. Several of the D(C) models, which have wingtip fairings for electronic equipment and bulbous nose and tail-radomes, are still in use in South Vietnam, however.

"Fortunately we don't draw much enemy fire from the VC," says Captain William Baird, a pilot who flies the RB-57 exclusively in the southern part of the country. "Charlie can tell a reconnaissance plane from a fighter-bomber. They know we are not going to shoot at them and they've been told not to shoot at airplanes unless shot at. They know if they shoot at us, we'll just pull up and call in a bomb strike."

The USAF has no Willy Fudd in Southeast Asia as the Navy has but it does have the Warning Star and the College Eye Task Force (CETF), which performs a similar reconnaissance role. Flying "alone, unarmed, and unafraid," crews and aircraft of the College Eye Task Force have played an important role in support of USAF combat operations in Vietnam since 1965. Using a modified Super Constellation designated the EC-121 and equipped with more than a ton of electronic devices including an airborne computer and a crew of up to thirty-one men, the College Eye Task Force has proven its adaptability in combat. The four-engined, triple-tailed "flying radar stations" track enemy fighters as they climb to intercept USAF fighter-bombers, assist in the rescue of pilots shot down by orbiting the area and dropping survival equipment until regular search and rescue forces arrive on the scene, and radar control the fighter-bombers to rendezvous with tankers for emergency refueling.

The CETF is a unit of the Aerospace Defense Command's 552d Airborne Early Warning and Control Wing at McClellan AFB, California, and all College Eye crew members, except the commander and a small contingent of staff officers who man the unit's headquarters, serve approximately four and a half months on temporary-duty status in Vietnam. The crews are formed at McClellan and often accumulate more than five hundred hours of combat flying time during a single tour. The normal crew complement on the EC-121 for a combat mission is eighteen personnel, made up of six officers and twelve enlisted men. The crew size varies, however, with the mission. A flight crew may consist of the aircraft commander and pilot, two navigators, two flight engineers, and a radio operator. The radar crew includes two officers, a senior director and weapons controller, an enlisted intercept control technician, and six enlisted search radar operators. Usually two radar in-flight maintenance technicians and a complete stock of electronic parts are carried so that the sensitive equipment can be kept operating throughout a mission.

Colonel William R. Nevitt was the commander of the College Eye unit when the milestone mission was flown marking three complete years of operations in the combat theater. He piloted the Warning Star aircraft himself on the trip north across the DMZ. In October 1968 Colonel James L. McCall arrived at Korat RTAFB, Thailand, to take command of that College Eye Task Force. Many of the officers and men of the organization have flown four complete tours of combat in Vietnam since the introduction of the new electronic reconnaissance technique into Southeast Asia and several have been credited with assists in the downing of enemy Migs by USAF fighter pilots.

The vital importance of the College Eye Task Force was summed up very clearly by Lieutenant Colonel John B. Mulherron, the radar staff officer of the Warning Stars operating out of Tan Son Nhut AB, Saigon, when he said, "They do a fine job of providing airborne surveillance where no ground radar exists in Southeast Asia. They are the 'Big Eye' of the fighter-bombers on a strike mission and have been instrumental in many Mig kills."

Without these flying radar units the loss ratio of USAF aircraft striking at targets in the north would be much higher. It is a new type of aerial reconnaissance which has proven its value during the Vietnam conflict and undoubtedly will be a part of the overall USAF reconnaissance setup from now on.

The guerrilla war in Southeast Asia has spawned many unique reconnaissance techniques, one of which is the "Blind Bat" operation. This is a night reconnaissance procedure involving the use of the C-130 aircraft carrying 250 two-million-candlepower illuminating flares. The C-130 crew is the hunter; fighters and fighter-bombers are the killers. For a seven-hour period between dusk and dawn the Blind Bat crews cover pre-determined areas seeking out the enemy in the blackness.

"Our mission is very simple," Captain Richard G. Knoblock of the 315th Air Division based at Ubon RTAFB, Thailand, said. "We just fly over selected areas along the enemy's major lines of communications and try to spot truck convoys or anything else that we can call in fighters to 'zap.' We also look for storage or parking areas concealed under the heavy foilage or canopied areas of the jungle.

"We have several methods available to achieve our mission. Usually we drop our flares in increments of two, three, or four, lighting a sector in which we are interested. If we then see a suitable target we call the control ship in the area for some strike aircraft. Within a matter of minutes the control ship has the fighter-bombers on the target. Sometimes, however, we fly blacked out and try to spot lights on the roads below us. If there is a lot of moonlight this method doesn't work very well because the VC and North Vietnamese spot us. During the period of a heavy moon we have to rely on more sophisticated equipment such as infrared or radar to detect the convoys."

Knoblock, who is aircraft commander and pilot of a Blind Bat crew, studies reconnaissance photographs taken only a few hours prior to his own mission before he takes off. As soon as he or one of his crew members spot anything that wasn't on the picture of the sector, they investigate with their flares, a combination of reconnaissance techniques that has proven very successful. The Blind Bat crews also act as forward air controllers when the fighter-bombers arrive in the sector and guide them to the target. Often the flare ships are asked to seek out enemy forces attacking Special Forces camps in the jungles or American airbases. During the seige of Plei Mei by the Vietcong, the illumination provided by the Blind Bat crews so harassed the enemy attackers that they finally withdrew. Sometimes just the appearance of the night reconnaissance C-130s over a camp is enough to deter the Vietcong from pressing an attack.

The development of the huge C-130 as a forward air controller aircraft at night is not as surprising as the use of the F-100F jet fighter as a "super FAC" in the project known as Commando Sabre. It was obvious to USAF planners that the O-1 and O-2 spotter aircraft that do most of the forward air controlling in South Vietnam were not suitable for such missions in North Vietnam, where the enemy areas were congested with antiaircraft guns and SAM sites. They were too slow, too vulnerable. Yet there was a need for some type of control of fighter-bombers attempting to hit targets in the north. They decided to experiment with a high-speed fighter to find out if it could be used as a FAC aircraft and the F-100F was chosen. After three months of tests at Phu Cat AB a Seventh Air Force report stated: "The F-100F program has proved highly successful in the location of targets and bomb damage assessment in areas where other FAC aircraft cannot operate."

Lieutenant Colonel Stanley M. Mamlock was chosen to lead the F-100Fs in actual combat operations over North Vietnam in the role of super FACs. It was his task to determine whether the F-100F pilots could survive over heavily defended targets while they directed the strike aircraft, whether the high-speed jets would permit the pilot to spot enemy activity above the DMZ. The answer was affirmative in both cases.

"The name of the game is hide-and-seek," Mamlock said. "We proved that we could find the supplies and other material the enemy tried to infiltrate into the south no matter where they hid the stuff."

A typical mission in the F-100F FAC, a two-seat version of the F-100D tactical fighter-bomber which can reach an airspeed of Mach 1.3, begins two and a half hours before takeoff with a preflight briefing on the up-to-date situation in the sector the crew is going to check. After the crew is in the air and headed toward North Vietnam, they make one in-flight refueling with a KC-135 tanker prior to crossing the DMZ. After reaching enemy territory they make a visual reconnaissance of their assigned sector, noting carefully the antiaircraft and SAM sites in the area and whether there are any new gun positions. These are usually easy to spot since the North Vietnamese gunners constantly try to knock the super FACs out of the sky unless they think their positions have gone completely unnoticed.

Once the F-100F crew have located a target they return to the tanker for another load of fuel, then lead the strike aircraft directed to them by the Airborne Command and Control Center to the enemy position. The FAC marks the target with a smoke rocket and the fighter-bombers take over. After the strike is completed, the crew still have one more dangerous task to perform. They assess the bomb damage despite the fact that they know the enemy gunners are waiting for them. Once this survey of the target area is completed and the information radioed to the Airborne Command and Control Center, the FAC heads for home. Back at the base, the crew are debriefed immediately, discussing and analyzing every detail of the mission no matter how insignificant certain facts may seem. Strike results are reported, new targets noted, and any new enemy gun positions are marked on a map of the area.

The Commando Sabre project has been very successful and was used daily until the bombing halt of 1968. In May of that year alone the jet FACs directed strikes that successfully destroyed ten SAM sites in the panhandle of North Vietnam and more than a hundred trucks and sank an equally large number of enemy sampans and other boats.

Another reconnaissance procedure that involves the F-100F is "back-seat" motion picture photography. Aerial motion picture photographers of the Military Airlift Command's Audio Visual Service use the rear set of the converted fighter-bomber to obtain film of air strikes that other aircrews can study for tactical and intelligence data. Later, after the combat crews have completed their study, some of the footage is cleared for television newscasts in the U.S. One of the best and most daring of the motion picture photographers serving in Vietnam was A1C Darry G. Winters. Winters was assigned to the 600th Photographic Squadron at Tan Son Nhut AB with his duty station located at Bien Hoa. The twenty-seven-year-old Californian flew more than three hundred missions during his year and a half in Southeast Asia, taking over 30,000 feet of combat air strike film for aircrews to study and intelligence officers to check for data. Two hundred and sixteen of his combat missions were in the F-100F. While some of his missions were over North Vietnam, most of them were in the south, where he documented nearly every major operation during his tour in the theater. When the Plei Me Special Forces camp in the central highlands was under heavy attack in October 1965, Winters flew three straight days filming the battle. When the enemy guerrillas set off a series of explosions at Bien Hoa which destroyed thirteen aircraft and killed thirty Americans, Winters recorded the disaster on film. Unfortunately, on his 217th mission in a F-100F, while taking combat film of a strafing attack against a Vietcong target fifteen miles west of Saigon, his plane crashed and Winters was killed. He was posthumously awarded the Distinguished Flying Cross.

Winters was one of less than a dozen official back-seat motion picture photographers in Vietnam. Their reconnaissance film, while not as plentiful as the film obtained by the Voodoos and Phantoms, serves an important purpose in the war besides providing intelligence data. It helps pilots who study the moving pictures of the mission to understand and develop the techniques necessary to survive and accomplish their assigned missions against the enemy.

The USAF has various other reconnaissance concepts under consideration and some of these are already under trial in Southeast Asia. Gliders, drones, SR-71s, U-2s, RF-111s—these are but a few of the vehicles that are in use or will be in operation in the near future. The Cuban crisis undoubtedly brought renewed interest in aerial reconnaissance and the war in Southeast Asia has kept that interest alive. No other single conflict has initiated as much research and development in the aerial reconnaissance field as the Vietnam War.

15

Reconnaissance of Tomorrow

IN A MAJOR arms-control policy statement shortly before he was elected President of the United States in 1968, Richard M. Nixon proposed establishment of an international satellite reconnaissance system to keep an eye on both the Soviet Union and the United States. He emphasized that in a world of rapidly changing technology the chief danger comes not from existing weapons so much as from a breakthrough that will rapidly alter the status quo of nations.

"Thus, a general openness which will permit rapid cooperation in coping with new developments in military technology is ultimately more important than detailed inspection agreements for existing armaments which may quickly become obsolete," he said.

President Nixon joined Presidents Eisenhower, Kennedy, and Johnson in stressing the need for an excellent aerial reconnaissance system for the security of the United States and the attainment of world peace. The need for new techniques and concepts has never been greater and the United States is constantly developing different ways and means of gathering the intelligence data it needs.

One element that always hindered the development of air reconnaissance was that there was no single department of the defense agency to serve as a focal point for reconnaissance activities. There was no one agency within USAF commands, for instance, to coordinate recommended program changes and to insure that lessons learned from past experiences were reflected in future reconnaissance requirements. At the conclusion of the Cuban crisis, during which aerial reconnaissance played such an important role, the USAF recognized the need for a central agency to keep reconnaissance forces fully prepared and updated and the Tactical Air Reconnaissance Center, Shaw AFB, South Carolina, was established.

The TARC is engaged at all times in a series of testing programs in support of worldwide reconnaissance forces. The new and complex equipment used by reconnaissance personnel must meet a predetermined set of requirements before it is recommended for use by the Air Force, and the TARC determines whether or not these requirements have been fulfilled. Brigadier General Robert W. Waltz, a World War II bomber pilot with many years of administrative experience in USAF units, became commander of the TARC in August 1966. He recently listed a series of projects that have been completed at Shaw AFB and among the new developments were testing of an in-flight processor; a split vertical camera; a photographic delivery system to drop film from a reconnaissance aircraft while it is still in flight; a new type of "thin" film that will double a camera magazine footage capacity; a new aerial color film; evaluation of an improved RF-101 navigation system; an oblique strobe for low-altitude night photography; and many others.

"I believe that one of the most important projects we completed," said General Waltz, "was the water conservation test. Wash water requirements for photo processing were reduced by more than 90 percent. This means that the water needed to process 40,000 feet of film is cut from 65,000 to 20 gallons per day. This is of vital importance in a combat area where water is in short supply. The water source can be swamps, rivers, or even the sea."

The USAF has a dominant role in aerial reconnaissance but the Navy and the Army also do extensive research. An Army liaison officer is stationed at the TARC and the two military forces have an arrangement for exchange of information. The Air Force reconnaissance personnel visit and coordinate with the Navy and both services have classified and unclassified publications which are exchanged. Another important factor in the three-service coordination is an organization named the Interservice Coordinating and Integrating Group, known as the ISCIG, which was established by the Department of Defense. The group works only in the reconnaissance-intelligence area and is responsible for the coordination and the avoidance of duplication in research and development. Under the ISCIG there are five technical panels, composed of specialists from each service, that deal with such subjects as photographic problems, infrared, radar, and photo interpretation. All together there are nearly 150 people involved in ISCIG affairs and they meet at least once a month, usually oftener.

Among the new manned aerial reconnaissance vehicles in use or planned for future use, two stand out prominently. One is the sophisticated SR-71, the USAF's only Mach 3 aircraft. At a television news conference in 1964, as the national elections neared, President Johnson announced that the United States had a new high-speed reconnaissance plane that "will go three times as fast as sound and fly at altitudes of 80,000 feet." Many of those who heard his unemotional announcement that day failed to realize that the United States had secretly built one of the most remarkable planes ever constructed. The SR-71 looks like a lethal stingray. It has a 90-foot-long fuselage and stubby swept-back wings that measure only 40 feet from tip to tip. Two huge engines at the rear of the fuselage and a cockpit for the two crewmen at its forward tip give it a strange, deadly look. While it has only about ninety minutes flight-time fuel capacity, during that period it can cover more than three thousand miles.

The SR-71, originally named the A-11, was planned while the U-2 was still making its secret flights over the Soviet Union. Richard Bissell, the CIA official who had instigated the U-2 operation, was also in charge of the new spy plane. When Francis Gary Powers was shot down in 1960, the SR-71 was well under way in Kelly Johnson's Skunk Works at the Lockheed Aircraft plant in Burbank, California. It and the satellites were ready to replace the U-2. However, the real mission of the SR-71 was camouflaged well. Not even all the members of the Joint Chiefs of Staff knew that it was intended to be a spy plane, and all news releases and other information given on the new aircraft always emphasized its role as an "interceptor." Not until President Johnson made his TV announcement in 1964 did the general public know that the SR-71 was actually a reconnaissance aircraft designed for worldwide operation.

On May 1, 1965, at Edwards AFB, California, Colonel Robert L. Stephens, the test force director and first military pilot to fly the new plane, established four of nine new world speed and altitude records in the delta wing SR-71. Colonel Daniel Andre flew in the second seat as his fire control systems operator. They averaged 2,070 miles per hour over a 17-kilometer straightaway course in opposite direction runs, then climbed to 80,257 feet to establish a new world absolute record for sustained horizontal flight. Their speed over a closed circuit was 1,688 miles per hour and they attained 1,642 miles per hour over a 500-kilometer circuit. These records erased any doubts as to the plane's capabilites. The J-58 engines, each capable of more than 42,000 pounds of thrust with afterburners, worked perfectly and the black paint on the aircraft helped reduce the skin temperature to a cake-baking level of 400-500 degrees.

Not that the SR-71 didn't have shakedown troubles. It did, although secrecy shrouded most of the test flights just as it now curtains the reconnaissance flights it obviously makes over Communist countries. In January 1966 test pilot Bill Weaver was flying one of the black-painted super spy planes over New Mexico when it exploded. Weaver ejected safely but his companion aboard the aircraft, Lockheed employee James T. Zwayer, died in the crash. A rancher who saw the smoking plane go down, Al Miller, flew to the scene in his helicopter and picked up Weaver. Miller later quoted the test pilot as saying the aircraft was traveling high and fast when something went wrong.

"Everything was going well but suddenly there was an explosion," Weaver was reported as saying.

Tight security measures were immediately imposed at the crash scene. Air police and airmen from Amarillo AFB and Cannon AFB, New Mexico, secured the entire area while other military and civilian personnel searched for the valuable equipment scattered by the crash. No official report was given for the cause of the crash or what type of test flight Weaver had been flying that winter day. Other crashes involving the SR-71 were treated similarly with very little information being released. Unofficially it was learned that the aircraft had two main problems during the early development stage: varying the flow of fuel for effective combustion at various altitudes, and controlling the flow of air into the engines at extreme heights. These bugs have since been eliminated.

Russia was quick to note the operational capabilities of the SR-71, which is loaded with the latest aerial cameras, side-view radar, and sophisticated electronic equipment. The fact that the plane was able to scan 60,000 square miles of the earth's surface per hour from an altitude of 80,000 feet obviously made it a spy plane with more potential than the U-2 which had overflown the Soviet Union earlier. The government newspaper *Izvestia* took official notice of the SR-71 and said that if it flew over the Soviet Union it would easily be shot down. Marshal Vladimir Aleksandrovich Sudets, commander-in-chief of Soviet antiaircraft defenses, emphasized that the new plane would meet the same fate as the U-2 if used for the same purpose.

Is the SR-71 overflying Red territory on spy flights? Undoubtedly it is, at least over Red China and the nations of Southeast Asia. SR-71s, flown by pilots of the Strategic Air Command, fly over North Vietnam regularly although they are not stationed in South Vietnam but operate from bases elsewhere in Southeast Asia. Most experts believe that the new planes range over the entire globe gathering intelligence data in conjunction with the satellites. The great advantage of the SR-71 over the satellite is that it can be dispatched quickly to take pictures of a specific area. A very brief announcement on June 5, 1968, stated that an SR-71 was missing over the Pacific. The plane had taken off from Okinawa but the USAF wasn't saying what had been its destination or its assigned mission. No further information was released, causing many persons to believe that the aircraft had been lost on a spy flight over Communist territory. Only time will tell whether or not the SR-71 is a vital factor in the security of the nation. Most experts believe that it is.

When Theodore H. Eklof, chief scientist at the TARC, was asked about future planned reconnaissance systems he immediately mentioned another manned aircraft in its operational infancy, the controversial F-111.

"I would say that there is a distinct possibility that there will be a reconnaissance version of the F-111," he said. "I would assume that eventually the tactical reconnaissance inventory will include, if not the RF-111, an aircraft with essentially the same characteristics."

While many opponents of the new aircraft call it McNamara's Folly because in 1962 the then Secretary of Defense overruled his own experts and chose the F-111 design over others submitted, there is no doubt that it is an amazing plane. During the Paris Air Show in June of 1967 Russian observers and photographers all but wriggled up the double tailpipes of the swing-wing F-111 taking pictures and measurements. There is little wonder that the Soviets are interested in the aircraft because its capabilities, if realized, can give the U.S. a very valuable vehicle for airborne reconnaissance as well as for bombing and interceptor duties.

The F-111 is a large plane. The Air Force version is 73 feet long and when its wings are cranked out straight they measure 63 feet. If the pilot of the F-111 has the wings folded back for supersonic flight, this span is cut to approximately 32 feet. Loaded with fuel and ready to fly, it weighs nearly 80,000 pounds including its two-man crew in side-by-side seating. The F-111 requires only a short takeoff run and can stop after landing within 2,100 feet of the point of touchdown. The RF-4, in comparison, needs twice as much runway for takeoff and more then 6,000 feet for landing even with a drag chute. The swing-wings of the F-111 make this possible. The pilot has them in a nearly straight-out position for takeoff, which gives him high lift. After he has the aircraft in the air, he pulls a lever and can swivel them to the rear to a maximum of 72.5 degrees to reduce drag and permit supersonic flight. The F-111 can reach a speed of Mach 2.5 at 60,000 feet and approximately Mach 1.2 or 800 miles per hour at treetop level.

Other features that will make it an outstanding spy plane are that it can take off and land in all kinds of weather; it handles as easily as a jet trainer; it has terrain-following radar that enables it to fly low, fast, automatically, under enemy radar tracking; and it has devices that permit it to score over a target with bombs or cameras four to ten times as effectively as anything the U.S. previously had in its inventory. The plane also has other equipment that is top secret but indicates that the F-111 is the most modern aircraft ever built—for instance, a small, bulbous infrared sensor on top of its rudder that detects heat-sensing missiles approaching the plane and enables it to throw out decoys to mislead them.

No details have been released on the RF-111 version of the

plane but it is obvious that it will be equipped with the latest cameras and electronic equipment. Despite the fact that the Navy is not satisfied with its model of the plane and that three of the F-111s that were sent to Takhli RTAFB to fly missions over North Vietnam were lost for unknown causes, the USAF pilots who have flown the aircraft like it very much.

"The difference between this and other airplanes is the difference between day and night," said Lieutenant Colonel Benjamin C. Murphy. "On all the combat missions we flew, the ground fire was way behind us. They didn't even know we were coming."

Reconnaissance pilots, who are required to get in to the target and out again without having any weapons to fire except cameras, appreciate the capabilities inherent in the F-111 and are convinced it will be the best spy plane yet produced.

It was announced early in 1969 by the Aerospace Defense Command that a new jet aircraft for electronic reconnaissance would also be added to its inventory. The craft will be either the Boeing 707 or Douglas DC-8 loaded with sophisticated electronic gear and will replace the EC-121 now in service. Atop the new plane will be a large, mushroom-shaped radar dome. With its higher speed and higher altitude capability, the new warning jet will give the U.S. a more efficient control system to deal with attacking high-speed missile-loaded bombers in event of a general war by detecting the enemy planes and directing the interceptors to them.

While other manned aerial reconnaissance vehicles are on the planning boards or in the discussion stage by the military, it is the unmanned vehicles that offer the brightest future for obtaining general intelligence data from the enemy and, as more sophisticated unmanned devices are developed, perhaps even specific data that now must be gathered by pilots in reconnaissance aircraft. These unmanned vehicles save lives, do an excellent job in most instances, and can aid a nation that needs information about the enemy but doesn't want to risk another

U-2 incident and its diplomatic consequences. Unmanned reconnaissance vehicles can "go out of control," "refuse to respond to remote-controlled signals," or otherwise "stray" over the territory of another country. Washington can't use the same statements when a manned reconnaissance plane is shot down over enemy areas. The Firebee drones used in Southeast Asia and over the Chinese mainland are examples of unmanned reconnaissance vehicles presently in use.

Publicized as primarily a jet target drone, the Firebee has been used for surveillance for a considerable length of time. The 23-feet-long drone stands nearly 7 feet high and has a wingspan of 13 feet. Using a J-69 jet engine with a rated thrust of 1,700 pounds, the 2,000-pound Firebee can attain speeds of 635 knots at 50,000 feet altitude. The drone can be ground launched or air launched and is controlled from a remote control station at either launching site. C-130 transports have been adapted to air launch up to four Firebees from wing pylons. Once launched, a beacon in the drone facilitates radar tracking from the remote control station and the Firebee's flight path is followed on a radar plotting board which enables the controller to fly a desired mission pattern. Thus the drone can be flown far beyond the line-of-sight distance from the control station.

The Firebee's automatic glide capability enables the remote control operator to maneuver it to a suitable recovery point when a mission is completed or the fuel depleted. For those drones programmed to fly reconnaissance missions at extremely low altitudes, an automatic power-off climb feature ensures adequate altitude for parachute deployment. A two-stage parachute sequence lowers the drone to a safe landing. A 6-foot-diameter drag chute first decelerates the Firebee and then the 81-foot main chute lowers it in a horizontal attitude to the ground or water at approximately 20 feet per second. Landing impact is absorbed by the nacelle keel which protects the equipment in the nose and fuselage compartments. Mid-air retrieval by helicopters is also a standard practice in some areas.

The sensory data acquired by the high-flying or low-level drone can be either photographic or infrared and it is excellent for use in sectors where the risk to manned aircraft is too high to be acceptable. With the introduction of new defensive weapons by the Communists, however, it is becoming increasingly difficult for even the drones to penetrate enemy territory. The Red Chinese claim to have shot down nine of them in the period 1964–1966 in the Yunnan, Kwangsi, and Kwantung provinces. Three of the Firebees are on display in Peking. Yet in 1968 a new $20-million contract was awarded to Ryan Aeronautical Company for additional Firebees, representing the largest single order ever placed for the unmanned drone. It is obvious that unmanned reconnaissance operations are included in future U.S. military plans.

Pilotless aircraft are so realistic and efficient that they are even causing American fliers trouble. One Navy pilot had a "dogfight" with an unknown bogie over North Vietnam only to discover later that he had shot down a Firebee drone. WO-1 Joseph E. Clark, a pilot with the Army's Americal Division, was flying a helicopter from Danang to Chu Lai, South Vietnam, early in 1969 when he suddenly saw "the strangest aircraft" he had ever seen.

"It was heading toward the sea at about 30 knots so I slowed our speed from 110 knots," Clark said, "dropped to 700 feet and pulled beside it. It was painted gray and white, was tailless and had no markings. It looked like a helicopter but it had no pilot. As I watched it, the strange bird flew under our chopper. Every time I tried to approach it, the plane would move away."

When he reported the "UFO," he was given quite a razzing from the radio station on the ground. Later, however, the "thing" was confirmed by the Naval Support Activity Detachment at Chu Lai as being a drone antisubmarine helicopter, radio-controlled from a destroyer providing security for the battleship *New Jersey*.

The Marines have a short-range battlefield reconnaissance

drone named the Bikini, so-called because it covers the bare essentials of the fighting area as the bathing suit of the same name covers the feminine body. The drone is 6 feet long, has an 8-foot wingspan, and is driven by a 4.5 h.p. chain-saw-type gasoline engine at a speed in excess of 100 miles per hour. The engine also drives a 28-volt alternator that operates a parachute recovery system, two control servos, and a camera. The Bikini has a maximum altitude of 10,000 feet and can remain airborne about thirty minutes. It carries a 70-mm camera with a shutter speed of 1/500 of a second which will take up to 70 exposures at the demand of the controller. An automatic exposure-control device allows dawn-to-dusk operation of the camera. Usually the drone is launched from a catapult on a jeep, using compressed air, and is controlled by an operator through radio equipment mounted on the back of the jeep. While the Bikini is not so sophisticated as other drones, it is very difficult to shoot down and can bring back photographs that are of value to the ground commander who needs to know what is ahead of him and needs to know it immediately.

In midsummer 1968 the Army announced the development of a new aerial reconnaissance vehicle that will carry a pilot but is not an airplane. It is a glider. Known as the QT3, the new surveillance glider will have a very small engine to power its own takeoff but over hostile territory the engine will be shut off and the pilot will glide silently through the night sky. Beneath their aluminum skin the gliders will be equipped with miniaturized infrared sensors to observe the trails used by the enemy for infiltration and cameras to photograph men and supplies detected. It is believed that the glider will be a modified version of the Model 232 sailplane built by the Schweizer Aircraft Corporation.

Conventional manned and unmanned aerial reconnaissance vehicles are under constant development and refinement yet the most revolutionary and probably the most overall efficient spy in the sky and certainly the one that promises the most for the future is the satellite. When Richard Bissell had the U-2 program at the peak of its operation, he realized that someday the Soviet Union would develop an antiaircraft weapon able to knock the spy plane out of the sky. Bissell and others therefore persuaded certain key Congressional figures to approve a secret sum of money for a satellite that could spy on enemy territory from high in space. So accurate was Bissell's foresight that in August 1960, only three months after the shooting down of Francis Gary Powers ended the U-2 program, the first surveillance satellite was recovered complete with pictures almost as detailed as those taken by Powers. Consequently there was no gap in the U.S. aerial reconnaissance program despite the embarrassing incident of the U-2.

President Johnson once said that reconnaissance satellites are the most important single device the U.S. has ever built. He explained his statement by pointing out that the satellites, by providing precise information on the armaments actually possessed by Communist nations, take the guesswork out of a President's most important decisions and eliminate the necessity of the nation's overbuilding its military arsenal at a cost of many billions of dollars. He estimated that by 1967 the U.S. had spent about $40 billion on space programs but that the nation would have gotten its money's worth even if the entire sum had been multiplied ten times and the only tangible results from the military and civil space programs had been reconnaissance satellites. Some experts say President Johnson's estimate was too conservative, that there is every evidence that observation from space is the most significant development in man's experience.

Tiros I, supposedly a weather-observation satellite, was launched on April 1, 1960, from Cape Canaveral by a Thor-Able rocket. In its nose were 9,200 tiny solar cells which were to supply the power to transmit magnetic-taped photo images back to earth from its orbit altitude of 450 miles in space. The 270-pound, drum-shaped weather satellite had two cameras. One was a wide-angle camera which utilized half a Vidicon tube and took a strip of overlapping photos at a resolution of about a mile and a half and covered an area about 135 miles long and 800 miles wide. A smaller, narrow-angle camera took pictures of an area about eighty miles wide—but it also, surprisingly, took "blip" photos of runways and missiles so sharp that even U.S. space experts were shocked. For a while NASA officials tried to emphasize the weather-observation role of Tiros I but finally on April 5 agency officials admitted that the satellite "might" be obtaining "blurry-eyed" photos of a rudimentary nature. Three days later Dr. Keith T. Glennan of NASA announced that Tiros I had successfully taken wide-angle pictures of the Soviet Union and Communist China but he also emphasized that a small timer in the satellite had failed and that the narrow-angle camera was no longer transmitting photos back to earth. This meant that no additional close-up pictures of military installations and missile bases could be taken.

Tiros I, whether it was planned as a space spy or not, inaugurated the use of reconniassance satellites. On May 24, 1960, the first MIDAS—Missile Defense Alarm System—satellite was launched. The MIDAS series were space reconnaissance spies designed to provide continuous, worldwide screening of ballistic-missile launchings through the use of infrared and thus to give maximum warning regarding a hostile missile attack on the U.S. At least one of these satellites was always over the Soviet Union, monitoring its missile bases. Later the SAMOS—Satellite and Missile Observation System—satellites were put in the sky, followed by many secret space spies that have never been publicized. These reconnaissance satellites have steadily stripped the Soviet Union and Red China of their most valuable military secrets.

It is estimated that the U.S. has launched more than two hundred classified reconnaissance payloads, most of them from Vandenberg Air Force Base, California. This site is excellent for putting the reconnaissance satellites into the desired polar orbit. The polar orbit is preferred because as the earth spins west to east, the north-south traveling satellite passes within sight of every spot on the surface at least once a day. The types and missions of these space devices vary greatly. Electronic eavesdropping that once was accomplished almost exclusively by ground listening stations near the borders of the Communist countries is now done by satellites called ferrets, like the manned aircraft serving the same purpose. One U.S. ferret makes two passes a day over Moscow monitoring secret transmissions from headquarters in that city to ships and submarines at sea, messages to their ground forces, and even signals from low-powered transmitters used by secret agents.

Dr. R. F. Taschek of the Atomic Energy Commission's Los Alamos, New Mexico, laboratory, reported in April 1968 that special U.S. military satellites have the capability of detecting nuclear tests as far away as 200 million miles—more than twice the distance to the sun. Named the Vela series, also called the Nuclear Detection Satellite Program, these spacecraft are deployed in widely separated positions in an orbit about seventy thousand miles above the earth and are primarily designed to detect any nuclear test blasts that might be touched off in space in violation of the limited test ban treaty. The treaty outlaws all nuclear weapons tests except those underground. Taschek said that the Vela satellites each contain about twenty thousand electronic components that enable them to detect distance space tests solely by the radiations a weapon blast emits—X rays, neutrons, and gamma rays. They must also be able to detect artificially produced radiations in space and report them. Otherwise the natural radiation from the sun, cosmic rays, and the Van Allen radiation belt would give false warning of enemy nuclear blasts. The Vela makes it possible to bargain with the Russians over nuclear treaties with confidence, safe in the knowledge that the Soviet Union cannot violate the treaty without being discovered.

Most of the reconnaissance satellites have a standard operating procedure regardless of their equipment differences or prime mission. As soon as the satellite passes over a designated, programmed target, its cameras and electronic equipment are turned on by a radio signal. Television instantly transmits photographs back to U.S. ground stations. The satellites also eject heat-resistant film cassettes to the earth on command. These 250-pound cassettes have small control rockets attached to them which guide their reentry path back to earth. The cassettes are tracked by radar sites and the information is relayed to Hickam AFB, Hawaii, where C-130 airplanes and their crews are standing by. After entering the earth's atmosphere, the cassettes release their heat shields, send out a radio signal, and automatically eject a bundle of aluminum chaff which the radar operators can track more easily. The aircraft are directed to the forecast drop area of the film capsule and after the cassette's chute opens at 50,000 feet, it is snared in mid-air by a long hook extending from the airplane. If the recovery should fail, there is an explosive device that destroys the cassette, preventing it from falling into enemy hands.

A key development in space reconnaissance is the ability of modern sensors aboard the satellite to see into the ocean. Reefs, mountains, fish, and various other objects submerged at great depths can be seen. In a report to Congress, NASA stated space studies will contribute greatly to the location of schools of fish and the study of fish migration. Military experts privately point out that if the multisensors on a reconnaissance satellite can detect and follow a school of fish 30 feet in diameter that is 200 feet under the surface, it would be much easier to detect and follow a nuclear submarine, which is much larger. Another factor involved in tracking a nuclear submarine from space is the large amount of sea water used to cool the submarine's reactor and the discharge of this hot water into its wake. Infrared detectors on reconnaissance satellites should have no difficulty picking up this "hot" wake since such detectors are sensitive to a temperature change of 0.1 degree Fahrenheit. If enemy submarines can be revealed in this manner—and unofficial military sources at the Pentagon insist they can—an effective antisubmarine operation is possible.

One of the main drawbacks to the use of reconnaissance satellites is the "model T" method of collecting the information from it. Valuable time, sometimes adding up to several days, is lost while the film is ejected in the cassette, hooked in mid-air, flown to a laboratory where it is processed, and then distributed to the various intelligence centers waiting for it. The data-handling systems in use can't move the quantity of information available in the satellite fast enough. However, experiments with the use of lasers for this communications role have proven very successful and offer a possible solution to the problem. The laser beam's very high frequency is ten times as great as any existing radar source and a particular percentage of modulation on the laser produces ten thousand times the volume of information that can be transmitted with a corresponding modulation of the radar source. In one experiment a laser light beam no thicker than a pencil relayed simultaneously the video and audio signals received from all seven television channels broadcasting from the Empire State Building. The laser can also be aimed precisely from one point to another, such as from a reconnaissance satellite to a ground receiving station, and it cannot be easily intercepted and monitored. Real-time transmission of reconnaissance data from space will be much closer with the laser.

One satellite reconnaissance concept under study would involve approximately a hundred unmanned orbital vehicles and four manned space stations such as the proposed MOLs—Manned Orbiting Laboratory—which are scheduled to fly about 1971. The unmanned satellites would provide continuous live reconnaissance of the entire globe by relaying their data to the manned space laboratories where superfluous information would be filtered out to reduce the volume of transmissions to the ground. This filtering would be accomplished by computers operated by astronauts in the manned vehicles. The vital data would then be transmitted to earth by lasers. Those who favor the new concept say that the U.S. could get such a system into operation by the late 1970's for far less money than has been spent to date on strategic missiles. Using the system it would be possible to obtain real-time data on enemy military inventories and daily reports on troop movements all over the world, border violations, or any other activity that might threaten the security of the nation.

New cameras and other sensors that can be used on reconnaissance satellites are, of course, key factors in the new concept or any other concept of reconnaissance from space. According to NASA reports, objects as small as garbage-can lids will be picked up on a routine basis by sensors that will be available for the reconnaissance satellites of the future. During World War II, focal lengths under twelve inches were common on aerial cameras. Today some cameras have 240-inch focal lengths and 960-inch focal lengths are under development. While ground resolution depends upon several factors, the focal length of the camera is one of the most important. By being able to increase the focal length and increase the sensitivity of the film so that the number of discernible lines per millimeter can be increased, the results are improved. The more lines, the more the film can be enlarged, and the more the picture can be enlarged, the smaller the object that can be revealed. The average human eye can see only about seven lines per millimeter and World War II film had about ten lines. The new modern films have a hundred or more.

Another important development in the field of space reconnaissance from both manned and unmanned vehicles is multispectral systems. These systems, instead of using a visible light camera, operate in the electromagnetic spectrum in which men, and the camera, are blind. The new sensors "see" radiation or spectral signals from objects under surveillance. These spectral signals may show up on one wavelength but not another. Consequently when a large number of photos, each taken on a different wavelength, are compared with one another, changes in the reflectivity of the target are revealed that are invisible to the naked eye or conventional camera. An expert photo interpreter can uncover an amazing amount of data from such "lightprints."

One such expert is Don Ross, a former Royal Canadian Air Force wing commander, who presently is a scientist specializing in multispectral analysis at Palo Alto, California. Utilizing his new technique, Ross can detect what previously was undetectable in pictures of land and water masses taken from space. He has pinpointed schools of fish in the ocean, uncovered earthquake faults, and differentiated between varieties of pine trees in a photograph taken from a satellite. His technique not only enables him to obtain such information from color photographs taken by sophisticated, newly developed cameras but also from ordinary black-and-white photographs taken previously by reconnaissance satellites using conventional cameras.

Basically, Ross enhances the contrast already present on a photographic print. A desert area might appear all gray on the picture but actually it consists of a series of subtle color changes because of differences in density and composition. The human eye can't separate these differences. Ross, however, assigns each of the gray color levels an arbitrary rating of yellow, red, blue, or orange. By filtering out the color levels as many as eighteen times on a single print, he creates a series of transparencies in vivid hues that show details that previously were not distinguishable. Using this method on a photo taken from Gemini 4, he was able to show schools of fish and lost shoals at the mouth of the Colorado River where it flows into the Gulf of California. This picture had been taken when the satellite was 120 miles above the ground.

Ross sees future earth-sensing reconnaissance satellites telemetering information in such huge volume that it will have to be stored in a computer for future use. He believes such satellites will map agricultural, marine, and other resources; track mineral strata; assist in the prediction of crop yields, in weather and pollution control, and in detection of forest fires—that they will analyze the health and wealth of the world.

William Fischer of the U.S. Geological Survey is another expert who thinks that sensors in reconnaissance satellites will be of great value to the ordinary citizen as well as to the military in the future. "The new sensors in space will be useful in predicting earthquakes and volcanic eruptions, I believe," he said. "A sensor camera revealed underground heat changes at the volcano Kilauea in Hawii. This may imply the buildup of forces before an eruption. If future research verifies this fact and thermal patterns can be established, we may be able to alert populations to dangerous earth movements before disaster strikes."

New prospects for photography and detection from space are under constant development. Many portions of the spectrum other than visible light, infrared, radio, and radar frequencies are being investigated. One such area involves millimeter wavelengths between infrared and radar. Devices called radiometers, similar in function to radio receivers, detect these millimeter waves being reflected and emitted from objects. The radiometers are used as the sensing element in an image-forming system. The main advantage of millimeter wave devices is that they cover the "blind area" in the infrared band. Objects that have nearly the same temperature as their background cannot be clearly detected by infrared but can be seen in the millimeter band.

There is even a method under development for taking pictures from space without a lens. In 1947 a Hungarian scientist, Dr. Dennis Gabor, discovered a way to take pictures by using light waves. Called the holographic process, the technique was not usable, however, because the results could not be put into image form for analysis. In 1960 an experiment with a laser beam applied to the holograms gathered by Gabor's process revealed that the various wavelengths and colors that radiated in all directions could be brought under control. By shining a laser beam through the jumble of holograms on a plate, it was discovered that an image of the target object stood out vividly in three dimensions. While the reovlutionary process is not yet perfected, it offers a great potential for the future.

Throughout history it is probable that more military and civilian leaders of the world have succeeded or failed as a result of their understanding of the situation than because of their ability to react. A fundamental requirement for understanding any situation is sufficient, valid, and timely information in a form easy to understand. During the Cuban crisis of 1962, it has been reported that the late President Kennedy constantly worried about making a miscalculation, a mistake in judgment that would lead to war. He kept referring to the misunderstandings that had directly led to World War I and World War II and he wanted to avoid such errors in the Cuban affair. Without the timely information delivered to him in a comprehensible form by the reconnaissance systems of the USAF and U.S. Navy, he would not have been able to make the correct decisions, decisions that avoided war with the Soviet Union.

President Johnson was able to declare a bombing halt prior to the elections in 1968, a move that very nearly cost Richard Nixon the Presidency, because reconnaissance planes and spy satellites were available to monitor North Vietnamese activities after the agreement went into effect. He was able to assure his military commanders that if the North Vietnamese took advantage of the moratorium by increasing their strength in the south he would order the bombing halt ended. Reconnaissance devices kept him informed daily on enemy adherence to the truce terms.

Aerial reconnaissance is justified and is a necessity for the self-defense and security of the United States. The need to know what is on the other side of the hill has never been more important if the nation is to survive. The technical feasibility for completely satisfying this need is near. The military value of real-time aerial reconnaissance of global range is beyond question. Unfortunately, the U.S. is not moving as fast toward this global reconnaissance concept as it should because of budget limitations. Landing a man on the moon is important but just as important is the fact that he will have a camera with him. The entire space program is adaptable to space reconnaissance . . . and so is the Soviet Union's space program. The race to outer space by these two great nations is also a race to a more complete aerial reconnaissance system that will furnish the data needed for Washington and Moscow to make their crucial decisions in future confrontations. It is imperative that the U.S. win this race, too.

Bibliography

BOOKS

ABEL, ELIE, *The Missile Crisis,* J. B. Lippincott Co., Philadelphia, 1966.

ALSOP, STEWART, *The Center,* Harper & Row, New York, 1968.

BABINGTON-SMITH, CONSTANCE, *Air Spy,* Harper & Brothers, New York, 1957.

BALL, EDMUND, *Staff Officer with the Fifth Army,* Exposition Press, New York, 1958.

BURLINGAME, ROGER, *General Billy Mitchell,* McGraw-Hill Book Co., New York, 1952.

BUESCHEL, RICHARD M., *Communist Chinese Air Power,* Frederick A. Praeger, New York, 1968.

CAGLE, MALCOLM W., AND MANSON, FRANK A., *The Sea War in Korea,* U.S. Naval Institute, Annapolis, Md., 1957.

CAIDIN, MARTIN, *The Ragged, Rugged Warriors,* E. P. Dutton & Co., New York, 1966; *Air Force,* Bramhall House, New York, 1957.

CASEY, ROBERT J., *Torpedo Junction,* Halcyon House, Garden City, N.Y., 1944.

CHENNAULT, CLAIRE LEE, *Way of a Fighter,* G. P. Putnam's Sons, New York, 1949.

CLAGETT, JOHN, *The U.S. Navy in Action,* Monarch Books, New York, 1963.

COX, DONALD W., *The Space Race,* Chilton Books, New York, 1962.

CRAVEN, W. F., AND CATE, J. L., *The Army Air Forces in World War II:* Vol. I, *Plans and Early Operations,* 1948; Vol. II, *Europe: Torch to Pointblank,* 1949; Vol. IV, *Pacific: Guadalcanal to Saipan,* 1950; Vol. V, *Matterhorn to Nagasaki,* 1953; Vol. VI, *Men and Planes,* 1955; University of Chicago Press, Chicago.

DOUGLAS, SHOLTON, *Combat and Command,* Simon & Shuster, Inc., New York, 1963.

DUGAN, JAMES, AND STEWART, CARROLL, *Ploesti,* Random House, New York, 1944.

DUPRE, FLINT O., *USAF Biographical Dictionary,* Franklin Watts, Inc., New York, 1965.

ESPOSITO, VINCENT J., *A Concise History of World War II,* Frederick A. Praeger, New York, 1964.

FARAGO, LADISLAS, *Patton: Ordeal and Triumph,* Ivan Obolensky, New York, 1963.

FOULIS, BENJAMIN D., WITH GLINES, C. V., *The Memoirs of Major General D. Foulis,* McGraw-Hill Book Co., New York, 1968.

FUTRELL, ROBERT, *The United States Air Force in Korea,* Duell, Sloan & Pearce, New York, 1961.

GLINES, C. V., *The Compact History of the United States Air Force,* Hawthorn Books, Inc., New York, 1963.

GOLDBERG, ALFRED, *A History of the United States Air Force,* D. Van Nostrand Company, Inc., Princeton, N.J., 1957.

GREEN, WILLIAM, *Famous Fighters of the Second World War,* Hanover House, New York, 1958.

GURNEY, GENE, *Journey of the Giants,* Coward-McCann, Inc., New York, 1961.

HAILEY, FOSTER, AND LANCELOT, MILTON, *Clear for Action,* Bonanza Books, New York, 1964.

History of the U.S. Signal Corps, G. P. Putnam's Sons, Editors of Army Times, ed., New York, 1961.

JABLOWSKI, EDWARD, *Flying Fortress,* Doubleday & Co., Inc., New York, 1965.

JOHNSON, STANLEY, *The Grim Reapers,* E. P. Dutton & Co., New York, 1943.

JOSEPHY, ALVIN M., JR., *American Heritage History of Flight,* American Heritage Publishing Co., Inc., New York, 1962.

KAHN, DAVID, *The Code Breakers,* The Macmillan Company, New York, 1967.

LEMAY, CURTIS, WITH KANTOR, MACKINLAY, *Mission with LeMay,* Doubleday & Co., Inc., New York, 1965.

LORD, WALTER, *Incredible Victory,* Harper & Row, New York, 1967.

MAJDALANY, FRED, *The Battle of Cassino,* Houghton Mifflin Co., Boston, 1957.

MAURER, MAURER, *Air Force Combat Units of World War II,* USAF Historical Division, Air University, Department of the Air Force, Washington, D.C., 1960.

MORENOFF, DR. JEROME, *World Peace Through Space Law,* The Mitchie Company, Charlottesville, Va., 1967.

MORGAN, WILLIAM, Ed., *The Complete Photographer,* National Educational Alliance, Inc., New York, 1942.

MORISON, SAMUEL ELIOT, *The Two-Ocean War,* Atlantic-Little-Brown, Boston, 1963.

MOSLEY, LEONARD, *Gideon Goes to War,* Charles Scribner's Sons, New York, 1955.

PARSONS, EDWIN C., *I Flew with the Lafayette Escadrille,* E. C. Seale & Company, Inc., Indianapolis, 1937.

REYNOLDS, QUENTIN, *They Fought for the Sky,* Holt, Rinehart & Winston, Inc., New York, 1957.

SMITH, S. E., *The United States Navy in World War II,* William Morrow and Co., New York, 1967.

SNYDER, LOUIS L., *The War,* Julian Messner, Inc., New York, 1964.

TOLAND, JOHN, *But Not in Shame,* Random House, New York, 1961.

TREGASKIS, RICHARD, *Invasion Diary,* Random House, New York, 1944.

TREGASKIS, RICHARD, *Guadalcanal Diary,* Random House, New York, 1943.

TULLY, ANDREW, *CIA: Inside Story,* William Morrow and Co., New York, 1962.

TULEJA, THADDEUS, *Climax at Midway,* W. W. Norton & Co., New York, 1960.

WHITE, WILLIAM L., *The Little Toy Dog,* E. P. Dutton & Co., New York, 1962.

WHITEHOUSE, ARCH, *The Years of the Sky Kings,* Doubleday & Co., Inc., New York, 1964.

WISE, DAVID, AND ROSS, THOMAS B., *The U-2 Affair,* Random House, New York, 1962.

UNIT HISTORIES

History of the 3d Reconnaissance Group, USAF Historical Division, Research Studies Institute, Maxwell AFB, Ala., 1957.

History of the 4th Reconnaissance Group, USAF Historical Division, Research Studies Institute, Maxwell AFB, Ala., 1957.

History of the 5th Reconnaissance Group, USAF Historical Division, Research Studies Institute, Maxwell AFB, Ala., 1957.

History of the 7th Reconnaissance Group, USAF Historical Division, Research Studies Institute, Maxwell AFB, Ala., 1956.

History of the 8th Reconnaissance Group, USAF Historical Division, Research Studies Institute, Maxwell AFB, Ala., 1957.

History of the 10th Reconnaissance Group, USAF Historical Division, Research Studies Institute, Maxwell AFB, Ala., 1956.

History of the 67th Tactical Reconnaissance Group, USAF Historical Division, Research Studies Institute, Maxwell AFB, Ala. 1956.

History of the 71st Reconnaissance Group, USAF Historical Division, Research Studies Institute, Maxwell AFB, Ala., 1956.

1st Aero Squadron Operational Report, Historical Report, Series E, Vol. I, Air Museum, Dayton, Ohio.

Index